A TRANSLATORS HANDBOOK

ON PAUL'S LETTER TO

THE PHILIPPIANS

Helps for Translators Series

Technical Helps:

Old Testament Quotations in the New Testament
Section Headings for the New Testament
Short Bible Reference System
New Testament Index
Orthography Studies
Bible Translations for Popular Use
The Theory and Practice of Translation
Bible Index
Fauna and Flora of the Bible
Manuscript Preparation
Marginal Notes for the Old Testament
Marginal Notes for the New Testament
The Practice of Translating

Handbooks:

A Translator's Handbook on the Book of Joshua
A Translator's Handbook of the Book of Ruth
A Translator's Handbook on the Book of Amos
A Translator's Handbook on the Books of Obadiah and Micah
A Translator's Handbook on the Book of Jonah
A Translator's Handbook on the Gospel of Mark
A Translator's Handbook on the Gospel of Luke
A Translator's Handbook on the Gospel of John
A Translator's Handbook on the Acts of the Apostles
A Translator's Handbook on Paul's First Letter to the Corinthians
A Translator's Handbook on Paul's Letter to the Romans
A Translator's Handbook on Paul's Letter to the Galatians
A Translator's Handbook on Paul's Letter to the Ephesians
A Translator's Handbook on Paul's Letter to the Philippians
A Translator's Handbook on Paul's Letters to the Colossians and to Philemon
A Translator's Handbook on Paul's Letters to the Thessalonians
A Translator's Handbook on the Letter to the Hebrews
A Translator's Handbook on the First Letter from Peter
A Translator's Handbook on the Letters of John

Guides:

A Translator's Guide to Selections from the First Five Books of the Old Testament
A Translator's Guide to Selected Psalms
A Translator's Guide to the Gospel of Matthew
A Translator's Guide to the Gospel of Mark
A Translator's Guide to the Gospel of Luke
A Translator's Guide to Paul's First Letter to the Corinthians
A Translator's Guide to Paul's Letters to Timothy and to Titus
A Translator's Guide to the Letters to James, Peter, and Jude
A Translator's Guide to the Revelation to John

HELPS FOR TRANSLATORS

A TRANSLATORS HANDBOOK

on

PAUL'S LETTER TO THE

PHILIPPIANS

by
I-JIN LOH
and
EUGENE A. NIDA

UNITED BIBLE SOCIETIES

London, New York,
Stuttgart

Books in the series of Helps for Translators may be ordered from a national Bible Society or from either of the following centers:

United Bible Societies
European Production Fund
D-7000 Stuttgart 80
Postfach 81 03 40
West Germany

United Bible Societies
1865 Broadway
New York, New York 10023
U.S.A.

L.C. Cataloging in Publication Data:

Loh, I-Jin, 1935-
    A translator's handbook on Paul's letter to the Philippians.

    (Helps for Translators)
    Bibliography: p.
    1. Bible. N.T. Philippians—Translating. 2. N.T. Philippians—Criticism, interpretation, etc. I. Nida, Eugene A., 1914-   . II. Title. III. Series.
BS2705.5.L64 1983   227'.6077   82-17585
ISBN 0-8267-0144-2

ABS-1984-800-4,500-3-CM-08528

PREFACE

This Translators Handbook on Philippians employs the same format that was used in other recently published volumes in the series. The texts of Today's English Version and the Revised Standard Version, representing two different principles of translation, are presented in parallel columns. The RSV text reflects rather closely some of the basic formal features of the Greek original, while the TEV text is a dynamic equivalence translation which attempts to bring out the meaning of the original Greek in a common form of English. These two translations are printed side by side in paragraph form in order to provide a basis for discussions of important features of the discourse structure. TEV is presented again verse by verse to serve as the base from which various difficulties in the text are pointed out and discussed.

As the primary running text, TEV is designed to serve only as a model, not the basis of translation. Frequent reference to other translations is made. This is to show how different interpretations of the Greek result in different renderings and to illustrate how various restructurings of the same interpretation of the original are possible. All of these, along with discussions on restructuring, are merely suggestions intended to alert the translators to the various possibilities and to sharpen their ability to come up with the closest natural equivalent of the original text in any given receptor language.

This Handbook deals with translational problems, and it is written specifically for translators. Exegetical comments are given only when they have direct bearing on translation. Where different exegetical possibilities exist, each is presented, and often a preference is indicated, but no attempt is made to provide original scholarly contributions. To achieve a limited goal such as this, what seems essential is simply to introduce the best insights of different commentators. Obviously, this Handbook is not meant to be a substitute for commentaries, and translators are urged to consult the standard works, for these alone can provide the additional background information necessary for a more exact understanding of the base text. Among the commentaries listed in the Bibliography, those by Lightfoot, Vincent, Michael, Beare, and Martin are especially useful, and the insights reflected in this Handbook are generally based on them.

The authors wish to express special appreciation to the members of the UBS Committee on Helps for Translators for reviewing various sections of the draft, to Lucy Rowe for typing various stages of the manuscript, and to Paul C. Clarke for editing and preparing this volume for the press.

I-Jin Loh
Eugene A. Nida

May 1977

CONTENTS

ABBREVIATIONS USED IN THIS VOLUME

Bible texts and versions cited (for details see Bibliography, page 153):

ASV	American Standard Version
Brc	Barclay
FrCL	French common language translation
GeCL	German common language translation
Gpd	Goodspeed
JB	Jerusalem Bible
KJV	King James Version
Mft	Moffatt
NAB	New American Bible
NEB	New English Bible
NIV	New International Version
Phps	Phillips
RSV	Revised Standard Version
Seg	Segond
SpCL	Spanish common language translation
TEV	Today's English Version
TNT	Translator's New Testament
TOB	Traduction Oecuménique de la Bible

Books of the Bible:

Col	Colossians	Jer	Jeremiah
1, 2 Cor	1, 2 Corinthians	Josh	Joshua
Dan	Daniel	1, 2 Kgs	1, 2 Kings
Deut	Deuteronomy	Lev	Leviticus
Eph	Ephesians	Matt	Matthew
Exo	Exodus	Num	Numbers
Ezek	Ezekiel	Phil	Philippians
Gal	Galatians	Psa	Psalms
Gen	Genesis	Rev	Revelation
Heb	Hebrews	1, 2 Sam	1, 2 Samuel
Hos	Hosea	1, 2 Thes	1, 2 Thessalonians
Isa	Isaiah	1, 2 Tim	1, 2 Timothy

Other abbreviations:

cf.	compare
ff.	and the following (verses)
LXX	Septuagint (see Glossary)
v.	verse
vv.	verses

INTRODUCTION

Paul's letter to the Philippians is no doubt one of the best loved of all his letters. Translators will be in a position to do a better job if they are aware of some of the particularly significant features of this letter.

1. This is an intensely personal letter. It lacks formality. Paul seems to set down ideas as they come to him, and to do so with frequent outbursts of unrestrained emotion. The chief of these is the refrain of joy. "May you always be joyful in union with the Lord. I say it again: rejoice!" (4.4). This is the keynote. The word "joy" in its verbal and noun forms appears sixteen times in the letter, proportionately more often than in any of Paul's other letters. What is even more remarkable is that this repeated call for joy comes from a prison cell where threats of death are always present. This radiant faith and confidence can come only from one whose life is centered in Christ (1.21; 3.8) and who has learned the secret of being content at all times and under all circumstances (4.10 ff.).

2. Writing to close friends, Paul is free to allow his personal feelings to become known. He is even driven to tears because of his adversaries (4.18), and about these persons he does not hesitate to use harsh words. He speaks of certain Judaizing Christians as "dogs" and people "who do evil things ... men who insist on cutting the body" (3.2). Christians whose conduct brings disgrace to the name they bear he describes as "enemies of Christ's death on the cross" and as people whose "bodily desires" are "their god" and who are bound "to end up in hell" (3.18-19). On the other hand, Paul is fond of using endearing terms when addressing his friends. They are always in his heart (1.7), the objects of his longing (1.8; 4.1), his "beloved" (2.12; 4.1), and his "joy and crown" (4.1).

3. Consistent with the general tone of the letter, great emphasis is placed on the corporate nature of the Christian community. This is clearly seen in the use of "you all" throughout the letter; of the word "participation" and its cognates (1.5, 7; 2.1; 3.10; 4.14, 16); of "in the Lord" (2.19, 24; 3.1; 4.1, 4, 10), "in Christ Jesus" (1.1, 26; 2.5; 3.3, 14; 4.7, 19, 21), "in Christ" (2.1); of phrases and compounds with the element "with" in Greek, for example, "partakers" (1.7), "rejoice together" (2.17, 18), "fellow worker" (2.25; 4.3), "fellow soldier" (2.25), "of the same nature" (3.10), "fellow imitators" (3.17), "yokefellow" (4.3), "to fight together" (4.3), "fellow partaker" (4.14), "one common purpose," "only one wish" (1.27), "having the same thoughts, sharing the same love, and being one in soul and mind" (2.2), etc. For Paul, oneness in Christ demands oneness in mission and oneness in the community.

4. The letter is also rich in figurative expressions taken from everyday life; those taken from the athletic arena, such as "win the prize" (3.12),

"run straight toward the goal to win the prize" (3.14), "to fight together" (4.3); those from commerce, for example, "profit" and "loss" (3.7, 8; 4.15), "account" (4.17), "receipt" (4.18); those from the battlefield, such as "progress" (1.12, 15), "stand firm together" (1.17), "the same conflict" (1.30), "win . . . lose . . . victory" (1.28); and those from the law court, for example, "defend and establish" (1.7, 16).

5. Finally, aside from repeated calls to "rejoice," the letter also contains several great themes. Paul expresses his spiritual last "will and testament" as "to live is Christ" (1.21). He explains how he regards his earlier "privileges" as "garbage" as the result of knowing Christ (3.4-11) and how he goes on trying to win the prize (3.12-14). And, above all, there is the famous Christological hymn (2.5-11). This is, no doubt, one of the earliest Christian hymns, and certainly the most beautiful and moving one preserved in the New Testament. It is written in solemn liturgical style, has rhythm and parallelisms, and contains some rare words. It combines two great themes, humiliation and exaltation, and shines as a jewel among the early confessions of faith.*

With the exception of the Christological hymn, which has some formal features, the letter as a whole is personal and informal in structure. Paul moves from one topic to another without a precise and formal outline. Nevertheless, one can detect a general movement of thought. The general plan is as follows:

I. Introduction
   A. Greetings 1.1-2
   B. Paul's Prayer for His Readers   1.3-11

II. Paul's Present Situation and Prospects
   A. To Live is Christ   1.12-26
   B. Stand Firm for the Faith of the Gospel   1.27-30

III. Call to Unity, Humility, and Witness
   A. Christ's Humility and Greatness   2.1-11
   B. Shining as Lights in the World   2.12-18

IV. Paul's Plans
   A. Commendation of Timothy   2.19-24
   B. Sending of Epaphroditus   2.25-30

*On the problem of translating poetry, see William A. Smalley, "Translating the Poetry of the Old Testament," The Bible Translator 26(2).201-211.

CHAPTER 1

Today's English Version	Revised Standard Version
PAUL'S LETTER TO THE PHILIPPIANS	**THE LETTER OF PAUL TO THE PHILIPPIANS**
1 From Paul and Timothy, servants of Christ Jesus—	1 Paul and Timothy, servants[a] of Christ Jesus,
To all God's people in Philippi who are in union with Christ Jesus, including the church leaders and helpers:	To all the saints in Christ Jesus who are at Philippi, with the bishops[b] and deacons:
2 May God our Father and the Lord Jesus Christ give you grace and peace.	2 Grace to you and peace from God our Father and the Lord Jesus Christ.
(1.1-2)	[a]Or *slaves* [b]Or *overseers* (1.1-2)

The title, Paul's Letter to the Philippians, may be rendered in some languages as "Paul Writes to the Christians (or, to the Believers) in Philippi." But in other languages it may be necessary to introduce a word for "letter" and to say, for example, "This is Paul's letter to the Philippians." "The Philippians" may need to be more specifically identified. Some translators refer to them as "the people living in Philippi," but such a rendering may give the impression that Paul is addressing his letter to all the inhabitants of that city. It may be better simply to say "the Christians..." or "the believers in Philippi."

Paul always opens his letters in the conventional Greek way of his time, starting with the name of the writer, followed by the name of the recipient, and then the greetings. To this formula a statement of the divine origin of Paul's apostleship is normally added (as in Romans, 1 and 2 Corinthians, Galatians, Ephesians, Colossians, 1 and 2 Timothy, and Titus), and sometimes a summary of his faith is included (as in Romans, cf. Galatians). The official title of "apostle" is omitted in this letter (as in his two letters to the Thessalonians and his personal note to Philemon). There is no need for Paul to mention his apostleship in the present letter because, of all the churches, the one at Philippi is closest to him. He is writing this letter, not as an apostle to his churches, but as a friend to his dear friends. The opening section sets the tone for the entire letter; it is personal, affectionate, and full of joy and gratitude.

1.1   From Paul and Timothy, servants of Christ Jesus—
        To all God's people in Philippi who are in union with Christ
    Jesus, including the church leaders and helpers:

Today's English Version (TEV) indicates the Pauline origin of the letter by beginning it with from Paul—so also the New English Bible (NEB) and the Jerusalem Bible (JB).* Although Timothy is mentioned as a fellow sender, there is no hint that he is a joint author of the letter; and it is unlikely that he served as Paul's amanuensis, or secretary, as some suppose. The first person singular pronoun "I" is used throughout the letter; and when Timothy is mentioned again (2.19-23), he is referred to in the third person. Apparently, his name is inserted at the beginning because of his constant and intimate relationship with the church at Philippi (cf. Acts 16.1,3; 17.14; 19.22) and also because Paul wanted to pave the way for his visit mentioned in 2.19-23.

In order to show the relationship of Timothy to Paul in this letter, it may be best to begin the salutation as "Timothy joins me, Paul, in sending this letter to all God's people...," or "I, Paul, together with Timothy, send this letter...." This suggested use of the first person singular pronoun "I" in apposition with "Paul" may be necessary so that the readers will understand that the Paul referred to in verse 1 is also the writer of this letter, and not another person. In the salutation of his letter to the Romans, Paul refers to himself as both "servant" and "apostle" (Rom 1.1).

Paul does claim one title both for himself and for his companion Timothy; they are servants of Christ Jesus. The word rendered "servants" is the ordinary Greek word for "slaves" (cf. Goodspeed [Gpd]; Bruce has "bond servants"). It is the correlative of "Lord." A servant is free to come and go, but a slave is not. When Paul identifies himself and Timothy as "servants," he means that they are the absolute possession of Jesus Christ, their Lord, and owe absolute obedience to him. Yet the kind of servanthood Paul has in mind is not that of complete servitude, utter absence of freedom; he is thinking, rather, of a cheerful and willing service which is inseparable from true freedom (cf. Rom 6.18,22). In the Old Testament the prophets are often spoken of as "the servants of the Lord" (Amos 3.7; Jer 7.25; Ezra 9.11; Dan 9.6); and the same title is applied to Moses (Exo 14.31; Josh 1.2), Joshua (Judges 2.8), and David (Psa 78.70; 89.3, 20). It is possible that Paul also has in mind the idea of a call to service, indeed an honor analogous to that of the Old Testament prophets and leaders. Thus "servant" in this context becomes a title of dignity, since God's "servant" is a chosen instrument entrusted with particular tasks.

It may be difficult in some languages to make the phrase servants of Christ Jesus an appositional qualifier of proper names such as Paul and

---

*Various versions and translations of the Scriptures are referred to throughout these notes. Each is identified by name the first time it is mentioned, and the letters in parentheses following the name give the abbreviated form in which it is cited thereafter. All such abbreviations are identified on page viii. Further information concerning the translations and versions cited can be found on pages 153-154.

Timothy, especially if personal pronouns such as "I" and "we" are used in connection with these proper names. It may be more appropriate to say "we are servants of Christ Jesus," or "we serve Christ Jesus." Or perhaps a relative clause can be employed, for example, "we who are servants of Christ Jesus." In the New Testament the word "servants" is applied, not to a select group of spiritual and moral elite, but to the rank and file of committed Christians who are set apart to belong to God and are dedicated to his service. They constitute the new and true people of God.

In some languages a verb must be introduced to indicate specifically the relationship of Paul to those to whom he writes. It may be useful to say "I, Paul, together with Timothy...am writing to all of you who are God's people living in Philippi," or "...this is my letter written to all of you who...." To connect the proper name with the qualifier, one may say "I, Paul, and Timothy are servants of Jesus Christ. We write this letter to...."

This letter is addressed, as some translations have it, "to all the saints" (Revised Standard Version [RSV] JB Moffatt [Mft]; New American Bible [NAB] "to all the holy ones"); but this rendering can be quite misleading, since the word translated as "saint" is equivalent to the Old Testament Hebrew word meaning "to separate" or "to set apart." Accordingly, Today's English Version (TEV) renders to all God's people (so also Gpd New English Bible [NEB] Bruce). In some languages the so-called possessive construction God's people, or "people who belong to God," may seem absurd. A more natural expression may be "people who worship God" or "people who are related to God."

The phrase in Philippi may sometimes be expanded to "living in Philippi" and also may be rendered as a restrictive clause, "who are living in Philippi." In some instances, it may be useful to specify Philippi by a classifier, for example, "in the town of Philippi" or "in the town named Philippi." The participle "living" would indicate permanent residence, expressed in some languages as "who have their homes in." If in Philippi is treated as a restrictive relative clause, it may be coordinated with the following relative clause by a conjunction such as "and," for example, "who are living in Philippi and who are in union with Christ Jesus."

God's people are the ones who are in union with Christ Jesus (TEV Gpd; NEB "incorporate in Christ Jesus"; Bruce "united in Christ Jesus"; Phillips [Phps] combines this phrase with the preceding and renders "true Christians"). In the Greek this is expressed simply as "in Christ Jesus." This phrase is the most characteristic expression used by Paul to describe Christians who have intimate communion with the living Christ, and who are, at the same time, members of the new community of which Christ is the Head. To be in union with the living Christ is to live continually in his presence just "as a bird in the air, a fish in the water, or the roots of a tree in the soil" (Vincent). TEV connects the phrase to God's people (so also NEB JB), not to the church leaders and helpers (see NAB).

Of all the expressions in the New Testament, the phrase "in Christ Jesus" is one of the most difficult to translate satisfactorily. In union with Christ Jesus is probably the closest natural equivalent in English, but in other languages one must use such expressions as "who are tied to Christ Jesus," "who are one with Christ Jesus," "who are related to Christ Jesus," or even "who stand together with Christ Jesus."

The letter is also addressed to the church leaders and helpers, literally "bishops and deacons" RSV NEB NAB). These terms seem to describe two kinds of church officials, but it is doubtful that they had acquired a specialized technical sense in Paul's lifetime. TEV employs more generic terms to describe them (cf. JB "presiding elders and deacons"; Knox "pastors and deacons"; Gpd "superintendents and assistants"). Church leaders were probably elders in the church at Philippi who were responsible for administrative duties, including financial ones. The helpers were probably their assistants, and their chief responsibilities seem to have been in financial matters. It is likely that these men are mentioned in the salutation because they were actually responsible for collecting and sending the gifts which Paul had received (cf. 4.10-13).

Including is literally "with," an ambiguous word in this context. A conjunction such as "and" before the phrase the church leaders and helpers, instead of including, may suggest in some languages that the church leaders and helpers were themselves not in union with Christ Jesus, thus separating the leaders and helpers as a distinct class from the believers. It may, therefore, be necessary to follow TEV and use a word such as including in rendering this phrase. Because of the particular emphasis placed upon these leaders and helpers, it may even be valid to add the word "especially" after including.

It is often necessary to define the relationship existing between the church on the one hand and the leaders and helpers on the other. The church leaders may be rendered as "the leaders among the believers" or "...in the congregation." Helpers must often be translated in a way that will indicate clearly who are being helped. Some translators, therefore, use expressions which imply "those who help the leaders," and to an extent this may be justified. Other translators use expressions which suggest "those who help the other believers."

1.2   May God our Father and the Lord Jesus Christ give you grace
           and peace.

As in all his salutations, Paul changes conventional Greek and Hebrew
greetings into a Christian benediction and couples God and Jesus Christ as
the sources of all blessings. Many translations render this benediction quite
literally, following the Greek word order, "Grace to you and peace from
God our Father and the Lord Jesus Christ" (RSV NEB cf. Mft Bruce
NAB), but TEV translates it in a more straightforward and more natural
manner (cf. Gpd "God our Father and the Lord Jesus Christ bless you and
give you peace").

The phrase grace and peace, combining the Christian concept of
"grace" with the Jewish view of "peace" (both terms either related to or
involved in standard greetings), is a formula often used in early Christian
greetings. Grace expresses God's love to sinful people who do not deserve
it — the love manifested in the life, death, and resurrection of Jesus. Peace
in this context means not simply an absence of troubles or anxieties, but
a state of total well-being, a wholeness of life resulting from forgiveness of
sins and reconciliation to God through Jesus. The ultimate source of grace
and peace is obviously God, whom Jesus revealed as Abba Father, but to
the extent that such blessing is made possible only through Jesus, who is
confessed as Messiah (Christ the anointed King) and exalted as Lord by
his resurrection (2.9), he too is to be acclaimed as the giver of grace and
peace. It is therefore better to render may God our Father and the Lord
Jesus Christ give you grace and peace, rather than "grace and peace to you
from God our Father, even the Father of the Lord Jesus Christ," as is
sometimes suggested.

This type of blessing or benediction must be identified in some languages as a kind of prayer, and so must be introduced by a verb specifically indicating prayer, for example, "I pray that God our Father and the
Lord Jesus Christ will give you grace and peace." In this context our is, of
course, inclusive — that is, including the Philippian believers as well as Paul
and Timothy. In some languages it is necessary to say "our Lord" rather
than the Lord, since it may be impossible to speak of a "Lord" without
indicating those to whom he is related as Lord.

In almost all languages Jesus Christ is treated simply as a proper name,
but the title Lord is often rendered as a description of function, for example, "the one who commands us" or "the one whom we obey."

The term grace is a highly technical expression, with special connotations in this type of greeting. Some languages have no close equivalent,
but one can often employ such a phrase as "show great kindness to" or
"be very good to." It may even be difficult to find an appropriate term

[8]

for <u>peace</u>, since the New Testament concept of peace is not the mere absence of conflict or anxiety. The closest equivalent in some instances may be "cause you to live well." This type of expression, however, may be understood in the sense of mere material prosperity, which, of course, is not what is meant. In some languages such an expression as "to feel real contentment" may be the closest equivalent.

TEV	RSV
Paul's Prayer for His Readers	
3 I thank my God for you every time I think of you; 4 and every time I pray for you all, I pray with joy 5 because of the way in which you have helped me in the work of the gospel from the very first day until now. 6 And so I am sure that God, who began this good work in you, will carry it on until it is finished on the Day of Christ Jesus. 7 You are always in my heart! And so it is only right for me to feel as I do about you. For you have all shared with me in this privilege that God has given me, both now that I am in prison and also while I was free to defend the gospel and establish it firmly. 8 God is my witness that I tell the truth when I say that my deep feeling for you all comes from the heart of Christ Jesus himself. (1.3-8)	3 I thank my God in all my remembrance of you, 4 always in every prayer of mine for you all making my prayer with joy, 5 thankful for your partnership in the gospel from the first day until now. 6 And I am sure that he who began a good work in you will bring it to completion at the day of Jesus Christ. 7 It is right for me to feel thus about you all, because I hold you in my heart, for you are all partakers with me of grace, both in my imprisonment and in the defense and confirmation of the gospel. 8 For God is my witness, how I yearn for you all with the affection of Christ Jesus. (1.3-8)

The section heading <u>Paul's Prayer for His Readers</u> must appear as a complete sentence in some languages, for example, "Paul prays for the believers in Philippi," or "This is what Paul prays for those who will receive his letter."

Continuing with the conventional style of Greek letter-writing of his day, Paul follows his greetings with an expression of thanksgiving to God for the recipients of the letter. But he goes beyond mere convention and reveals his affectionate feelings for his Christian friends. Coupled with his expression of affection, there is a note of joy, and this note of joy is dominant throughout the letter.

1.3   I thank my God for you every time I think of you;

Although he has included Timothy's name in the opening greeting, Paul begins his thanksgiving with the first person singular "I," and the first person singular is maintained throughout the letter. The thanksgiving

[9]

is offered to <u>my God</u>, reflecting Paul's profound personal relationship to God (cf. Acts 27.23). In Greek the occasion for this thanksgiving is stated rather ambiguously, literally "upon all remembrance of you." It is possible to take "you" in a subjective sense, meaning "on the basis of your remembering," with the resultant rendering "for all your remembrance of me" (Mft). On the basis of this view, Paul is expressing appreciation for his Philippian friends' gift of money. But this interpretation does not seem to represent his real meaning. For one thing, the words "of me" are not found in the Greek text. Furthermore, the word translated "remembrance" occurs frequently in the opening verses of Paul's letters (Rom 1.9; Eph 1.16; Philemon 4). In every instance it is closely associated with "thanksgiving" and is used in the sense of "mentioning in prayer" or "remembering in prayer." Consequently, most translations render this clause as <u>every time I think of you</u> (TEV NAB cf. NEB JB "whenever I think of you"), correctly suggesting that, whenever Paul thinks of his Christian friends at Philippi, he gives thanks to God.

In many languages an expression such as <u>my God</u> cannot be used, for one cannot really possess God. Accordingly, this expression must be rendered as "the God whom I worship" or "the one who is God to me."

The phrase <u>for you</u> must be understood in the sense of "because of you" or "because of what you have done."

In some languages it may be necessary to place <u>every time I think of you</u> at the beginning of verse 3, so as to read "Every time I think of you I thank my God for you." <u>Every time</u> may be rendered in many languages as "whenever"; <u>every time I think of you</u> must be expressed in some languages as "whenever you come into my thoughts," "whenever I think about what you have done," or "whenever what you did speaks to my mind."

1.4   **and every time I pray for you all, I pray with joy**

This verse is sometimes regarded as parenthetical because Paul's thanksgiving is not mentioned again until verse 5 (cf. Luther), but this conclusion is unnecessary, for the following reasons. First, there is no need to mention the object of thanksgiving in verse 5, since it is already implicit in the phrase "every time I think of you" (v. 3). TEV makes the object explicit by supplying "for you," thus "I thank my God for you every time I think of you." Secondly, there is no evidence that verse 4 is a digression, since it connects rather naturally both with what precedes and with what follows. Both "thanksgiving" (v. 3) and "supplication" (v. 4; the word translated <u>pray</u> in TEV) are essential components of prayer. Furthermore, verse 5 gives the reason for the "joy" mentioned in verse 4. Finally, the sense of "joy," being the dominant tone in this letter (1.18,25; 2.2,17,18,28,29; 3.1; 4.1,4,10), is not likely to be parenthetical in Paul's thought.

The word translated pray (a noun in Greek) is not the usual word for prayer. Its essential component is "supplication" (American Standard Version [ASV] "in every supplication of mine"). The supplication Paul continuously makes is for you all. One cannot fail to be impressed by the repeated use of "all," "each," or "every" in this letter, especially when the Philippian church is referred to (1.4,7,8,25; 2.17; 4.21). The word seems to be related to Paul's constant exhortations to unity (1.27; 2.1-4; 4.2,3,5,7,9). The repeated reference to all the members of the Philippian church is intended to remind them of the danger of divisions, which is the one negative element in Paul's general feeling of satisfaction with respect to that group of believers. One should not conclude that the use of "all" is meaningless and may be left untranslated (cf. Phps NAB).

In verse 3 the phrase for you must be understood in the sense of "because of you," but in verse 4 for you all must be understood in the sense of "on behalf of you all." I pray for you must be expressed in some instances as "I pray to God that he will help you'" but in others it may be sufficient simply to say "I speak to God about you."

The semantic elements in the expression I pray with joy must be reversed in some languages, for example, "I am happy when I pray" or "I feel joy in my praying." In some languages this joy may be expressed idiomatically as "my heart dances as I pray," or "my abdomen is content as I talk with God."

1.5   because of the way in which you have helped me in the work of the gospel from the very first day until now.

Paul now gives the reasons for his "joy" (not for his "thanksgiving" in verse 3, as RSV suggests). The way in which you have helped me translates a Greek noun phrase "your partnership" (RSV) or "your fellowship" (King James Version [KJV]). The basic meaning of the word translated "partnership" is "participation in something with someone," but it can have a more restricted meaning, that of "contributions" or "gifts" (cf. Rom 15.26; 2 Cor 9.13; Mft "what you have contributed to the gospel"). For this reason some commentators suggest that Paul is here referring to the Philippians' tangible expression of Christian partnership, their gift of money. This interpretation may well be true, but the context seems to indicate that Paul is using "partnership" in a wider sense and hence refers to all the cooperation and share in the work of the gospel which the Philippians have shown, whether it be in the spreading of the gospel, in sympathy, in suffering, or in generosity.

[11]

Because of the way in which you have helped me may be rendered in some languages as "because of how you helped me," "... how you made it easier for me," or "... how you made it possible for me."

In the work of the gospel is literally "into the gospel." The word "gospel" originally meant a reward for bringing good news, but later it came to be used for good news itself, often the joyous news of victory in war. In the New Testament it always means good news itself and refers to the salvation that God has made possible through the death and resurrection of Jesus Christ. The word appears nine times in Philippians and is used in a variety of ways. It is the message about Jesus Christ that is proclaimed (1.5; 4.15), defended (1.7, 16), promoted, spread, and advanced (4.3; 1.12; 2.22). It is also the standard of Christian living and the basis of faith (1.27). The phrase in this context is not a reference to the Philippians' sharing in accepting Paul's preaching, but rather to their active participation in the work of the gospel. It may therefore be expressed as "in proclaiming the good news to others," or "in the telling of the good news to others."

The phrase from the very first day is obviously a reference to the beginning of Paul's mission to Philippi (cf. Acts 16.12 ff.), and it may be essential to indicate this temporal relation. It may be rendered in some languages as "from the first day I was in Philippi until now," or, perhaps better, "from the very first day you believed until now."

1.6   And so I am sure that God, who began this good work in you, will carry it on until it is finished on the Day of Christ Jesus.

And so I am sure that is literally "being sure of this very thing" and may be rendered as "and therefore I am sure of what follows," or "... this that I am going to say." It may, however, be better in some languages to combine the first part of verse 6 with the substance of what is referred to, as in TEV. Fom the context it is clear that the one who initiated the good work among the Philippians and who would carry it to completion is God. Therefore TEV translates explicitly God, who began this good work. The expression good work may refer to the part taken by the Philippians in the work of the gospel, but more naturally it points to the activity of God at the time of their conversion. The outward cooperation in the work of the gospel is, of course, the outcome and expression of the inward change made at the time of conversion.

It may be necessary to restructure rather radically the clause who began this good work in you. The verb began simply indicates an aspect of the more central activity indicated by the noun work. Therefore one may need to render this clause as "who began to work in you in this good way," or even ". . . for good." One may also express the proper relations by a rendering such as "who began to do in you what was good."

A single Greek word meaning "will complete" (future tense), in combination with a preposition, is rendered in TEV as a verbal phrase <u>will carry it on until it is finished</u>. The verb, as used in this particular context, has the sense of continuance and consummation (Mft "will go on completing"; Bruce "will go on bringing it to completion"). It may also be possible to render this verbal clause as "will continue to work in you until he has finished what he has planned," or ". . . accomplished his purpose."

<u>The Day of Christ Jesus</u> is not a reference to the day of one's death, but to the Parousia, or the return of Christ (Knox "the day when Jesus Christ comes"), and so TEV capitalizes the word Day. It is the Day of judgment as well as the Day of salvation (1 Thes 1.10). Apparently the early return of Christ is very much in the apostle's mind as he writes this letter. In some languages a literal translation of <u>the Day of Christ Jesus</u> may be quite misleading; one may need to indicate clearly the idea of the Parousia and so render this expression as "on that Day when Christ Jesus returns."

1.7   You are always in my heart! And so it is only right for me to feel as I do about you. For you have all shared with me in this privilege that God has given me, both now that I am in prison and also while I was free to defend the gospel and establish it firmly.

This verse involves several historical and translational problems. The Greek itself is ambiguous, and accordingly many translations show disagreements as to the meaning. Although TEV begins with <u>you are always in my heart!</u>, one can reverse the pronouns and render "I am close to your heart" (Knox footnote), or "I have a secure place in your heart" (Bruce cf. NEB "you hold me in such affection"). However, in the light of the Greek word order, as well as of the context (especially v. 8), it seems best to follow the TEV rendering (cf. RSV JB). Unlike other translations, TEV moves this sentence to the beginning of the verse. This restructuring has two advantages: (1) It immediately focuses attention on the central thrust of what Paul is going to say in the following sentences; and (2) it avoids the involved and clumsy sentence constructions which would otherwise result (cf. other translations).

<u>You are always in my heart!</u> may be expressed in some instances as "I am always thinking of you with happiness," "you constantly make me think gladly of you," or "you are very dear to me."

It is only right for me to feel as I do about you may be expressed as "I am completely justified in feeling as I do about you," or "it is entirely proper that I should feel as I do concerning you."

You have all shared with me may be expressed as "you have all helped me," "you have all worked along with me," or even "you have all been my partners."

This privilege that God has given me is an attempt to reflect the sense of a single Greek noun, "the grace." The absolute use of the word "grace" with a definite article points to its divine origin. In the present context it refers both to Paul's imprisonment and to his defending and establishing the gospel. To be able to do these things is regarded by him as a God-given privilege (cf. 1.29). This privilege that God has given me may be expressed in some languages as "this work that God has specially given to me," or "this task which God has been so good as to give to me." By indicating clearly that God's goodness was involved in giving Paul his ministry, one may indicate something of the meaning of "grace" as suggested in the TEV translation privilege.

It may be necessary in some languages to render I am in prison as "I am tied in prison," or "I am locked up here in prison." Otherwise, a reader might get the impression that Paul was merely visiting a prison at the time.

Also while I was free to defend the gospel and establish it firmly translates a Greek prepositional phrase "in the defense and confirmation of the gospel" (RSV). The word translated to defend often carries a judicial sense, meaning "to stand for a defense against a charge in court" (cf. Acts 25.16; 2 Tim 4.16). The term rendered establish it firmly occurs only here and in Heb 6.16. It can also be used in a technical legal sense of "to defend" or "to guarantee legally." The phrase can be taken as having to do with Paul's imprisonment, in which case these two words are legal terms describing Paul's trial before the imperial court or a provincial judge. Accordingly, the phrase can be translated "appear in court to vouch for the truth of the gospel" (cf. NEB Mft NAB). TEV, however, interprets the circumstances differently, as the translation shows. It gives specific temporal references to Paul's activities: now that I am, indicating that his imprisonment is a present reality, and while I was free, suggesting that his defense and his establishing the gospel were things done prior to the present imprisonment.

While I was free may be expressed as "while I was able to go about," "while I was unhindered," or "while there was nothing to stop me."

It may be difficult to express succinctly the idea in the phrase to defend the gospel. In most languages one can speak of "defending a person" but to defend the gospel may require some modification, for example, "to answer those who speak against the gospel," or "to show clearly that the gospel is true."

It may be even more difficult to render the expression establish it firmly. In a sense it is people's faith in the gospel which is made secure and firm, rather than the gospel itself. It may therefore be necessary to render this expression as "to cause people to believe the good news firmly," "... to believe with no uncertainty what the good news says," or "... what the good news is about."

1.8   God is my witness that I tell you the truth when I say that my deep feeling for you all comes from the heart of Christ Jesus himself.

In the Greek God is my witness that I tell you the truth is simply "God is my witness." This expression is used by Paul to convey solemn, intense, personal emotion (cf. Rom 1.9; 2 Cor 1.23; 1 Thes 2.5, 10). He appeals to God as the One who knows and who can testify to the truthfulness of his innermost feelings. It may be expressed in some instances as "God knows that what I say is true," or "... this that I am going to say is true."

Comes from the heart of Christ Jesus himself translates a Greek prepositional phrase, literally "with the entrails of Christ." The entrails consist of the heart, liver, and lungs. In biblical times these were collectively regarded as the seat of feelings and affections, the equivalent of "heart" in modern usage. Paul identifies himself so closely with Christ that the deep feeling he has towards his Christian friends appears to be nothing other than the love of Christ himself (JB "loving you as Christ Jesus loves you").

The final clause of verse 8 may be very difficult to render, for it contains two metaphorical expressions, deep feeling and heart. Furthermore, it is impossible to say in some languages that "a feeling comes." The meaning here is, of course, that the true source of Paul's feelings is Christ. But the emphasis is upon the similarity of his affections to Christ's, and therefore this clause may be rendered as "I love you in the same way that Christ Jesus himself loves you." Or it may be possible to render this clause as "my love for you all results from the kind of love which Christ Jesus himself has shown."

TEV	RSV
9 I pray that your love will keep on growing more and more, together with true knowledge and perfect judgment, 10 so that you will be able to choose what is best. Then you will be free from all impurity and blame on the Day of	9 And it is my prayer that your love may abound more and more, with knowledge and all discernment, 10 so that you may approve what is excellent, and may be pure and blameless for the day of Christ,

Christ. 11 Your lives will be filled with the truly good qualities which only Jesus Christ can produce, for the glory and praise of God. (1.9-11)

11 filled with the fruits of righteousness which come through Jesus Christ, to the glory and praise of God. (1.9-11)

Paul's affection for his friends now passes into prayer for them. For Paul love is the key to <u>true knowledge and perfect judgment</u>. He now proceeds to give the substance of his prayer to which he has already referred in verse 4. Verses 9-11 are one sentence in Greek, but to make the thoughts of the sentence clear, it must be restructured.

1.9   I pray that your love will keep on growing more and more, together with true knowledge and perfect judgment,

The Greek has the word "this" before the content of Paul's prayer ("I pray this: that . . ."), but normally this addition would be superfluous in translation.

<u>Your love</u> should not be restricted to the Philippians' love for God, for Paul, or even to their love for one another. It is much more likely that Paul has in mind the most comprehensive Christian love. In some languages <u>your love</u> may seem too abstract, and this expression may be better rendered as "your loving heart."

Furthermore, in some languages it is not possible to speak of "love growing more and more," although one may say "I pray that you will keep on loving more and more." Again, it may be necessary to indicate in some languages who is loved, and therefore one may need to translate "that you will love one another more and more."

<u>True knowledge</u> and <u>perfect judgment</u> are essential elements of love. "Love" should <u>keep on growing</u> (present tense), that is, it should develop into and be accompanied by spiritual and moral insights. The word translated <u>true knowledge</u> is frequently used by Paul to convey the idea of a mental grasp of spiritual truth and especially that practical and experiential knowledge of God which is available to those who have become Christians. <u>Perfect judgment</u> (literally, "all insight" or "all perception") appears only here in the New Testament. It refers to a person's ability to make moral decisions. The adjective "all" is not intensive, but extensive; that is, it signifies "every form of" <u>perfect judgment</u> (NEB "insight of every kind").

<u>True knowledge and perfect judgment</u> may be viewed as the result of increased love, and so they may be indicated in some languages as result, and in other languages as purpose. On the basis of this type of interpretation, one may translate "that you may love one another more and more, and as a result have true knowledge and perfect judgment." On the other hand, one may understand <u>true knowledge and perfect judgment</u> as an

[16]

accompanying feature of love and accordingly translate "that you may love one another more and more, and at the same time have true knowledge and perfect judgment."

In a number of languages it is necessary to translate <u>knowledge</u> and <u>judgment</u> as verbs, and this requires syntactic restructuring, with resulting expressions such as "that you may know what is true and judge perfectly," or ". . . judge in a completely right way."

1.10   so that you will be able to choose what is best. Then you will
            be free from all impurity and blame on the Day of Christ.

Paul now goes on to define the purpose of his prayer in verse 9. The same Greek expression translated <u>to choose what is best</u> appears also in Rom 2.18, where TEV renders it as "to choose what is right." The Greek term here translated <u>to choose</u> is sometimes used in the technical sense of testing coins to determine whether they are genuine. Thus the TEV rendering carries the force of accepting or choosing what is proved to be right or best or essential in religion (Mft Gpd "to have a sense of what is vital"; NEB footnote "may teach you by experience what things are most worthwhile"). The phrase <u>what is best</u> means literally "things which differ" or "things that excel." The latter meaning seems to suit the context better. It is a reference to the ability, not so much to distinguish right from wrong or good from bad, but to determine what is best among all that is good.

<u>What is best</u> is a general qualification which it is not always possible to employ. Certainly it is not a reference to particular things or objects, but rather to behavior and experience. It may be necessary to render the first part of verse 10 as "so that you will be able to choose what is best to do," or ". . . how you should best behave."

<u>Then you will be free from all impurity and blame on the Day of Christ</u> (literally, "so that you may be pure and blameless with a view to the Day of Christ") is taken as the result of having the ability to discriminate what is best. The adjective rendered <u>free from all impurity</u> occurs elsewhere in the New Testament only in 2 Peter 3.1. It means "unmixed," "genuine," or "unadulterated." It may be rendered in some languages as "not having anything bad about you," or "without any wrong." The adjective translated <u>free from . . . blame</u> can mean either "not causing others to stumble" or "not stumbling." Paul seems to have in mind the fitness of the Philippians to stand before Christ on the Day of judgment. In this context it is better to adopt the meaning of "blameless." This concept may be expressed in some languages as "without having done anything for which you could be blamed," or "without having done what was wrong."

On the Day of Christ, as in verse 6, refers to the Parousia, so it is possible to render it more explicitly as "on the Day when Christ comes back."

1.11   Your lives will be filled with the truly good qualities which only Jesus Christ can produce, for the glory and praise of God.

In Greek this verse is a participial (perfect passive) phrase connected with verse 10, but TEV supplies your lives to make it a separate sentence.

Truly good qualities which only Jesus Christ can produce is literally "fruit of righteousness which is through Jesus Christ." TEV changes Jesus Christ from a secondary to a primary agent (Mft "harvest of righteousness which Jesus Christ produces"; JB "the perfect goodness which Jesus Christ produces"). The Greek word rendered "righteousness" in some translations (RSV Mft) is used with several different senses in the Pauline letters. It is sometimes used in the sense of "the requirements of God," at other times in the sense of "what is right." It is also used to refer to an attribute of God. Most significantly, this term is used by Paul to convey the idea of the saving activity of God whereby he puts men in a right relation to himself through Jesus Christ. In the present context, however, "righteousness" refers to a person's inner status, or, as TEV renders it, the truly good qualities of Christians (JB "perfect goodness"; Phps "true goodness"). These are the natural consequences of being restored to a right relationship with God. Paul is careful to add that this quality is not something that a man can acquire for himself; it is something which only Jesus Christ can produce.

In some languages one cannot speak of "lives being filled with good qualities." One can say, however, "that all that you do may be truly good." In this context the noun lives refers to one's behavior, and the verb filled suggests the totality of such activity.

The qualifying clause, which only Jesus Christ can produce, may be rendered as "only Jesus Christ can cause you to do this," or ". . . to have such goodness."

The supreme end of Christian life is the glory and praise of God. The word glory is an important term in the Bible. In the Old Testament it means basically "weight" or "importance," and it is often associated with a revelation of the majestic character of God. The same thought appears often in the New Testament also. In the Pauline letters glory appears many times as an ascription of praise (Rom 4.20; 2 Cor 1.20, etc.), and it is prominent in the doxologies (Rom 11.36; 16.27; Gal 1.5; Eph 3.21). In these contexts, glory is equivalent to praise. The phrase can sometimes be rendered "to give glory and praise to God," but it must often be expressed as a separate sentence, for example, "all of this is for the glory and praise of God." However, implied in both glory and praise is an underlying causative relation, for it is people who must give these things to God. Therefore one may need to translate this final phrase as "in order that people may honor and praise God." In some languages an expression such as "praise God" must be indicated as a type of discourse, either direct or indirect, for example, "say how great God is," or "say, God is truly great."

TEV	RSV
To Live Is Christ	
12 I want you to know, my brothers, that the things that have happened to me have really helped the progress of the gospel. 13 As a result, the whole palace guard and all the others here know that I am in prison because I am a servant of Christ. 14 And my being in prison has given most of the brothers more confidence in the Lord, so that they grow bolder all the time to preach the message*a* fearlessly.	12 I want you to know, brethren, that what has happened to me has really served to advance the gospel, 13 so that it has become known throughout the whole praetorian guard*c* and to all the rest that my imprisonment is for Christ; 14 and most of the brethren have been made confident in the Lord because of my imprisonment, and are much more bold to speak the word of God without fear.
*a*the message: *some manuscripts have* God's message. (1.12-14)	*c*Greek *in the whole praetorium* (1.12-14)

The section heading To Live Is Christ suggests several meanings and implied relationships. In a number of languages it will be necessary to expand it and say, for example, "For a person to live is to serve Christ," or "only in serving Christ can one truly live." These suggestions, however, by no means exhaust the possible relationships implied in To Live Is Christ.

In these verses Paul moves on to the subject matter of his letter. He informs his readers about his present situation (vv. 12-17), reflects on his hopes and expectations (vv. 18-26), and proceeds to give some practical exhortations on Christian living (vv. 27-30). He regards his whole existence as determined and controlled by Christ (v. 21), and consequently his utmost concern is that the message of Christ be proclaimed regardless of the motives of those who preach it (v. 18). Only the progress of the gospel gives joy to the apostle (vv. 12, 25).

1.12   I want you to know, my brothers, that the things that have happened to me have really helped the progress of the gospel.

My brothers is Paul's favorite way of describing his fellow believers in the Christian community. Though in a number of languages it is possible to identify fellow believers by such a phrase, in other languages a different kinship term with practically the same meaning may be employed, for example, "my close relations" or "you of the same family with me." In some

[19]

languages, however, one may need to use such a phrase as "my fellow believers" or "you who also believe together with me."

The things that have happened to me is sometimes translated as "my present situation" (Bruce). It refers to the apostle's arrest and imprisonment and may be expressed as "what I have experienced" or even "what I have suffered."

The word translated progress, which appears again in verse 25, is a military metaphor describing a scout who identifies and, if possible, removes obstacles before an advancing army. This word signifies advancement in spite of the dangers and obstacles which block the way of the traveler.

The progress must often be stated in terms of the greater number of people hearing or believing. The verb helped in this context indicates primarily a causative relation, and for that reason one can translate "caused more and more people to hear," or ". . . to believe."

1.13   As a result, the whole palace guard and all the others here know that I am in prison because I am a servant of Christ.

As a result indicates that what follows in verses 13-14 is the consequence of the progress of the gospel (cf. Bruce "the upshot of it all has been this"). Even though the phrase has been discarded by many translators, it is best to have it for a better connection. As a result may also be rendered as "because of this" or "because of what has happened."

TEV restructures the sentence by making the phrase the whole palace guard and all the others the subject, instead of "my imprisonment" (NEB NAB; JB "my chains") or the impersonal "it" (Gpd RSV). The word rendered palace guard, literally "praetorium" (a Latin word borrowed into Greek), refers either to a particular residence or to a particular group of men. If the former is meant, it would be a reference to the imperial palace in Rome (KJV "palace") or to the ruler's residence (cf. Mark 15.16; Acts 23.35). In such a case, it could be translated as "the house where the emperor lives."

The context, however, indicates that "praetorium" refers to a body of men, thus the palace guard (so also Phps; Gpd "Imperial Guard"). One can also use a more generic term such as "headquarters guard" (NEB "all at headquarters") and leave the place of Paul's imprisonment an open question. The whole palace guard may be expressed as "all of the soldiers who are guarding the palace," or ". . . the house where the emperor lives."

There is no need to restrict the meaning of all the others here to "the rest of the soldiers"; it may be understood as "the public at large" (NEB), "everyone else here," "all the other people here," or simply "everyone here."

Because I am a servant of Christ (literally, "in Christ") explains the cause of the apostle's imprisonment (NEB NAB "in Christ's cause"; Gpd "for the sake of Christ"). TEV employs "servant," the only title Paul claims in this letter (v. 1), to focus upon the apostle's relation to Christ. As in verse 1, a servant of Christ may be made a verbal expression, for example, "because I serve Christ," "because I work on behalf of Christ," or "because all I do is to help Christ."

1.14   And my being in prison has given most of the brothers more confidence in the Lord, so that they grow bolder all the time to preach the message*a* fearlessly.

*a*the message; *some manuscripts have* God's message.

In Greek the first clause is literally "most of the brothers having confidence in the Lord because of my bonds." TEV restructures this by changing "because of my bonds" (dative of cause) into the subject and "most of the brothers" (subject of the participle) into the direct object, thus my being in prison has given most of the brothers more confidence in the Lord (cf. Mft "my imprisonment has given the majority of the brotherhood greater confidence in the Lord"). My being in prison constitutes the cause for Paul's fellow believers' becoming more confident. This relation must be expressed in some languages by a clause of cause, for example, "because I am in prison, most of my fellow believers have more confidence in the Lord."

The exact relation of the phrase in the Lord to the context is debated. In Greek it lies between "the brothers" and "having confidence," and it is therefore grammatically possible to connect it with either. KJV and ASV connect it with "the brothers." NEB favors this construction by rendering "fellow Christians" (Gpd "Christian brothers"; NAB "brothers in Christ"). But this exegesis is questionable. In 2.24 Paul uses the same verb with "in the Lord." Besides, whenever he speaks of "brethren" he always means "Christians," and so to add "in the Lord" is really redundant. Consequently, to connect in the Lord with confidence, as TEV does, makes better sense (cf. Mft; Phps "taking fresh heart in the Lord"). The Lord is the basis of confidence and hope. That being the case, in a number of languages this relation must be expressed as one of cause, for exmaple, "are more confident because of the Lord," or even of agency, "the Lord has caused them to be more confident."

They grow bolder may be expressed negatively as "they do not fear so much," or "they fear less and less." The fundamental change expressed in grow bolder all the time must be rendered in some languages as "become bolder constantly," or "are constantly more and more bold."

[21]

To preach the message is literally "to speak the word." The earliest manuscript reading supports the TEV rendering without adding "of God" after "the message" (but see RSV NEB NAB "the word of God"). The fact that the genitive qualifier "of God" appears in different positions in various manuscripts and the fact that it has a variant reading "of Lord" suggest that it was not in the original.

TEV	RSV
15 Of course some of them preach Christ because they are jealous and quarrelsome, but others from genuine good will. 16 These do so from love, because they know that God has given me the work of defending the gospel. 17 The others do not proclaim Christ sincerely, but from a spirit of selfish ambition; they think that they will make more trouble for me while I am in prison. (1.15-17)	15 Some indeed preach Christ from envy and rivalry, but others from good will. 16 The latter do it out of love, knowing that I am put here for the defense of the gospel, 17 the former proclaim Christ out of partisanship, not sincerely but thinking to afflict me in my imprisonment. (1.15-17)

1.15   Of course some of them preach Christ because they are jealous and quarrelsome, but others from genuine good will.

Paul now speaks of two classes of preachers with different motives. Of course is used in the sense of "it is true" (Gpd JB NAB) or "indeed" (RSV NEB). Some of them seems to refer to a segment of most of the brothers mentioned in the previous verse (it may be useful to render this phrase as "some of the brothers" or "some of our fellow believers"). However, it is sometimes argued that Paul is here referring to preachers in general on the ground that jealous and quarrelsome motives can hardly be compatible with the attitude of confidence in the Lord which some of them apparently had. It is very difficult to determine who these preachers are. That they are Jewish Christians who insist on going back to Jewish ways seems unlikely, since Paul does not accuse them of any false teachings. In any case, they are "pro-Christ" but "anti-Paul" preachers.

The word translated preach is the standard New Testament word for the preaching of the gospel. It has substantially the same meaning as the word translated proclaim in verse 17 and as preached in verse 18. The latter is a compound verb which may signify "to proclaim with authority," but the two words are used interchangeably in this context (cf. vv. 15, 17,

18). It may be impossible to translate <u>preach Christ</u> literally, since in many languages one can only "preach about Christ" or "tell people about Christ." To indicate clearly that this is a proclamation of the good news about Christ, it may be useful to render <u>preach Christ</u> as "tell the good news about Christ."

<u>Because they are jealous and quarrelsome</u> (literally, "on account of envy and strife") explains the motives of the preachers (NAB "from the motives of envy and rivalry"; NEB "in a jealous and quarrelsome spirit"). One may find it necessary to indicate the so-called "object" of <u>jealous</u>, in which case it is probably best to say "because they are jealous of me." Yet one must be cautious in the use of a term such as "jealous," for it may imply meanings which do not fit this context. Hence one may need to use such an expression as "they are unhappy because of what I have been able to do," or "they are envious because of my success." <u>Quarrelsome</u> may be rendered as "they quarrel with others," "they habitually quarrel with people," or "they quarrel with me." In some languages "to quarrel" is "to fight with words."

The meaning of the biblical word translated <u>good will</u> varies greatly according to the context. It is used of God's "choice and pleasure" in Matt 11.26; Luke 10.21; and Eph 1.5. It is sometimes used in the sense of a person's "wish" or "desire" (e.g. Rom 10.1). In the present context it means "good will" or, as JB renders it, "right intention" (Phps "good faith"). It is possible that the meaning here refers to good will toward Paul, since Paul is speaking of the preachers' attitude toward him in the context. "Good will" toward the gospel which he proclaims is, of course, presupposed.

If <u>good will</u> is understood to refer to the attitude of these preachers toward the gospel, then one may translate <u>from genuine good will</u> as "because they like the gospel," or "because they are fully in favor of the gospel." Similarly, if one understands that the good will is directed toward Paul, one may translate "because they are favorably disposed toward me." One may, however, wish to emphasize, in rendering <u>good will</u>, the concept of "right intentions," in which case one may translate <u>from genuine good will</u> as "because their purposes are altogether good," or "because what they want to accomplish is perfectly right."

1.16   These do so from love, because they know that God has given me the work of defending the gospel.

KJV follows the Received Text in reversing the order of verses 16 and 17. This change seems to have been made to conform the text to the order of the two classes of preachers mentioned in verse 15; but the change is

[23]

not supported by the best textual witness, and it is not followed in most translations. The authentic text has a chiastic (crisscross) order; that is, verse 16 discusses what is mentioned in verse 15b, and verse 17 refers to the content of verse 15a.

These do so from love is literally "the ones on the one hand out of love." Paul does not say for whom. One possibility is "out of love for him," meaning Christ (so German common language translation [GeCL]). The context indicates, however, that love is directed to the apostle, for he is dealing with the influence of his imprisonment on the preaching of the gospel. Mft translates explicitly "the latter do it from love to me" (NEB "moved by love for me"; Phps "out of their love for me").

In rendering these do so from love, it is important to make certain that these points to the last mentioned group, namely, the others who preached Christ from genuine good will. It may be necessary to say "these latter do so from love."

TEV renders a Greek causative participle by a finite verb: because they know (Gpd Phps "for they know"; Knox "because they recognize").

God has given me the work translates a single Greek verb which literally means "I recline" or "I am set" (Barclay [Brc] "I am lying in prison"). It is a military term describing a soldier posted as a sentinel (Bruce "I am posed here"), but the term can also be used figuratively with the meaning of "to be appointed" or "to be chosen" (cf. Luke 2.34). The appointment to defend the gospel comes from God, and TEV makes this fact explicit: God has given me the work. If this interpretation is adopted, the word defending may have the sense of "vindicating."

God has given me the work implies that God had assigned the particular work to Paul by way of a direct command. It may be appropriate to indicate this in some languages in the form of direct discourse, for example, "God has said to me, This is your work," or "God said to me, Your work is to defend the good news."

As in verse 7, of defending the gospel may be rendered as "to show that the good news is true," or "to prove that the good news is right."

1.17   The others do not proclaim Christ sincerely, but from a spirit of selfish ambition; they think that they will make more trouble for me while I am in prison.

TEV restructures this sentence to present the thoughts in a more logical order and to make the contrast with the previous verse more apparent. The others refers to the preachers mentioned in verse 15a (RSV; Bruce "the former"). This phrase must be rendered in a way that will show clearly that it refers to those who preached Christ out of jealousy and quarrelsomeness.

It may be possible in some languages to use such an expression as "the former," but frequently one must repeat part of the identifying elements in verse 15, for example, "the others, who are jealous, do not proclaim Christ sincerely."

Not ... sincerely is literally "not purely," in the sense of "from mixed motives" (NEB). The translator must make certain that the negative not qualifies the sincerity with which the preaching is done. A literal rendering of the others do not proclaim Christ sincerely may suggest that they do not proclaim Christ at all. Those persons did, in fact, proclaim Christ, but they did not do so with pure motives. One must often translate the first part of verse 17 as "the others proclaim Christ, but they do not do so sincerely." Not ... sincerely may be rendered in some instances as "with bad motives," "but what they want to accomplish is not right," or "but their purposes are personal." This meaning is brought out more clearly in the phrase which follows; from a spirit of selfish ambition is an amplification of not ... sincerely.

From a spirit of selfish ambition is literally "out of partisanship." The word "partisanship" originally meant "working for pay." Since a man who works solely for pay works from a low motive, the term later acquired a bad sense – describing a person who serves in an official position for his own selfish purposes and to that end creates a "partisan spirit" (Phps; Mft "for their own ends"). From a spirit of selfish ambition may be rendered as "because they simply want things for themselves," "because they themselves want to get ahead," or "because they want to surpass."

TEV changes a participle with a force of purpose into a finite verb, they think (Mft "intending"; Phps "hoping"; NEB "meaning"; Gpd "imagining"). The word translated think occurs only here in the Pauline letters. It connotes the sense of thinking with a purpose which is based on wrong judgment or conceit (cf. the context of James 1.7).

They will make more trouble for me translates an infinitive construction meaning literally "to raise up affliction." TEV supplies for me, making explicit the goal of their malicious action (NEB "meaning to stir up fresh trouble for me"). They will make more trouble for me is clearly causative, and the closest natural equivalent, in many instances, is "they will cause me to suffer more," or "they will cause me to have more difficulties."

Since while I am in prison refers to Paul's condition at the time, it may be useful to add an adverbial expression such as "here," for example, "while I am here in prison."

TEV	RSV
18 It does not matter! I am happy about it—just so Christ is preached in every way possible, whether from wrong or right motives. And I will continue to be happy, 19 because I know that by means of your prayers and the help which comes from the Spirit of Jesus Christ I shall be set free. 20 My deep desire and hope is that I shall never fail in my duty, but that at all times, and especially right now, I shall be full of courage, so that with my whole being I shall bring honor to Christ, whether I live or die. 21 For what is life? To me, it is Christ. Death, then, will bring more. 22 But if by continuing to live I can do more worthwhile work, then I am not sure which I should choose. 23 I am pulled in two directions. I want very much to leave this life and be with Christ, which is a far better thing; 24 but for your sake it is much more important that I remain alive. 25 I am sure of this, and so I know that I will stay. I will stay on with you all, to add to your progress and joy in the faith, 26 so that when I am with you again, you will have even more reason to be proud of me in your life in union with Christ Jesus. (1.18-26)	18 What then? Only that in every way, whether in pretense or in truth, Christ is proclaimed; and in that I rejoice. 19 Yes, and I shall rejoice. For I know that through your prayers and the help of the Spirit of Jesus Christ this will turn out for my deliverance, 20 as it is my eager expectation and hope that I shall not be at all ashamed, but that with full courage now as always Christ will be honored in my body, whether by life or by death. 21 For me to live is Christ, and to die is gain. 22 If it is to be life in the flesh, that means fruitful labor for me. Yet which I shall choose I cannot tell. 23 I am hard pressed between the two. My desire is to depart and be with Christ, for that is far better. 24 But to remain in the flesh is more necessary on your account. 25 Convinced of this, I know that I shall remain and continue with you all, for your progress and joy in the faith, 26 so that in me you may have ample cause to glory in Christ Jesus, because of my coming to you again. (1.18-26)

Paul here describes the attitudes of others, both those who are for him and those who are against him. Now he proceeds, with serene nobility, to speak of his reactions to all of them.

1.18   It does not matter! I am happy about it—just so Christ is preached in every way possible, whether from wrong or right motives. And I will continue to be happy,

Some translations interpret this verse as a summary of the author's reaction to the situation described in verses 12-17, and so include it in the preceding paragraph (so Mft). It is, however, awkward to begin a new paragraph with verse 19. As the particle "for" at the beginning of verse 19 clearly indicates, the verse is meant to explain what is said in verse 18b. For this reason a number of translations introduce a new paragraph at verse 18b (so Spanish common language translation [SpCL], New International Version [NIV]; RSV also begins a new paragraph here, but makes it a part of verse 19). However, the author's style in repeating the note of "joy" makes the break at verse 18b unlikely. A third possibility is to introduce a new paragraph at the beginning of verse 18. It does not matter! then would serve both as a summary of Paul's reaction to what is said in verses 15-17 and as a transition to what comes after. This interpretation, which is favored by a greater number of translations (so Gpd TEV GeCL French common language translation [FrCL] NAB), is probably the one to be preferred.

Paul will not allow himself to be troubled by those preachers who proclaim Christ from impure motives and in open hostility toward him. In Greek the verse begins with a rhetorical question without supplying an answer, literally, "What then?" (Gpd "What difference does it make?"). The TEV rendering It does not matter! is an explicit answer to what is already implicit both in the context and in the question.

The significance of the pronoun it in It does not matter! may be obscure if this sentence is rendered literally into another language. One may find it preferable to render the sentence as "What they want to do to me does not matter," "What they are doing does not really concern me," or "...cause me anxiety." Similarly, I am happy about it may be rendered as "I am happy about what has happened."

In this verse the verb translated happy (RSV "rejoice") occurs twice. In some translations the two verbs are separated only by a comma (ASV "and therein I rejoice, yea, and will rejoice"; cf. KJV), making the second clause an echo of the first. But most modern translations put a full stop (NAB Phps Gpd) after the first instance of the verb and a comma after the second, thus connecting the second half of the sentence with verse 19. RSV and NEB rearrange the location of the verse numbers and make the second "happy" clause part of verse 19. TEV offers yet another alternative; it moves the first "happy" clause to the beginning of the sentence, thus completely separating it from the second "happy" clause.

I am happy about it, that is, about the fact that Christ is being proclaimed regardless of motives. Just so has the sense of "the one thing that really matters is," or "my only concern is" (Gpd "all that matters is"; Bruce "this is all that matters").

Expressions for joy or happiness frequently require elaborate idiomatic structures. I am happy may, for example, be rendered in some languages as "my abdomen is sweet," "my insides are cool," or "I dance within."

Since what does matter for Paul is that Christ is preached in every way possible, it may be important in some languages to relate this statement more closely to the initial negative statement, It does not matter! For example, one may render verse 18 as "What they are doing to cause me trouble is not important. What is important is that Christ is preached in every way possible, regardless of whether men's purposes are wrong or right. That Christ is preached is what causes me to be happy, and I will continue to be happy."

Whether from right or wrong motives (literally, "whether in pretense or in truth") further expands and defines in every way possible. The word rendered "pretense" in some translations is a noun meaning "ostensible (usually insincere) reason." Paul is not suggesting here that the preachers do not really believe what they preach, but rather that they use the name of Christ as a cover or pretext for selfish ends; thus they have wrong... motives (JB "dishonest motives"; cf. Mark 12.40; Acts 27.30). The Greek expression rendered as right motives in TEV is translated by Mft as "honestly" and in NEB as "sincerely." Whether from wrong or right motives may require considerable expansion, especially in languages where motives must be expressed by a verbal form, for example, "whether what they want is right or wrong," "whether what they expect to gain from such preaching is right or wrong," or "whether they are preaching for the sake of Christ or only for their own sake."

Paul is assured that the future will bring fresh reasons for happiness: And I will continue to be happy (future tense in Greek). The reason is given in verse 19. And here has the force of "yes" (RSV NEB Phps) or "indeed" (NAB).

1.19   because I know that by means of your prayers and the help which comes from the Spirit of Jesus Christ I shall be set free.

I know here has the force of "know for sure" or "know well" (NEB "knowing well").

The help which comes from the Spirit of Jesus Christ is literally "the supply of the Spirit of Jesus Christ." There are two genitive constructions here, and their meaning may be explained in a variety of ways. The first one, "the supply of the Spirit," can be taken as an objective genitive, making the Spirit that which is given (so Mft "as I am provided with the Spirit of Jesus Christ" and NEB "the Spirit of Jesus Christ is given me for support"). Another possibility, which appears to suit the context better, is to take the construction as a subjective genitive. In this case, the Spirit would be the giver, thus "the help which the Spirit of Jesus Christ gives," or, as TEV renders it, the help which comes from the Spirit of Jesus Christ (cf. NEB alternative rendering "the Spirit of Jesus Christ supplies me with all I need").

The second genitive construction, "the Spirit of Jesus Christ," occurs only here in the New Testament. Some take the phrase as in apposition, meaning "the Spirit, which is Jesus Christ." This interpretation does not seem to fit the context well. Others take it to mean "the Spirit that is promised or given by Jesus Christ" (cf. Mark 13.11; Luke 12.12; John 16.7). However, in the Pauline letters the Spirit is usually said to be given by God the Father (cf. 1 Cor 6.19; 2 Cor 1.22; 5.5; Eph 1.17; Gal 3.5; 1 Thes 4.8). We are left, then, with another possibility. Just as the Holy Spirit is referred to as "the Spirit of Christ" (Rom 8.9; cf. 1 Peter 1.11) and "the Spirit of his Son" (Gal 4.6), it may well be that the expression is used in this context simply as another name for the Holy Spirit.

Help translates a Greek word which means "rich provision" (cf. Phps "resources").

Your prayers and the help which comes from the Spirit of Jesus Christ are essentially the means by which Paul is set free. This relation may be expressed in some languages as cause, for example, "your prayers and the help which comes from the Spirit of Jesus Christ will cause me to be set free." In other languages it may be indicated as "because of your prayers and because of the help which comes from the Spirit of Jesus Christ, I shall be made free."

I shall be set free is literally "this to me shall turn out to be salvation." The exact meaning or reference of the term "salvation" in this context is debated. Some take it in its fullest sense, that is, final salvation in the Day of Christ. Others interpret it in the general sense of a person's total well-being (Gpd "highest welfare"; Knox "soul's health"; Phps "good of my own soul"). Still others maintain, on the basis of the Septuagint of Job 13.16 which Paul apparently quotes, that the reference is to the ultimate vindication of the apostle's stand for Christ. In view of Paul's prospect of seeing his Christian friends again (see v. 26 and 2.24), the TEV rendering, which favors this interpretation, seems preferable. Paul is thinking of his vindication and the resulting release from prison (Mft "the outcome of all this, I know, will be my release"). NEB employs the more generic term "deliverance," which could cover all the interpretations.

I shall be set free may be rendered as "I shall be delivered," or "I shall be untied." In some languages an active expression is required, often with a kind of indefinite subject, for example, "men shall cause me to be free," or "men shall unbind me."

1.20   My deep desire and hope is that I shall never fail in my duty, but that at all times, and especially right now, I shall be full of courage, so that with my whole being I shall bring honor to Christ, whether I live or die.

Deep desire translates a vivid Greek word meaning "waiting or watching with outstretched head," indicating an intense desire or eager expectation to catch sight of someone or something (cf. Rom 8.19). Since deep

[29]

desire and hope are bound together by one article, NEB takes the two nouns as a reference to one event, and so translates "I passionately hope." Only rarely can one translate deep desire literally. In some languages it is possible to speak of "great desire," and one may often use a verbal expression such as "I desire very much." If desire and hope are seen as being essentially a single expression of emotion, one may translate "I hope with all my heart."

I shall never fail in my duty is a straightforward rendering of the literal "in nothing shall I be ashamed" (KJV). JB brings out the apostle's confidence by rendering "I shall never have to admit defeat." Any failure to stand firm in loyalty to Christ would, for Paul, be "shame." A literal translation of "in nothing shall I be ashamed" may present serious difficulties in some languages, since "ashamed" may suggest certain connotations which would not fit this particular context. Accordingly, I shall never fail in my duty provides a more satisfactory basis for a dynamic equivalence of the Greek expression. However, it may be more satisfactory to express the goal of Paul's desire and hope in a positive rather than a negative way, for example, "that I shall always do what I should," or "...do what is right for me." If the negative expression I shall never fail in my duty is transformed into a positive expression "shall always do what I should," the following conjunction but must be changed to "and."

At all times, and especially right now is more vivid than a more literal "as always, so now" (Mft "that now as ever"). And especially right now seems to imply that the time of crisis is very near. I shall be full of courage translates a prepositional phrase, "with all boldness." The dominant idea is boldness or confidence in speaking openly; hence NEB has "shall speak so boldly" (cf. 2 Cor 3.12; Eph 6.19; 1 Thes 2.2). Rarely can one translate literally I shall be full of courage. One can often say "I shall be very courageous," but in some instances a translator may find it more useful to retain the figure of speech suggested by the Greek text, that is, "I shall speak up boldly," or "I shall speak without fear of anyone."

The literal meaning of the phrase rendered with my whole being is "in my body." A number of other translations understand the expression in the same sense as TEV (NEB "in my person"; Mft "in my own person"; Phps "the way I live"). It refers to the apostle's total person, which was always at the Lord's disposal (1 Cor 6.19-20), whether in life or in death (Rom 14.8). It may be rendered as "in everything that I do," "by means of all that I do," or even "in everything that I say and do."

I shall bring honor to Christ is a restructuring of a passive construction, "Christ will be magnified." Some translators retain the original Greek form on the ground that Paul deliberately shrinks from making himself the primary agent. But a literal translation of the sentence structure is rather clumsy in most languages. I shall bring honor to Christ is essentially a causative construction; that is, Paul will cause people to honor Christ. It may be useful to restructure the clause in a way that will indicate this fact clearly, for example, "I shall cause people to honor Christ." In some languages "to honor" may be expressed as "to recognize as great." Therefore the entire expression may be translated as "I shall cause people to recognize Christ as being great."

Whether I live or die is rather loosely attached to what immediately precedes. The connection may be expressed in some languages as "it makes no difference whether I continue to live or whether I die." In other cases one may express the connection by "I shall cause people to honor Christ, either by what I do as I continue to live, or by my dying," or ". . . by my being killed."

1.21   For what is life? To me, it is Christ. Death, then, will bring more.

The mention of life and death in the preceding verse leads the apostle to state what these things mean to him. TEV restructures the whole verse, making the apostle pose a rhetorical question and then answer it. Life translates a Greek verb meaning "to live." The verb is in the present tense, denoting the process of continuous living, not the principle of life (cf. Rom 8.12; 2 Cor 1.8).

To me is emphatic in the Greek text. It has the force of "according to my own experience" (Gpd "as I see it"). The rhetorical question what is life? may be rendered more explicitly "what does it mean to live?" The question is answered by it is Christ. This phrase is translated by some as "life means Christ" (Knox, Bruce) and by others as "Christ is my life" (Luther, Tyndale). Life to Paul has no meaning apart from Christ. His life is not his own; it is totally devoted to Christ (Gal 2.20). In some languages a literal rendering of this important saying may be wrongly understood as equating me with Christ. To avoid this misconception one may have to render the last clause "it is for Christ," even at the expense of losing some of the impact found in the original Greek.

For what is life? is obviously a rhetorical question. Paul is not asking for information; he is only highlighting the purpose of his own life. This question must be semantically amplified in some languages, for example, "what is the purpose of living?" or "what is to be gained in continuing to live?" It may even be useful to render this question as "what do people live for?" Paul indicates clearly that for him it is Christ. For languages which do not employ rhetorical questions, it may be necessary to recast the question and its answer to read "for the very purpose of my life is Christ." In some languages, however, it would be utterly meaningless to

[31]

say that "life is Christ," but it is usually possible to say "the purpose of my living is to serve Christ."

Death translates a Greek aorist infinitive which denotes the event of dying, not the process. Will bring more translates a single word in Greek, literally "gain." "Death is gain" in two respects. First, it is the gateway to the immediate presence of Christ (v. 23). This would mean gain for the apostle personally (JB "death would bring me something more."). Second and more important, his death by martyrdom would produce the promotion and progress of the gospel. Hence, death would be gain for the proclamation of the gospel; this seems to be what the phrase will bring more is intended to communicate.

In a number of languages one cannot speak of "death bringing something." Since in this context death refers specifically to the possibility of Paul's own death, it may be necessary to render the second part of this verse as "if I die, then, it will be an advantage to me," ". . . I will profit from that," or ". . . it will help spread the good news."

1.22   But if by continuing to live I can do more worthwhile work, then I am not sure which I should choose.

At this point Paul's language becomes rather obscure. He seems to waver between alternatives, unable to reach a decision. The general idea, however, is clear enough. He is weighing the advantages of a continued life on earth against those to be gained by death.

In Greek the verse has three clauses, literally "but (a) if to live in the flesh, (b) this to me fruit of work, (c) and what I shall choose I do not know." The extent of the "if" and "result" clauses is taken differently by various interpreters. TEV and RSV represent two major interpretations: TEV takes (a) and (b) together as the "if" clause and (c) as the "result" (so also JB NEB FrCL Traduction Oecumenique de la Bible [TOB]), whereas RSV has (a) as the "if" clause, (b) as the "result," and (c) as a separate sentence (so also Brc NIV cf. NAB).

It is generally agreed among commentators that the "if" clause used here is not really conditional in meaning. Paul assumes that he will survive the ordeal of the trial. "To live" in Greek is a present infinitive, signifying a continuous process of living, as in the preceding verse. "In the flesh" is added to emphasize that natural or physical life is meant. The TEV rendering continuing to live seems to be sufficient to bring out the original thought. One may, of course, follow a more literal translation, such as "living on in the body" (NEB) or "living on in this mortal body" (Knox). One may also stress the idea of cause and means and render this phrase as "because I continue to live," or "by means of my continuing to live."

[32]

The interpretation and translation of the second clause (literally, "this to me fruit of work") is more difficult. There are two major interpretations. (1) According to some interpreters, Paul is saying that he will be able to reap the fruit of the work he has been obliged to leave incomplete because of his imprisonment. Knox obviously favors this interpretation. Giving "if" an interrogative force, he renders the clause "But what if living on in this mortal body is the only way to harvest what I have sown?" Gpd appears also to follow this line of interpretation but phrases it differently: "But if living on here means having my labor bear fruit." (2) According to other interpreters, however, rather than thinking about reaping the harvest of his previous work, Paul is here looking toward more productive or fruitful missionary work in the future. The term "fruit" is thus used in the sense of winning "converts" in Rom 1.13. Work is a term frequently used by Paul to refer to his missionary labor (Rom 15.18; 2 Cor 10.11; Phil 2.30). TEV prefers the latter interpretation. By combining the two clauses and making "I" the subject, TEV thus has but if by continuing to live I can do more worthwhile work (cf. JB). To translate this rather obscure sentence in a more general way leaves it almost void of meaning (cf. NEB "but what if my living on in the body may serve some good purpose?"; Phps "for me to go on living in this world may serve some good purpose").

If one adopts the first interpretation outlined in the preceding paragraph, the conditional clause in this verse may be rendered as "but if by my continuing to live I can complete the work I have begun." However, if one assumes the second interpretation (that followed by TEV), it is possible to translate "but if by means of continuing to live I can do further work," or ". . . can accomplish something more."

In the last clause of this verse, Paul declares his inability to decide whether he should choose life or death, literally "and what I shall choose I do not know." The Greek verb translated "I know" usually means "I make known" or "I declare," and some commentators believe it should be translated in that way even in this context; that is, the apostle dares not venture to decide between the alternatives, but the choice must be left to the Lord. This interpretation does not seem necessary, however. The context makes it clear that Paul is faced with a real dilemma. So "I know not" is to be taken in the sense of "I am not sure," or "I cannot tell" (NEB Knox Mft Gpd). It may be difficult to indicate clearly the alternative choices. One may wish to translate the final clause of this verse as "in that case, I am not sure whether I should choose to continue living or to die." It may, however, be necessary to specify that the death anticipated is not a natural death, and therefore one may need to use such a term as "undergo execution" or "be executed."

1.23   I am pulled in two directions. I want very much to leave this life and be with Christ, which is a far better thing;

The Greek verb translated I am pulled is a vivid word picturing a traveler on a narrow road with walls of rock on both sides, unable to turn either way. One can readily imagine the kind of pressure suggested by this verb. Though TEV changes the image from one of pressure or of being hemmed in to one of being torn apart, it still correctly represents the dilemma involved. The same verb is translated in Luke 12.50 as "distressed" (cf. Luke 19.43 "your enemies... close in on you from every side"). In two directions translates "from the two." A number of picturesque expressions are used to translate this verb, for example, "I am hemmed in on both sides" (Knox); "I am torn in two directions" (Phps); "I am caught in this dilemma" (JB). Other possible renderings are "I do not know what direction to turn," or "I want to go in two directions at once."

Paul proceeds to give his personal preference with a participial phrase, literally "having the desire to depart and be with Christ." TEV changes this to a finite statement, I want very much to leave this life and be with Christ. The Greek word translated "desire" is sometimes used in the bad sense of "lust," "passion," or "covetousness." Here it is used in the sense of "strong desire" (Mft cf. Bruce "great desire"), and it is given a verbal form, I want very much.

The verb translated to leave this life occurs elsewhere only in Luke 12.36. It may have a military sense of breaking up an encampment or a nautical sense of releasing a vessel from its moorings. It is often used as a euphemism for death.

To leave this life and to... be with Christ are closely connected. These two infinitives have only one article in the Greek. Apparently Paul is thinking of an immediate union with Christ directly after death (cf. 2 Cor 5.6, 8; Luke 23.43). Elsewhere Paul describes death as sleep from which the believers will arise to be with Christ at his return (cf. 1 Cor 15.51-52; 1 Thes 4.13-17).

It is seldom possible to translate literally to leave this life. A more satisfactory rendering is normally "to die," though in some languages it may prove more satisfactory to translate "to not continue to live."

There is a subtle problem involved in rendering the phrase be with Christ. Since this is associated with a previous expression for dying, readers might assume that what is meant is that Paul wishes to die and thus be with Christ in the state of death. To avoid this implication, it may be necessary to translate "I want very much to stop living here in this world, and to live with Christ."

A far better thing is a triple comparative used by Paul to express the superior excellence of being with Christ, literally "much rather better" (Knox "a better thing, much more than a better thing"). Which is a far better thing must be clearly specified in some languages as being related directly to Paul's experience, for example, "this would be far better for me," or "which would be to my advantage."

1.24 **but for your sake it is much more important that I remain alive.**

In this verse Paul states the other side of the dilemma. But here has the force of "on the other hand" (Phps Bruce).

The Greek comparative translated it is much more important can also be rendered "it is more urgent" (NAB cf. JB Knox), "it is probably more necessary" (Phps), or "there is greater need" (NEB). I remain alive represents a Greek expression which is literally "to remain in the flesh." Obviously, "to remain in the flesh" in this context does not mean "to live in sin" (cf. Rom 7.5, 18).

For your sake may be expressed in some cases as "in order to help you." This may be combined with the rest of the verse as "but in order to help you, it is much more important that I remain alive," or ". . . continue to live."

1.25 **I am sure of this, and so I know that I will stay. I will stay on with you all, to add to your progress and joy in the faith,**

Verses 25 and 26 form one sentence in Greek, but TEV breaks it into two shorter sentences to produce a clearer rendering. Since in Greek there is no punctuation mark after I am sure of this, it is possible to interpret this phrase in two different ways. (1) It is sometimes taken adverbially to modify the following verb I know, thus with the meaning "of this I am confidently persuaded," or "this I know confidently." NEB appears to favor this interpretation with "this indeed I know for sure." This would then refer to I will stay. (2) However, several translations (TEV RSV Gpd Mft etc.) understand the clause to refer to the preceding verses. That is to say, Paul is sure that to stay alive for his Philippian friends' sake would be his duty if the choice were left to him, because he is convinced that his remaining would be for their good. On the basis of this interpretation, it may be necessary to translate "I am sure that I would choose to continue to live."

I know reflects Paul's personal conviction. This conviction is vividly expressed by employing a play on words. The verb rendered stay on is a compound of the simple verb translated stay. It means to stay or wait beside a person, so as to be ready to help and to serve (NEB "I shall stay,

[35]

and stand by you all to help"; Gpd "I shall stay on and serve you all"). A literal rendering of I will stay on with you all can be misinterpreted, since it may seem to imply that Paul would continue to stay with the Philippians for some period of time. It may therefore be useful to translate this clause as "I will continue to live and to help you all." In a sense, this anticipates the final clause of the verse.

To add to your progress and joy in the faith is literally "into your progress and joy of the faith." Here "into" has the force of to add (Gpd "to help"). Progress and joy share one article, so they should probably be taken closely together with faith. Phps appears to miss the point in taking them to mean two separate ideas: "to help you forward in Christian living and to find increasing joy in your faith." On the other hand, it seems unnecessary to take them so closely together as to merge them into a single idea as Knox does: "happy furtherance." Progress is the same word used in 1.12, but here it applies to the progress of the Philippians' faith. The word faith here stands for experience based on trust in God and on Christ and his redeeming work. For Paul, joy is an indispensable element of that experience.

Despite the close association of progress and joy, it may be necessary to dissociate them in view of their relation to the verb add to and the final purpose, namely, the faith. In the first instance, it may be necessary to translate "so as to cause you to have more and more faith." The final expression, dealing with joy, may then be rendered as "to cause you to have more happiness in your faith," or "...as you trust Christ."

1.26   so that when I am with you again, you will have even more reason to be proud of me in your life in union with Christ Jesus.

So that (or "in order that") marks the ultimate end of Paul's staying on with his Philippian friends. Because of the rather complex relation of the clauses, it may be necessary to introduce verse 26 with a separate sentence, for example, "The purpose of all this is that when I am with you again...," or "I will do this so that when I am with you again ..."

When I am with you again is literally "by means of my coming to you again." "Coming" is the very word which Paul uses of the coming of Christ at the day of judgment (1 Cor 15.23; 1 Thes 2.19; 3.13; 4.15; 5.23; 2 Thes 2.1, 8). In this context it refers to Paul's visiting again with his friends (Knox "when I come once again to visit you"; Phps "when I come to see you again").

Since the Greek here is somewhat obscure (literally, "that your pride may abound in Christ Jesus in me"), interpreters differ as to whether Christ or Paul is the object of "pride." Some translators understand the object to be Christ: "so that in me you may have ample cause to glory in Christ Jesus" (RSV); "and so you will have another reason to give praise to Christ Jesus on my account" (JB); "thus you will have ample cause to glory in Christ Jesus over me" (Mft). Others, however, regard the immediate cause of pride as being Paul himself. This is the position taken by TEV: you will have even more reason to be proud of me (NEB "your pride in me may be unbounded"; cf. Gpd Phps). If one follows the first interpretation, one may translate "in this way you will have every reason to honor Christ Jesus," or ". . . give praise to Christ Jesus." If, on the other hand, one follows the second interpretation, the rendering may be "you will have even more reason to be proud because of what I have done."

In your life in union with Christ Jesus is an attempt to bring out the meaning of a characteristic Pauline expression, "in Christ Jesus" (cf. 1.1). Even a glance at various translations will show how difficult it is to translate this formula adequately. Gpd makes it an adjectival expression, "Christian exultation." Phps takes it to mean "as your minister in Christ." Apparently Paul is saying that the Philippian Christians' pride in him is developed in the sphere of Christ Jesus. The basic meaning is one's intimate union or fellowship with Christ.

It is not easy to relate clearly the expression in your life in union with Christ Jesus to what precedes. Furthermore, in many languages life must be expressed by a verb. Therefore, the final phrase may be rendered in some languages as "as you live your life joined to Christ Jesus," or ". . . as one with Christ Jesus."

TEV

27 Now, the important thing is that your way of life should be as the gospel of Christ requires, so that, whether or not I am able to go and see you, I will hear that you are standing firm with one common purpose and that with only one desire you are fighting together for the faith of the gospel. 28 Don't be afraid of your enemies; always be courageous, and this will prove to them that they will lose and that you will win, because it is God who gives you the victory. 29 For you have been given the privilege of serving Christ, not only by believing in him, but also by suffering for him. 30 Now you can take part with me in the battle. It is the same battle you saw me fighting in the past, and as you hear, the one I am fighting still. (1.27-30)

RSV

27 Only let your manner of life be worthy of the gospel of Christ, so that whether I come and see you or am absent, I may hear of you that you stand firm in one spirit, with one mind striving side by side for the faith of the gospel, 28 and not frightened in anything by your opponents. This is a clear omen to them of their destruction, but of your salvation, and that from God. 29 For it has been granted to you that for the sake of Christ you should not only believe in him but also suffer for his sake, 30 engaged in the same conflict which you saw and now hear to be mine. (1.27-30)

1.27

Paul now gives some practical exhortations. He urges his readers to stand firm with one common purpose and to fight together for the gospel. Verses 27-30 constitute one sentence in Greek. Most recent translations break it into several shorter sentences and so attempt to make Paul's meaning more comprehensible.

1.27   Now, the important thing is that your way of life should be as the gospel of Christ requires, so that, whether or not I am able to go and see you, I will hear that you are standing firm with one common purpose and that with only one desire you are fighting together for the faith of the gospel.

Now, the important thing is is an idiomatic equivalent of a single word in Greek (literally, "only"). This clause also serves to bring out the emphatic nature of the imperative statement which follows (Bruce "see to it that"; Phps "make sure that"; Knox "you must"). The adverb now should not be understood merely in a temporal sense. Rather, it serves as a transition from what is said in the preceding verses to the implications which must be drawn from it. In some languages an appropriate transitional would be "and so accordingly the important thing is . . . ," or "and so what is important is that . . . ."

Your way of life should be translates a Greek verb which means literally "behave as citizens." Elsewhere in the New Testament the verb occurs only in Acts 23.1. The verb originally meant "to live the life of a citizen" or "to live as a member of a community." Later it came to be applied to all moral conduct within a community. Paul usually uses another Greek word (meaning literally "to walk about") for Christian conduct (e.g. Eph 4.1; Col 1.10; 1 Thes 2.12). He uses a more distinctive term here probably to emphasize his Philippian friends' mutual duties as members of a local Christian community. Your way of life may be rendered as "the way in which you live," "how you behave," or simply "what you do."

As the gospel of Christ requires is literally "be worthy of the gospel of Christ." The gospel of Christ is best taken objectively, meaning "the good news about Christ" (1 Cor 9.12; 2 Cor 2.12; 1 Thes 3.2). It may be awkward in some languages to speak of "the gospel requiring" anything. Only people can be said to require certain kinds of behavior. However, it may be possible to say "as the gospel about Christ says you should live." One may then translate this rather complex relation as "what is important is that you live in the way that the good news about Christ says you should live," or ". . . that you live in accordance with the demands in the good news about Christ."

[38]

There is no doubt that so that should go with I will hear that you are standing firm etc., with the clause whether or not ... introduced between the two elements.

Whether or not I am able to go and see you translates a Greek phrase with three participles (literally "whether coming and seeing you or remaining absent"). Because of the somewhat irregular construction in the Greek, some commentators suggest an emendation. They would change the finite verb I will hear into a participle and link it with the third participle in the series ("remaining absent"), which they would take adverbially. This suggestion is followed by some translators, for example, "whether I come and see you for myself or hear about you from a distance" (NEB); "whether I come and see for myself, or stay at a distance and only hear about you" (JB cf. NAB Phps Knox Gpd). If this emendation is followed, one has to supply a finite verb, such as "I may know" or "I may learn," for the following clause. The meaning seems quite clear, however, even without the emendation (cf. TEV RSV).

A translator may find it particularly difficult to embed the clause whether or not I am able to go and see you within the purpose clause introduced by so that. Accordingly, it may be better to continue with the purpose clause and then reintroduce certain aspects of that clause in order to relate it more clearly to the conditional expression introduced by whether, for example, "so that I will hear that you stand firm ... ; I want to hear that whether or not I am able to go and see you." In some languages there is no convenient way of indicating succinctly a positive or negative condition such as may be introduced in English by "whether or not." The closest equivalent may simply be "if I am able to go see you, that is fine; and if not, that is also fine," or "if I am able, or if I am not able, to go see you ...."

I will hear is literally "I may hear the things concerning you," but since the details of "the things" are mentioned in the following clause, this phrase is omitted in TEV. The basic meaning of the verb translated are standing firm is simply "to stand" (Mark 3.31; 11.25), but in Pauline contexts it usually has the added component of firmness (2 Thes 2.15; 1 Cor 16.13). The metaphor could be that of soldiers standing firm in battle or of condemned believers fighting for their lives in a Roman amphitheater (Eph 6.13; 1 Cor 4.9). In a number of languages the positive idiom "to stand firm" must be expressed negatively as "not to be moved," "not to change," or "not to give up."

With one common purpose is literally "in one spirit" (RSV). It is sometimes argued that Paul is here referring to the divine Spirit. But the context seems to indicate clearly that the united purpose of the Philippian Christians is meant (NEB "one in spirit"; Knox "common unity of spirit";

JB "unanimous"). With one common purpose may be expressed in some languages as "by all intending the same way," "by all of you having the same goal in mind," or "by all of you wanting to do the same." With one common purpose is essentially equivalent to with only one desire.

The order of the Greek allows some ambiguity in the phrase with only one desire (literally "one soul"). It can be interpreted as in apposition with the "one spirit" which immediately precedes it (so NEB "one in spirit, one in mind" and Gpd "with one spirit, one purpose"), or it can be interpreted as modifying the following participle fighting together. TEV chooses the latter alternative and clarifies its choice by supplying and that. Another means of clarification is used by NAB, which supplies the connective "and" and rearranges the word order ("and exerting yourselves with one accord"). "Spirit" and "soul" are sometimes used almost interchangeably in the New Testament (Luke 1.46-47; John 11.33; Acts 4.32; 1 Cor 16.18). If a distinction must be made, "spirit" would be used of the mind with its activities of thought and reflection, whereas "soul" would be used of the seat of inward feelings, affections, passions, and desires. The term "soul" in this context is rendered in various fashions by various translators: NEB "one in mind"; Mft "like one man"; Bruce NAB "with one accord" (cf. JB "united by your love").

You are fighting together translates a Greek participle which means literally "striving together with." The compound verb used here is used elsewhere only in 4.3. The simple verb, from which the word "athletics" is derived, occurs in 2 Tim 2.5 in the sense of "contesting in the games." The metaphor is taken from an athletic contest or from war. The present context seems to favor the latter. Both Mft and Gpd render the participle as "fighting side by side" (NEB "contending as one man"). In rendering fighting together, it is essential to employ a form which will not suggest "fighting against one another." It may be useful to employ such as expression as "join together in fighting for." In some languages, however, the metaphor of "fighting" would be inappropriate in this type of context. It may be preferable to use such an expression as "to work hard for," or "to put all one's strength in order to help."

The expression the faith of the gospel appears only here in the New Testament. Faith is in the dative case in Greek and this can be taken as an instrumental dative, resulting in the rendering "with the faith of the gospel" (Knox). TEV, however, along with most translations, takes it to be a dative of interest and so renders for the faith of the gospel. The word faith seems to be used here in the semitechnical sense of the content of the gospel (Eph 4.5).

The genitive construction the faith of the gospel can be taken as in
apposition, that is, "the faith which is the gospel." It can also be interpreted as an objective genitive, "the faith in the gospel." It seems better,
however, to take it in the sense of "the faith which is appropriate to the
gospel," or "the faith which is based on the gospel." If it is interpreted
this way, "the gospel" may have an attributive force, thus "the gospel
faith" (NEB). It is important to note that Paul is urging his readers to
fight for "the faith appropriate to the gospel," not for "the gospel which
is believed."

A more or less literal translation of the faith of the gospel leads almost inevitably to a misunderstanding which makes faith essentially equivalent to the good news or the content of the good news. If, however, one
interprets the faith of the gospel in terms of faith which is appropriate to,
or based upon, the gospel, it may be necessary to make the relation quite
explicit, for example, "fight for the kind of trust which results from the
good news," or ". . . the kind of faith which those who believe the good
news have."

1.28   Don't be afraid of your enemies; always be courageous, and
         this will prove to them that they will lose and that you will
         win, because it is God who gives you the victory.

The first clause of this verse, don't be afraid of your enemies, is sometimes connected with the previous sentence (NEB "contending as one man
for the gospel faith, meeting your opponents without so much as a trem-
or"; cf. RSV JB Phps). For the sake of clarity, TEV makes this somewhat
obscure clause (literally, "and not being frightened in anything by your
opponents," cf. RSV) into two clauses: Don't be afraid of your enemies;
always be courageous. The addition of always be courageous makes the
transition to the next clause smoother and more natural. The verb translated be afraid occurs nowhere else in the New Testament. It is used of
the shying of a horse when it is startled (cf. NAB "do not be intimidated
by your enemies"). The enemies are probably the heathen inhabitants at
Philippi, who would use persecution, or the threat of it, to intimidate
the believers.

Some languages have quite distinct terms for various types of enemies. In this verse the term enemies does not refer to enemies in war, but
to those who cause difficulty through persecution. Accordingly, it may be
necessary to indicate clearly the type of enemies involved, for example,
"Don't be afraid of those who are persecuting you," or ". . . those who
are causing you trouble."

Always be courageous may be expressed in some languages in rather idiomatic form, for example, "always have a hard heart," or "do not be afraid to show your faith to those who oppose you." In other languages being courageous is expressed negatively, for example, "do not run away," or "do not wish to hide yourselves."

And this will prove to them that they will lose is literally "which is to them an omen of destruction." The addition of the connective and makes it immediately obvious that this refers to the preceding idea of courageousness. This is a relative pronoun with explanatory force (cf. Eph 3.13; Col 3.5). "Omen" represents a rare Greek word found in the New Testament only here, in Rom 3.25-26, and in 2 Cor 8.24. It signifies a proof based on factual evidence, so it is not simply a "foreshadow" (NAB), but a "sure sign" (NEB JB Gpd) or "clear omen" (Mft RSV). TEV makes it a verbal statement, this will prove.

A literal rendering of this will prove to them may be awkward or even impossible in some receptor languages, since the pronoun this would have to refer to a particular kind of behavior, namely, being courageous. A verb such as "prove" may require a personal agent, and therefore one may sometimes say "by doing this, you will prove to them." In other languages proof may be expressed in terms of convincing, for example, "if you do this, they will be convinced that they will lose."

The verbal statement they will lose translates a Greek noun which means literally "perdition" or "destruction." Some commentators take this to mean the loss of eternal life at the day of judgment. However, since the imagery of war and contest is evident in the context, it is possible to take it in the sense of defeat in war or contest, thus they will lose (so also JB).

You will win renders a Greek noun, meaning "salvation." Here again, the word is often taken to mean the gaining of eternal life at the last judgment. But, in contrast to they will lose, one can interpret the word in the sense of victory in war or contest, thus you will win. You is in an emphatic position in Greek. Paul adds an explanatory phrase: literally, "and this from God." "This" refers to win, and God is the one who makes the winning possible. The phrase is thus rendered explicitly because it is God who gives you the victory.

You will win may be expressed as "you will be victorious," or "you will come out ahead." The rendering of this expression should be in direct contrast to the rendering of the previous clause, they will lose.

It is God who gives you the victory is an expression of causation. God becomes the primary agent, and you experience the victory. Therefore it may be useful to render the expression in some languages as "because God is the one who causes you to be victorious," or "... causes you to win."

1.29   For you have been given the privilege of serving Christ, not only by believing in him, but also by suffering for him.

<u>For you have been given the privilege of serving Christ</u> (literally, "because to you it hath been granted in the behalf of Christ" ASV), can be made into an active statement, as in JB "that he (God) has given you the privilege ...." However, since <u>you</u> is in an emphatic position corresponding to the "you" in verse 28, it is better to keep the original passive structure in the receptor language if it is possible to do so.

The final clause of verse 28 introduces an immediate cause, expressed characteristically in English by the conjunction <u>because</u>. A more remote type of cause is expressed in English by the conjunction <u>for</u>. The clause introduced by <u>because</u> gives a specific reason for the immediately preceding expression <u>you will win</u>. The cause introduced in verse 29 is related to the entire content of verse 28. One might argue that the content of verse 29 is simply the cause of God's giving the believers the victory, but it seems more satisfactory to understand verse 29 as relating to all that has preceded. The relation, however, is of a more general nature. To represent these two levels of causal relations, it is useful to find two different conjunctions in a receptor language which can specify the different degrees of cause and effect relations, just as "because" and "for" do in English. If, however, the receptor language has only one such expression, one can say at the beginning of verse 29: "All this will happen because you have been given the privilege ...."

The verb rendered <u>you have been given</u> (literally, "it has been granted [to you]") is formed on the stem of the noun meaning "grace." It denotes a free, unmerited favor or kindness from God (Eph 4.32; Rom 8.32); therefore it is a <u>privilege</u>. Most recent translations try to make this meaning explicit, for example, "for you have been granted the privilege" (Gpd NEB); "for it is your special privilege ..." (NAB); and "for you have received the privilege of serving Christ" (Brc). "In behalf of Christ" is to be taken in the sense of <u>serving Christ</u> (so also Brc).

In some languages one may wish to change the passive clause <u>you have been given the privilege</u> into an active one, for example, "God has given you the privilege," "God has made it possible for you," "God has been good to you in causing you to," or "... giving you the task of."

<u>Serving Christ</u> may be rendered as "working for Christ" or "helping Christ." This type of expression occurs frequently in the New Testament.

Both believing and suffering are present infinitives in Greek, thus indicating that the privilege of believing Christ and suffering for him is not a once for all action but is continuous.

In rendering not only ... but also, it is important to avoid expressions which would imply direct negation. The relation is strictly additive, rather than what may be called adversative. Accordingly, in many languages one will need to translate "you may serve Christ by believing in him, and you may also serve him by suffering on his behalf." In rendering suffering for him, it is important to avoid the implication of "suffering because of him," that is, because of what Christ has done. The suffering in this context is suffering for the advancement of the cause of Christ.

1.30   Now you can take part with me in the battle. It is the same battle you saw me fighting in the past, and as you hear, the one I am fighting still.

The Greek of this verse is somewhat obscure. It means literally "having the same conflict such as you saw in me, and now hear in me." The participle "having" agrees with "you" of the previous verse; so "you" is the logical subject of the participial clause. The emphasis is on the word "same," and several translations (including TEV) make this fact explicit: now you can take part with me in the battle; "take your part in the same struggle" (Gpd); "you and I are together in the same fight" (JB); "you and I are engaged in the same contest" (NEB). The Greek word translated battle applies originally to athletic contests in the arena, but it is also used of any inward or outward struggle (Col 2.1; 1 Thes 2.2; cf. 1 Tim 6.12; 2 Tim 4.7; Heb 12.1).

As already suggested in connection with the term fighting in verse 27, it may not be possible to preserve the metaphor of battle in verse 30. Sometimes, however, one can speak of "struggle" or "conflict," and in other instances the closest equivalent may be "severe opposition." Since the conflict is essentially one in which Paul is defending the gospel, it may be important to make this aspect more specific. For example, verse 30 may be rendered as "Now you can join me in my struggle to defend the good news. This is the same struggle which you saw me having in the past, and I am continuing in my struggle to defend the good news even as you now hear."

For a smoother connection, TEV repeats the battle (in the battle ... the same battle). The Greek verb rendered you saw is in the aorist tense, referring to incidents in the past. Most translations make this information explicit: you saw me fighting in the past (TEV); "you saw me fighting before" (JB); "you saw how I fought it once" (Knox). The fight to which these words refer is recorded in Acts 16.19-24 (cf. 1 Thes 2.2). Since the

[44]

emphasis is on the same kind of fight which the Philippians are encouraged to engage in, TEV uses the word <u>same</u>.

As you hear ... I am fighting still is literally "now you hear in me." "In me" is to be taken in the sense of "in my person," that is, <u>I am fighting still</u> personally, a reference to Paul's present imprisonment as he awaits trial.

CHAPTER 2

TEV

RSV

Christ's Humility and Greatness

1 Your life in Christ makes you strong, and his love comforts you. You have fellowship with the Spirit,*b* and you have kindness and compassion for one another. 2 I urge you, then, to make me completely happy by having the same thoughts, sharing the same love, and being one in soul and mind. 3 Don't do anything from selfish ambition or from a cheap desire to boast, but be humble toward one another, always considering others better than yourselves. 4 And look out for one another's interests, not just for your own. 5 The attitude you should have is the one that Christ Jesus had:

6 He always had the nature of God,
   but he did not think that by force
   he should try to become*c*
   equal with God.
7 Instead of this, of his own free will he
   gave up all he had,
   and took the nature of a servant.
He became like man
   and appeared in human likeness.
8 He was humble and walked the path
   of obedience all the way to
   death—
   his death on the cross.
9 For this reason God raised him to the
   highest place above
   and gave him the name that is
   greater than any other name.
10 And so, in honor of the name of Jesus
   all beings in heaven, on earth, and
   in the world below*d*
   will fall on their knees,
11 and all will openly proclaim that Jesus
   Christ is Lord,
   to the glory of God the Father.

1 So if there is any encouragement in Christ, any incentive of love, any participation in the Spirit, any affection and sympathy, 2 complete my joy by being of the same mind, having the same love, being in full accord and of one mind. 3 Do nothing from selfishness or conceit, but in humility count others better than yourselves. 4 Let each of you look not only to his own interests, but also to the interests of others. 5 Have this mind among yourselves, which you have in Christ Jesus, 6 who, though he was in the form of God, did not count equality with God a thing to be grasped, 7 but emptied himself, taking the form of a servant,*d* being born in the likeness of men. 8 And being found in human form he humbled himself and became obedient unto death, even death on a cross. 9 Therefore God has highly exalted him and bestowed on him the name which is above every name, 10 that at the name of Jesus every knee should bow, in heaven and on earth and under the earth, 11 and every tongue confess that Jesus Christ is Lord, to the glory of God the Father.

*d*Or *slave*   (2.1-11)

*b*You have fellowship with the Spirit; *or* The Spirit has brought you into fellowship with one another.

*c*become; *or* remain.

*d*WORLD BELOW: *It was thought that the dead continued to exist in a dark world under the ground*

(2.1-11)

It may be very difficult to render the section heading <u>Christ's Humility and Greatness</u> as succinctly as it is rendered in TEV. In some languages one may say "Christ is humble and also great," or "Christ becomes humble and then becomes great"; but such an expression might be taken to imply that in his earthly life Christ was not great. One may prefer, therefore, to use rather different expressions, for example, "Christ became like man, and God raised him to the highest place above." Or one may wish to select from the hymn in verses 6-11 an expression which would characterize the exalted position of Jesus, for example, "All beings will worship Jesus, " or "Christ is the Lord."

In the section of the letter extending from verses 1 to 18, Paul deals with the character of Christian living. First, he makes a moving appeal for unity and humility in a church somewhat beset by internal divisions and rivalries (vv. 1-4). Then he proceeds to point the believers to the supreme example of Christ's humility depicted in what is regarded as the most beautiful hymn of early Christianity (vv. 5-11). Finally, he calls his Philippian friends to shine as lights in the world, which is full of crooked and mean people (vv. 12-18).

Verses 1-4 consist of a single sentence in Greek. In order to clarify the thought, this sentence should be restructured into shorter sentences.

2.1   Your life in Christ makes you strong, and his love comforts you. You have fellowship with the Spirit,^b and you have kindness and compassion for one another.

^bYou have fellowship with the Spirit; *or* The Spirit has brought you into fellowship with one another.

Paul begins the chapter with a series of four conditional clauses which are true to fact. That is, while it is true that in Greek each clause begins with a term corresponding to "if" in English, these "if" clauses are equivalent in force with an affirmative statement. By rendering these clauses literally with "if," one might get the impression that Paul makes this fourfold appeal with an element of doubt; that is contrary to what he means to say. A number of translations attempt to bring out the intended emphasis in the Greek clause structure. Thus Mft begins these clauses with "by all ... by every"; Gpd "by whatever"; NAB "in the sense of." TEV renders these clauses by a series of positive statements, and these are then taken as the sure basis of his appeal in the following verses (cf. Rom 2.17 ff.).

A literal translation of these conditional sentences almost inevitably destroys the personal character which is so much a feature of this letter. It may also make the meaning of the verse extremely obscure. It is therefore desirable to identify all the participants and specify their relationships. A comparison of various translations shows that this task is by no means easy. NEB and JB identify "we" (Paul and his readers) as the principal participants (NEB "if then our common life in Christ..."; JB "if our life in Christ..."; cf. Gpd "in our relation to Christ"). Phps makes "you" (the Philippians) the principal participants and clearly identifies "Christ" as the source of "encouragement and love" ("now if you have known anything of Christ's encouragement and of his reassuring love..."). SpCL goes a step further in consistently making "Christ" the primary agent and participant and "you" (the Philippians) the secondary participants ("if Christ ... if his love ... if his Spirit..."). The pattern in TEV, in the order of primary and secondary participants, is: you—Christ, Christ—you, you—Spirit, and you—you (one another).

The first clause is literally "if there be therefore any encouragement in Christ" (cf. KJV). The formula "in Christ" is rendered in various ways, such as "our life in Christ" (JB), "our common life in Christ" (NEB), "your faith in Christ" (FrCL), and your life in Christ. The noun rendered "encouragement" by most translators can also mean "consolation" (KJV), "comfort" (ASV), or "exhortation" (the sense suggested by many commentators). But the context seems to favor the meaning of "helping," "encouraging," or "strengthening." TEV changes this noun into a verb, makes you strong (cf. NEB "stir the heart").

In many languages it is difficult to translate literally your life in Christ. In the first place, a noun such as life must often be rendered as a verb meaning "to live." But it may make no sense to speak of "living in Christ." The concept of a supernatural being living within a human being (for example, "Christ living in us") is not too difficult to understand, since this can be done by means of Christ's Spirit; but for a person to "live in Christ" may seem utterly meaningless. The closest equivalent in some languages is "your living completely on behalf of Christ," or "your living completely controlled by Christ." It may be equally difficult to relate "your life in Christ" to the concept of "making you strong." In some languages the closest equivalent may be "the fact that Christ commands all that you do in your living makes you strong," "...causes you to be strong," or "your living in such a way as to be controlled completely by Christ causes you to be strong." One must avoid, however, a term such as "strong" which applies only to physical strength. In this type of context, one would wish to use such an expression as "causes you to be courageous," or "causes you to stand firm."

His love comforts you translates the second "if" clause in Greek, which means literally "if any comfort of love" (KJV). It is not likely that "love" here refers to the apostle's love for his friends at Philippi as has sometimes been suggested; rather it is Christ's love. The word meaning "comfort" occurs only here in the New Testament. It can also mean "persuasion" (JB), "consolation" (ASV), and "incentive" (RSV).

His love comforts you poses problems of translation in some receptor languages because "love" in them may occur only as a verb; therefore his love must be translated as "the fact that he loves you." Sometimes one can say "the fact that Christ loves you comforts you." In other languages one may use a passive expression, for example, "you are comforted because Christ loves you." In some languages comforts is expressed negatively as "takes away your anxieties," or "causes you not to worry any longer."

Fellowship with the Spirit is literally "if any fellowship of the Spirit" (KJV). Since the Spirit is without the article in Greek, it is sometimes taken to mean the spiritual gift of love, joy, peace, etc. (NAB "fellowship in spirit"; Bruce "spiritual fellowship"). But most modern translators and commentators take it to be a reference to the Holy Spirit (cf. 2 Cor 13.13). The genitive construction "fellowship of the Spirit" should not be interpreted in the subjective sense of "fellowship made possible by the Spirit" (cf. Brc), but in the objective sense of "participation in the Spirit" (Mft RSV) or fellowship with the Spirit. Both Phps and SpCL render specifically "his Spirit," meaning Christ's Spirit (cf. Rom 8.9b).

In some instances one may translate you have fellowship with the Spirit as "you share with Christ's Spirit," or "you have something in common with Christ's Spirit." In certain languages fellowship is expressed quite idiomatically, for example, "you and Christ's Spirit talk together," "you and Christ's Spirit go hand in hand," or "there is a oneness between you and Christ's Spirit."

The meaning of the last "if" clause in Greek is obscure (literally, "if any bowels and mercies" (KJV). The noun rendered "bowels" occurs also in 1.8, where it is translated heart by TEV. It is regarded collectively as the seat of deep feelings, affections, and passions, and is translated "affection" (Gpd RSV NEB), "tenderness" (JB), "compassion" (NAB), "kindness" (Phps). TEV renders it in a verbal form, have kindness.

The noun rendered "mercies" in KJV signifies the outward expression of deep feelings in compassionate yearnings and actions. It is usually rendered "sympathy" (Gpd RSV JB) or compassion (TEV NEB). On the analogy of Col 3.12, where the two nouns appear together, it is sometimes suggested that they have to be taken together here, with the resultant meaning "affectionate sympathy" or "affectionate tenderness" (so Mft). TEV makes clear that the feelings of kindness and compassion are for one another, that is, among the members of the Philippian church.

You have kindness . . . for one another is better expressed in some languages as "you are kind to one another," or "you are good to one another."

You have ... compassion for one another may be expressed simply in some languages as "you feel for one another," or "you share the same feelings with one another." In some instances this expression of sympathy or compassion must be indicated more explicitly, for example, "you feel sorry for one another when anyone suffers."

2.2   I urge you, then, to make me completely happy by having the same thoughts, sharing the same love, and being one in soul and mind.

TEV supplies I urge you, the sense implied in the imperative "complete" (RSV). Mft and NAB try to bring out the sense of appeal by adding "I pray you" and "I beg you" respectively. Then (cf. JB Bruce) is supplied to make clear that Paul is here basing his urgent appeal on the four statements made in the previous verse. He has no doubt whatever that the things on which he bases his appeal are definite realities in the experience of the Philippian Christians.

To make me completely happy (so also JB) represents a restructuring of the more literal "complete my joy" (RSV). The verb in its original sense means "to make full." This verbal phrase is rendered "give me the utter joy" by Mft and appears in Gpd Knox NEB as "fill up my cup of happiness." Paul's choice of this particular verb indicates that the Philippians are already a source of joy to him (1.4-5; cf. 4.1). Still his joy is incomplete because of disputes among the members of the church. It may not be possible in some languages to speak of being completely happy. One may, however, indicate an extreme degree of happiness by saying "cause me to be very, very happy," or, somewhat idiomatically, "cause my heart truly to sing."

By having the same thoughts is literally "that you think the same thing." "That" here has the force of "so as to," not the usual sense of "in order that." Most translators render this term as by, emphasizing the means of achieving happiness. The verb translated "think" (which also occurs in 1.7; 2.5; twice in 3.15) should not be taken primarily in an intellectual sense; it denotes rather an "inward disposition" or "state of mind" (JB "be united in your convictions"; Brc "by being in perfect harmony of mind").

The expression of means indicated by the preposition by followed by the participial constructions having the same thoughts, sharing the same love, and being one in soul and mind must be expressed in many languages as cause, literally, "because you think the same way ...." In some languages having the same thoughts is expressed as "thinking together," "sharing one another's thoughts," or "having only one set of thoughts."

Sharing the same love (literally, "having the same love" KJV RSV) means the mutual love among the Philippians (JB "united in your love"; NEB "with the same love for one another"). This concept must be expressed in some languages as "loving in the same way," but since in many languages it is essential to indicate the goal of an emotion such as love, it may be necessary to translate "having the same kind of love for one another," or "loving one another in the same way."

And being one in soul and mind literally means "(being) one-souled, thinking the one thing." It is best to take these two expressions (one adjective and one participial phrase) together as TEV and various other translations do. The adjective rendered one in soul occurs here only in the New Testament, but a similar expression appears in 1.27 (rendered with ... one desire by TEV). Paul repeats a thought which appears earlier in the verse in a stronger form, "thinking the *one* thing." Apparently the apostle is concerned to produce among the Philippians a unity in purpose and sentiment (JB "with a common purpose and a common mind"). In some languages the phrase can be rendered "being one in heart and will."

Being one in soul and mind must be radically restructured in certain instances, especially if soul and mind are better expressed as verbs rather than as nouns, for example, "desiring the same thing and thinking precisely the same thing," or "being concerned for the same things and being agreed."

2.3 Don't do anything from selfish ambition or from a cheap desire to boast, but be humble toward one another, always considering others better than yourselves.

In Greek, no verb appears in the first half of this verse, yet the construction (literally, "nothing according to partisanship nor according to vainglory") carries an imperative force (cf. Gal 5.13). On the basis of the preceding verse, some commentators suggest that one should supply the verb "think" or "contemplate," that is, "think nothing" or "contemplate nothing." However, don't do anything or "do nothing" (RSV cf. Phps NAB "never act") seems to bring out the sense more forcefully. From has the sense of "on the principles of," "from motives of" (cf. Phps Brc). The noun rendered selfish ambition has already appeared in 1.17. It describes a desire to do things for selfish purposes which result in creating a partisan spirit. From selfish ambition may be expressed as "simply because you

[51]

want things for yourselves," or "because of what you yourselves desire."

A cheap desire to boast translates a single Greek noun which means "vainglory." It appears only here in the New Testament (the corresponding adjective is used in Gal 5.26, where it is rendered "be proud" by TEV), and suggests a conceit that is groundless (cf. Brc "the conceited desire for empty prestige"). In some languages from a cheap desire to boast may be expressed as "simply because you wish to show off," "because you are so proud of yourselves," or "because you want people to know how great you think you are."

The antidote to a cheap desire to boast is to be humble toward one another (literally, "in lowliness of mind"). "Humility" is one of the most important Christian moral attitudes. The Greek moralists regarded humility as the subservient attitude of a lower-class person, an attitude of abject self-abasement. But in the New Testament, based on the example of Christ (cf. 2.8), humility acquires a positive meaning, connoting the lowly service done by a noble person. Humility before God, a recognition of one's utter dependence on him, leads to humility in one's relations with his fellowmen (1 Peter 5.5-6). One aspect of humility is selflessness. Be humble toward one another is sometimes expressed negatively as "do not be proud of yourselves." In some instances one may introduce a verb of activity and so translate "act toward each other in a humble way," or ". . . as a humble person."

The final phrase of verse 3 defines essentially what humility is, always considering others better than yourselves. In some instances the translation may require an expression of direct discourse, for example, "always think, Others are better than I am." Again, however, the meaning may sometimes be expressed by a negative formulation, for example, "never think that you are better than others are." This particular rendering is really not as strong as the original text would imply.

2.4   And look out for one another's interests, not just for your own.

Just as "humility" is the opposite of "vainglory," so the consideration of others' interests is the antithesis of harboring partisanship to achieve one's selfish ambition (v. 3). Look out for one another's interests, not just for your own restructures a Greek participial phrase with the force of an imperative (literally, "not looking each of you to his own things, but each of you also to the things of others" ASV). NEB also restructures, but in a different manner: "You must look to each other's interest and not merely to your own." The participle translated look out means basically "to look attentively," that is, to fix one's attention on something with deep interest in it (Brc "concentrate"; cf. 2 Cor 4.18; Gal 6.1). There is a danger of translating look out for one another's interests, not just for your own in such a way as to suggest a wrong interpretation. From some translations readers receive the idea that one is to concentrate attention on other people's affairs even to the neglect of his own, and not necessarily for the advantage of the other person, but rather to take advantage of that person. Therefore it may be important to translate this verse as "Be sure to protect the interests of others, and not just your own."

The phrase "each of you to his own things" is sometimes interpreted in a way that brings it into closer harmony with the disposition of humility mentioned in the preceding verse. According to this interpretation, Paul is here speaking of the "good qualities" of others; he is urging his readers to seek out the virtues of their fellow members. Most recent translators, however, understand Paul as urging the Philippian Christians to consider one another's interests (cf. 1 Cor 10.24, 33).

To give greater force to the plea which Paul has just addressed to his readers, he now introduces one of the earliest Christological hymns. This hymn embodies the essence of early Christian faith, the faith which acclaims the humiliation and exaltation of Christ. It powerfully demonstrates that the lordship of Christ was attained only by way of his servanthood. The message is crystal clear: "no cross, no crown." In citing this hymn, Paul's aim is to persuade the Philippians to live a life devoid of discord and personal ambition. They are to live in unity and humility with the model of Christ as their most powerful incentive.

The stately and solemn ring of the words of this hymn are unmistakable even in English translation. The passage has a liturgical style, with its majestic rhythms, balanced clauses, and artful parallelisms. The hymn may be pre-Pauline, since it contains some uncommon words and ideas not found in other Pauline writings. It is best arranged in two stanzas, the first (vv. 6-8) portraying Christ's humiliation, and the second (vv. 9-11), his exaltation.

The background thought in this hymn is debated. Some trace it to Hellenistic myths. It is more likely, however, that the imageries of the creation and rebellion of Adam in Genesis 1—3 and of the Suffering Servant of the Lord in Isaiah 52.13—53.12 contributed most to the author's composition of the hymn. In either case, the hymn is not a piece of speculative theology; it is a dramatic and poetic rendition, proclaiming the obedience and triumph of the historical figure Jesus.

2.5   The attitude you should have is the one that Christ Jesus had:

This verse functions as an introductory formula for the hymn (cf. Eph 5.14; 1 Tim 1.15; 3.16; 2 Tim 2.11).

[53]

The Greek of this verse is somewhat cryptic; it is literally "this you think in you which also in Christ Jesus." "This" does not refer back to what has been said in verses 2-4, but rather introduces what comes after. The verb translated "you think" (which has already appeared in 1.7 and 2.2) connotes more than mere thinking (it is rendered feel by TEV in 1.7). It denotes primarily, not an act of thinking, but a state of mind, an inward disposition. It signifies sympathetic interests and concern, reflecting the action of the "heart" as well as the "head." In this context the verb is best rendered "have the attitude" (TEV Gpd NAB Brc). The mood of the verb is present imperative.

"In you" in this context is best taken in the sense of "among you" or "within your Christian community," not "within you" in the sense of "in your hearts." The exact sense of the clause can best be brought out by restructuring; thus TEV has the attitude you should have is . . . , and NAB "your attitude must be . . . ." Since the action implied in the verb is continuous, the clause can also be translated "the attitude you should always have is . . . ." Brc is even more explicit: "try always to have the same attitude . . ." (cf. GeCL).

The second half of the verse presents translators with two problems. Since the clause is without a verb, the first problem is to determine what verb to supply. One solution is to supply the main verb used in the first part of the verse, that is, "think among yourselves that which also you think in Christ Jesus." The resulting meaning then would be "have among yourselves the disposition which you experience in Christ Jesus," or "adopt toward one another the same attitude you adopt towards Christ Jesus." This interpretation is followed by Mft: "treat one another with the same spirit as you experience in Christ Jesus." Another suggestion is to supply the verb "was," with the resulting meaning "have this mind in you, which was also in Christ Jesus" (cf. KJV ASV). NEB appears to adopt the latter interpretation as an alternative rendering: "have that bearing towards one another which was also found in Christ Jesus." This solution seems to suit the context better.

Closely related to this problem is another: how to interpret the expression "in Christ Jesus." It is argued by several commentators that the regular Pauline sense of "in communion with Christ Jesus," or more specifically "in your Christian fellowship," is the meaning in this context also. Paul would then be urging the Philippian Christians to put into practice in their common life the disposition or attitude (described in vv. 2-4) proper to those who are members of Christ's church.

However, the context seems to indicate that the characteristic Pauline sense of the expression should not be pressed in this particular instance. It is rather to be interpreted in the sense of "that belonged to

Christ Jesus" or, as TEV renders it, that Christ Jesus had (cf. Gpd Brc). With this interpretation, the transition to the Christological hymn becomes natural. Paul is here making an appeal to Christ as the supreme example of humility—an act of utter self-negation. The past tense "Christ Jesus had" is significant, since Christ's attitude of humility is exemplified in his accomplished saving acts. Note that in Greek all the verbs (except verse 11) and participles (except the first) used in the hymn are in the aorist tense. Christians are only called upon to tread the path already trodden by Christ himself (cf. 1 Peter 2.21-25).

In a number of languages the closest equivalent of attitude is "thinking." Therefore verse 5 may be rendered as "You should think the same way that Jesus Christ thought." However, in the hymn which follows more is involved than mere thinking. The emphasis is on what Jesus Christ did, and attitude must be understood in a broader sense than mere thinking. This may be expressed in some languages as "What you do should be the same as what Jesus Christ did."

2.6   He always had the nature of God,
                  but he did not think that by force he should try to become*c*
                  equal with God.

          *c*become; or remain.

The hymn proper begins here.

He always had the nature of God is literally "who, being in the form of God" (KJV ASV). "Who" points to Christ as the subject. The word rendered "being" is not the common Greek word for "being," but it denotes one's essential and unchangeable nature. The participle is either present or imperfect. In either case, it signifies a continuing state, so it is best rendered he always had, or "was his from the first" (NEB).

The Greeks had two separate words for "form," and both are used in the hymn. One denotes an essential form of something which never alters, a form which corresponds to an underlying reality. The other suggests an outward form which may change from time to time and from circumstance to circumstance. The former, which appears in verses 6-7 (elsewhere in the New Testament only in Mark 16.12), is translated nature. The latter, which is used in verse 7 (elsewhere in the New Testament only in 1 Cor 7.31), is rendered likeness. When the author says that Christ existed in the "form of God," he implies that Christ had the nature of God. This is the sense adopted by Gpd "he possessed the nature of God," Mft "he was divine by nature," Phps "who had always been God by nature," and NEB "divine nature was his."

[55]

One must realize that in a poetic passage like this a precise metaphysical sense cannot be pressed. To say he always had the nature of God is not equivalent to saying that "Christ is God" or that "Christ is of one substance with God." Similarly he . . . took the nature of a servant (v. 7) does not imply that Jesus was basically only a "servant." Here nature should be taken in the general sense of "one's inherent character or quality" which is manifested and expressed in actions. And so it is in Jesus' humble and obedient ministry that the early church sees God himself working.

In a number of languages there is no abstract term such as nature. The closest equivalent would be an expression of "likeness," and therefore the first line of this hymn may be rendered as "He has always been just like God." One must obviously avoid an expression which would be equivalent to saying "He has always been God himself."

The meaning of by force he should try to become is to some extent conditioned by the next phrase equal with God. It is therefore best to consider the meaning of the latter expression first. Equal with God is probably better taken in the sense of "to exist in a manner equal to God." The structure of the hymn (synonymous parallelism, cf. v. 7) suggests that "equality with God" is closely related in meaning to "having the nature of God," though not necessarily identical. The former is a natural accompanying consequence of the latter. By virtue of the fact that Christ had the nature of God, he naturally had the divine prerogative, that is, a unique privileged status in relation to God. Both expressions signify Christ's unparalleled affinity with God. The primary focus of had the nature of God is in Christ's sharing God's "inherent character and quality," while the emphasis in equal with God is to the relation with God's "rank" or "status." Taken in this sense, "equality with God" is not a reference to equality of attributes or powers, nor is it alluding to a higher dignity which Christ could achieve in the future; it is an honored status Christ already had.

The Greek word rendered by force he should try to become is a noun which appears only here in the New Testament and which occurs only rarely in Greek literature. Because of its rarity, its meaning has been debated. The form of the noun suggests an active meaning. It is so understood by KJV ("thought it not robbery to be equal with God"). From this point of view, Christ did not regard his claim to equality with God as something unlawful; it was something rightfully his. But this interpretation does not seem to be suitable in the context. The general consensus of scholarly opinion is that the noun should be taken in a passive sense. Three possible meanings have been suggested:

1. It can mean "a prize to be seized." This is the meaning adopted by TEV (so also RSV "did not count equality with God a thing to be

grasped," NEB "he did not think to snatch at equality with God," NAB "he did not deem equality with God something to be grasped at"). On this understanding, "equality with God" is not something already possessed by Christ. He declined to do what he could have done.

2. It can also mean "a prize to be held tight." This is the sense favored by JB "yet he did not cling to his equality with God," and Brc "but he did not regard his equality to God as a thing to be clutched to himself" (cf. the alternative renderings of TEV and NEB). The implication is that "equality with God" is something which Christ already possessed and which he might have held on to, but he resolved not to do so. This interpretation appears to suit the context better, for it is difficult to conceive that Christ could have given up what he did not have (cf. v. 7).

3. Another meaning has much to commend itself in this context; that is "a lucky find," "a piece of good fortune." The sense is that Christ held a privileged status which could open up the future possibility of advantage, but he refused to utilize this status or to exploit his privileges. This interpretation also implies that "equality with God" is something Christ already had, but it has the added advantage of giving full value to the basic sense of the noun "snatching" instead of "holding." If this interpretation is adopted, the phrase can be rendered "he did not utilize equality with God as a gain to be exploited," or "he did not exploit equality with God for his own advantage" (Bruce).

In order to distinguish clearly between the nature of God and equal with God, it may be necessary to speak of the first as "being just like God," and of the second as "ranking as high as God." In other languages equality may be expressed idiomatically as "sitting on God's feet," "standing as high as God," or "having God's own power."

2.7   Instead of this, of his own free will he gave up all he had,
          and took the nature of a servant.
        He became like man
          and appeared in human likeness.

Instead of this, of his own free will he gave up all he had is literally "but emptied himself." "Himself" in Greek is emphatic by position, indicating that it was his own doing, so TEV makes this explicit: of his own free will. This may be expressed in some languages as "he was happy to . . . ," "he was glad to . . . ," or "he was willing to give up all he had."

The verb "to empty" has given rise to the so-called "kenotic" theory of incarnation. Undue theological exploitations have cast a heavy shadow on its meaning. It should be said at the outset that the verb must be understood metaphorically, not metaphysically. It says nothing about Christ stripping himself of his divine attributes as has sometimes been suggested. While it is probable that the Suffering Servant passage in Isaiah has some bearing on the present hymn, it is not necessary to see in "to empty" an allusion to Isa 53.12 ("he poured out his soul to death") and make it refer to the death of Christ. The event of Christ's death is referred to later, in verse 8.

The verb "to empty" is used elsewhere in the Pauline Epistles four times (Rom 4.14; 1 Cor 1.17; 9.15; 2 Cor 9.3), and in each instance it is used metaphorically in the sense of "to bring to nothing," "to make worthless," or "to empty of significance." Context should always determine the meaning; and in the present context the verb refers back to what immediately precedes and its action is explained by the words which immediately follow. Instead of holding onto his privileges, Christ gave up his divine rank by taking on the nature of a servant. The TEV rendering brings out this meaning, he gave up all he had (Gpd "but laid it aside"; Phps is even more explicit, "but he stripped himself of every advantage"). What was given up is not simply the opportunity to become equal with God, but the equality with God itself, namely Christ's divine status or rank of dignity and glory (John 17.5). Unless one is careful in the translation of he gave up all he had, the implication may be that Jesus lost completely all of his divine attributes. Accordingly, some translators prefer to use as a substitute for the phrase all he had such a phrase as "his status" or "his high position."

And took the nature of a servant translates a participial phrase, literally "taking the form of a slave." The aorist participle denotes that the action is simultaneous or contemporaneous with that of the main verb "he emptied." It has also an explanatory force; that is, Christ surrendered his divine rank "by taking" the nature of a servant. The word rendered nature in this clause is the same as the one used in verse 6. Obviously the nature of a servant is intended as a sharp contrast to the nature of God. Christ did not disguise himself as a servant; he became a servant, expressing in his deeds complete and absolute submission to the will of God. The heart of the matter is to show that Christ gave up the highest possible status and took on the lowest possible role. Christ did not merely exist in a servant's condition; he lived in humble service. In order to make the expression took the nature of a servant contrast with had the nature of God, it is important that the two expressions be as parallel in form as is possible. For example, if had the nature of God is rendered as "was just like God," one may then translate took the nature of a servant as "he was just like a servant." In such an expression, of course, one must avoid any terminology which would suggest mere pretense.

The author of the hymn goes on to define the path of humiliation which Christ took with a pair of synonymous parallelisms. He became like man is literally "becoming in the likeness of men." Both participles, namely "taking" and "becoming," involve a change in status and role. "Becoming" here can also be taken in its so-called "etymological" sense of "being born" (RSV NAB "being born in the likeness of men"). The word "likeness" suggests similarity, but this does not mean that Christ's humanity is unreal (cf. Rom 8.3; Heb 2.7, 14). In Greek, the plural form of man is used, emphasizing the fact that Christ became like a member of the human race in general, not like any particular individual. In order to emphasize the concept of "humanity" in the term man, it may be important to translate he became like man as "he became just like people."

Many translations place and appeared in human likeness in verse 8. But the structure of the hymn suggests that the verse division followed by TEV and JB is to be preferred.

To stress Christ's likeness to other men, the author of the hymn goes on to say and appeared in human likeness (literally, "and being found in the form as a man"). Likeness translates the other word for "form," denoting outward shape and appearance rather than inherent nature. The compounds of these two "forms" bring out vividly the difference between the inward and the outward aspects (see Rom 8.29; 12.2b; 2 Cor 3.18; Gal 4.19; Phil 3.10 for inner, spiritual process; Rom 12.2a and 1 Peter 1.14 for a process affecting that which is outward). It should be noted, however, that Paul is not here suggesting a discrepancy between appearance and underlying reality. What he means to emphasize is that Christ's likeness to men in general is a real likeness: "he came as man in the world and lived as a man" (GeCL).

In many languages a verb such as appeared is expressed in a quite different manner: someone "sees" who or what appears. Therefore appeared in human likeness may need to be expressed in such languages as "people saw him just like a man."

2.8   He was humble and walked the path of obedience all the way to
       death—
       his death on the cross.

This verse concludes the first stanza of the hymn. It reaches the climax in Christ's supreme humility and obedience. It is this act of humility which is urged on the Philippian Christians (vv. 3-5).

Note the word order in Greek: in 2.7 we have "but *himself* he emptied," with the emphasis on the person; whereas here we have "he *humbled* himself," with the emphasis on the act. Note also that the Greek verb is in the aorist tense, describing an act, not a disposition. To reflect this emphasis, he was humble is best taken in the sense of "he abased himself" or "he humiliated himself" (Knox "he lowered his own dignity"). To indicate the role of Jesus in "humbling himself," one may say in some languages "he caused himself to be humble," "he himself lowered his own status," or "he caused himself to become low." (For the meaning of "humility," see the discussion under verse 3.)

Walked the path of obedience all the way to death translates a participial phrase which means literally "becoming obedient to the extent of death." The action of the aorist participle "becoming" is simultaneous or contemporaneous with the main verb "he humbled," and it is also explanatory. Christ humbled himself "by becoming" obedient even to the extent of death; in other words, "obedient to death" defines the measure of Christ's humbling himself (cf. also John 10.17; Heb 5.8; 12.2). The obedience is rendered to God, as implied in verse 9. A contrast with Adam appears to be in the author's mind (Rom 5.12-21). The act of self-humbling and obedience sums up the whole course of Christ's life on earth. TEV attempts to make this fact explicit by rendering walked the path of obedience all the way to death. Christ humbled himself by living a life of complete obedience which culminated in death (cf. Phps). Paul hastens to add that Christ's death was not a normal death, but the cruel, torturous, shameful death on the cross. It was an accursed death, the death of a common criminal (Gal 3.13).

Two principal problems are involved in the expression walked the path of obedience all the way to death. In the first place, many languages do not permit the metaphorical use of such an expression as walked the path. In the second place, some languages require an indication of the person to whom another is obedient. It may be more satisfactory to render walked the path simply as "becoming," although one can also say "in what he did he became obedient." When it is necessary to indicate the person to whom Christ was obedient, that person must, of course, be God. Therefore one may say "he was obedient to God even to the point of dying," or "... giving his life."

The final phrase in verse 8, his death on the cross, may be introduced as an explanation of precisely what kind of dying was meant, for example, "He was obedient to God even to the point of dying, that is to say, dying on a cross," or "... that is to say, being crucified."

2.9 For this reason God raised him to the highest place above
    and gave him the name that is greater than any other name.

This verse marks the turning point in the drama. Two contrasts govern the transition: (1) humiliation vs. exaltation, and (2) servant vs. Lord.

Up to this point attention has been focused on the humility and obedience of Christ. But now God takes the initiative in conferring on Christ the highest honor.

The phrase <u>for this reason</u> introduces the result. Exaltation is the natural consequence of humiliation (Matt 18.4; 23.12; Luke 14.11; 18.14; cf. 2 Cor 11.7; Phil 4.12). In some languages <u>for this reason</u> may be rendered as "because of what he did."

<u>God raised him to the highest place above</u> is literally "God hyperexalted him." This rare compound verb occurs only here in the New Testament. The force of "hyper" is not simply "more than before," but rather "in superlative measure." The idea is not that God exalted Christ to a higher rank than the one he held before. The contrast is between the lowest point of his earthly role (servant—obedience—criminal death) to the highest heavenly honor (cf. Isa 52.13). It is possible that the exaltation includes the resurrection and especially the ascension, as understood by a number of commentators (Acts 2.23-24, 33; Rom 1.4; Heb 1.3); but the context seems to suggest that the reference is primarily to status, namely, the highest honor, the lordship.

<u>The highest place above</u> may be rendered more or less literally as "the highest place in heaven." But this could be understood merely in a locative sense in some languages. Therefore one may prefer such a rendering as "to the greatest place of honor in heaven." Or, <u>raised him to the highest place above</u> may simply be rendered as "caused him to have the greatest possible honor," or ". . . status."

The verb <u>gave</u> has the sense of "granted as an act of grace" (see 1.29). NEB has "bestowed," Mft "conferred." <u>Name</u> is not simply a designation to distinguish one person from another. In its biblical sense, it carries the idea of one's character, position, role, rank, dignity, etc. (cf. Eph 1.21; Heb 1.4). <u>The name that is greater than any other name</u> (literally, "the name that is above every name") could then mean "the highest rank or dignity of all." The reference is most probably to <u>Lord</u> in verse 11.

In languages in which reference to a "name" implies status or distinction, it may be possible to preserve the second part of this verse, namely, <u>gave him the name that is greater than any other name</u>. However, in many languages the use of the term "name" in such a context would be meaningless, if not misleading. Since the second part of verse 9 is really parallel to what is said in the first part, it may be better in some instances to translate the second part as "gave him a position that was higher than any other position." Similarly, <u>in honor of the name of Jesus</u> (v. 10) would be rendered as "in honor of the position which Jesus has."

2.10   And so, in honor of the name of Jesus
            all beings in heaven, on earth, and in the world below*d*
            will fall on their knees,

> *d*WORLD BELOW: *It was thought that the dead continued to exist in a dark world under the ground.*

The words in verses 10-11 are adapted from Isa 45.23, a passage quoted in Rom 14.11. The context in the Isaiah passage is the proclamation of the unique greatness of the God of Israel and of the universal worship that would be paid to him.

And so states the purpose of the exaltation. Most translations render the particle as "so that."

In honor of the name of Jesus is literally "in the name of Jesus." "At the name of Jesus," as rendered in several translations (RSV NEB JB etc.) may be misleading, for it seems to suggest that, whenever the name of Jesus is mentioned, everyone would bend in reverence. The meaning, however, is that to Jesus is given the honor that is proper only to God, because Jesus bears the name that carries with it the highest honor. TEV makes this meaning explicit. There is no need to interpret this expression in the sense of "through the name of Jesus," thus making Jesus the mediator through whom all creatures offer their homage to God. The drift of the passage makes it clear that Jesus is the direct object of worship.

In those languages in which a term such as "name" has no value as a symbol of status or as a substitute for the person himself, it may be useful simply to eliminate any mention of the name. Therefore, in honor of the name of Jesus may be rendered as "in honor of Jesus" or "in order to show honor to Jesus."

Paul now describes the cosmic and universal power and authority of Jesus Christ by what in Greek are three adjectives which here function as nouns. KJV and ASV understand the adjectives to be neuter, that is, "things" ("every knee should bow, of things in heaven, and things in earth, and things under the earth"), but it is more likely that the reference is to rational beings. TEV makes this interpretation explicit and restructures the clause into all beings in heaven, on earth, and in the world below will fall on their knees (cf. JB Brc). It is not necessary to identify these rational beings exclusively as "spirits." It is quite possible that beings in heaven refers to the angels, and those on earth to human beings. The world below refers most likely to the residence of the dead known as Hades. Its equivalent in the Old Testament is Sheol. In ancient times, people believed that there was an underworld where the spirits of the dead carried on a shadowy existence. In any case, the author intends to show that the lordship of Jesus Christ is cosmic and universal (cf. Eph 4.10; Rev 5.3, 13).

In some languages there is no generic term equivalent to beings. The closest natural equivalent may be such a pronoun as "those," for example, "all those who are in heaven, and on earth, and below the earth."

It may be misleading in some languages to speak of the world below. This would suggest that there is "an earth beneath the earth." It may therefore be necessary to say "in the space beneath the earth," or "in the region below the ground."

The phrase will fall on their knees is an idiomatic expression referring to reverence and worship, and sometimes prayer (Rom 11.4; Eph 3.14).

2.11   and all will openly proclaim that Jesus Christ is Lord,
        to the glory of God the Father.

All is literally "every tongue." This expression, like "every knee," is a poetic way of saying "everyone" or "all." The verb translated openly proclaim usually indicates an open profession of faith (cf. 1 Tim 3.16). It can also be rendered "confess" (RSV NEB), "acclaim" (JB), or "openly declare" (Brc). Note that verses 10-11 express the purpose of the exaltation: "and so (so that) . . . will openly proclaim (future indicative)." In some languages openly proclaim is best expressed as "will say to everyone," or "will say when everyone is listening."

The content of the acclamation is Jesus Christ is Lord. Here we have one of the earliest Christological confessions of the church preserved in the New Testament (cf. Rom 10.9; 1 Cor 12.3). Lord is the most common title applied to Jesus by the early church. It is the word employed in the Septuagint to translate the Hebrew "Yahweh." It can be used in the general sense of "master" or "sir," but when it is applied to Jesus, it has a unique Christological significance. When Jesus Christ is acclaimed as Lord, he is installed in the place which properly belongs to God alone. This means that Jesus Christ has sovereignty over the entire universe. Lord is emphatic by its position in the sentence. Since this is a creedal statement, the words may be placed within quotation marks (so GeCL NEB TNT).

In many languages the equivalent of Lord must occur with a so-called possessive pronoun, since it is impossible for anyone to be merely Lord; he must be Lord of certain persons, that is, "the one who controls" or "the one who gives orders to" those persons. Therefore Lord must be rendered in many instances as "their Lord."

The ultimate purpose in giving homage to Jesus Christ and in acclaiming him as Lord is to be to the glory of God the Father. This is equivalent to saying "so that all will praise God." (For the fuller meaning of "glory," see the discussion under 1.11.) With these words the hymn draws to an appropriate close. The authority of the Son is derived from the Father.

2.11

Only God the Father has the ultimate sovereignty (1 Cor 15.28; Rev 3.21; John 13.31; 17.1).

In order to show quite clearly how to the glory of God the Father relates to what has immediately preceded, it may be necessary to make the connection more specific, for example, "in saying this about Jesus, they will be showing honor to God the Father." In some languages the equivalent of glory in this type of context is simply "to show honor to" or "praise to." In certain languages, however, it is possible to use idiomatic equivalents, for example, "to lift up the name of," or "to show how magnificent God is."

As in the case of Lord, it may also be necessary in some languages to indicate the relation of Father to those who claim him as Father. That is, a term such as "Father" is obligatorily possessed. In this context it may be necessary to say "God their Father," or, perhaps in a more general sense, "God our Father."

TEV	RSV
Shining as Lights in the World	
12 So then, dear friends, as you always obeyed me when I was with you, it is even more important that you obey me while I am away from you. Keep on working with fear and trembling to complete your salvation, 13 because God is always at work in you to make you willing and able to obey his own purpose.	12 Therefore, my beloved, as you have always obeyed, so now, not only as in my presence but much more in my absence, work out your own salvation with fear and trembling; 13 for God is at work in you, both to will and to work for his good pleasure.
14 Do everything without complaining or arguing, 15 so that you may be innocent and pure as God's perfect children, who live in a world of corrupt and sinful people. You must shine among them like stars lighting up the sky, 16 as you offer them the message of life. If you do so, I shall have reason to be proud of you on the Day of Christ, because it will show that all my effort and work have not been wasted.	14 Do all things without grumbling or questioning, 15 that you may be blameless and innocent, children of God without blemish in the midst of a crooked and perverse generation, among whom you shine as lights in the world, 16 holding fast the word of life, so that in the day of Christ I may be proud that I did not run in vain or labor in vain. 17 Even if I am to be poured as a libation upon the sacrificial offering of your faith, I am glad and rejoice with you all. 18 Likewise you also should be glad and rejoice with me.
17 Perhaps my life's blood is to be poured out like an offering on the sacrifice that your faith offers to God. If that is so, I am glad and share my joy with you all. 18 In the same way, you too must be glad and share your joy with me. (2.12-18)	(2.12-18)

Shining as Lights in the World is a useful heading for this somewhat heterogeneous section, but it may be necessary to make some alterations in the grammatical structure, for example, "You will shine as lights in the world," or ". . . to people in the world." It is possible, moreover, to employ some of the other phrases within this section as indicative of important aspects of these three short paragraphs, for example, "Complete your salvation," or "Being God's perfect children."

The keynote of the first stanza of the hymn is Christ's humble obedience (v. 8). Paul now applies this supreme example to the Philippian situation by urging his friends to be obedient to him as God's messenger, even as they did when he first appeared among them (Acts 16.12 ff.). Furthermore, they are to become blameless children of God and to shine as lights in the world (v. 15).

The present passage is reminiscent of Moses' farewell speech to the Israelites (Deut 32.1-5), but there is a difference. While Moses' speech is clouded with rebuke for the Israelites' past disobedience, Paul addresses his readers with confidence in their unbroken obedience.

2.12   So then, dear friends, as you always obeyed me when I was with you, it is even more important that you obey me now while I am away from you. Keep on working with fear and trembling to complete your salvation,

Verses 12 and 13 represent a long sentence in Greek. For the sake of clarity it is best broken into several shorter sentences.

With the connective so then Paul established the link between the Christological hymn and the practical exhortation. The Philippian Christians must have the attitude that Christ had (v. 5); thus, as Christ obeyed, so should they. The readers are addressed as dear friends (literally, "my beloved," "my dear friends," Gpd JB). This expression, which appears again twice in 4.1, shows the warmth of the apostle's affection toward his converts. It is a favorite expression, often used by Paul to introduce earnest appeals to his readers (1 Cor 10.14; 15.58; 2 Cor 7.1; 12.19, etc.).

In many languages the expression of direct address would come naturally at the beginning of the section. Therefore one may need to shift the order of so then, dear friends, employing such an expression as "dear friends, therefore, as you always obeyed me . . . ."

In some languages, however, dear friends may seem out of place since the term friends itself would include a component of endearment, and the addition of an adjective such as dear would imply that there were other friends who were not dear. An equivalent expression of dear friends may in some languages be "you who are so friendly to me," or "you who are so loved by me."

[65]

The references to Paul's presence and absence (literally, "not as in my my presence only but now much more in my absence" KJV) can be taken several ways. (1) A number of translations connect them with "work out your own salvation" (Gpd NAB Brc Segond [Seg]). (2) Another possibility, though less likely, is seen in the Phps rendering: "as you have always obeyed me—and that not only when I was with you—now, even more in my absence, complete the salvation . . . ." Here he appears to connect <u>pres-ence</u> with "obeyed" and <u>absence</u> with "work out salvation." (3) A third possibility is to connect them both with "you have always obeyed" (Brc GeCL NIV). The Greek word order indicates that this is preferable to (1). However, there is a difficulty in connecting the sense of "but now" with "obeyed." (4) To avoid this difficulty NEB offers a variation of (3) by making the sentence into an imperative rather than a statement, thus ". . . must be obedient, as always; even more, now that I am away, than when I was with you." (5) Still another variation is suggested by TEV (so also SpCL FrCL TNT). It supplies a command, <u>you obey me</u>, to the reference to Paul's absence, thus: <u>it is even more important that you obey me now while I am away from you.</u>

The aorist verb <u>obeyed</u> is used without an object in Greek. A number of translations accordingly render the verse without supplying an object (including Gpd Mft RSV NEB Brc). Some commentators suggest "God" to be the object, but the sense is probably that of obedience to Paul as God's messenger and to his instructions and guidance (cf. 2 Cor 7.15; 10.6; Philemon 21), and TEV makes that explicit: <u>as you always obeyed me</u> (so also Bruce Phps TNT; cf. NAB "obedient as always to my urging"; JB "continue to do as I tell you").

In some languages a literal rendering of <u>as you always obeyed me when I was with you</u> might suggest that when Paul was with the Philippian believers he was constantly commanding them to do certain things. It may be better, therefore, to render this clause as "in the same way as you always took my advice when I was with you."

There may be some complications in the introductory part of this verse because of the three different connectives before the principal clause, namely, <u>so then</u>, <u>as</u>, and <u>when</u>. In many languages, this cluster of connectives would be too heavy a "preposed" set of structures. However, one can make certain modifications, for example, "Dear friends, when I was with you, you always took my advice. Therefore, it is even more important for you to obey me now, while I am away from you," or ". . . take my advice now, while I am not with you any longer."

To bring out properly the emphasis in the Greek text, TEV restructures the following phrase (literally, "but now much more in my absence") into <u>it is even more important that you obey me now while I am away</u>

from you. This rendering makes it clear that the contrast of presence and absence is not to be taken in the sense of "during my life" and "after my death," as is, in fact, advocated by some comentators.

The compound Greek present imperative, rendered "work out" by most translators, has the sense of continuing a work to its conclusion, thus keep on working...to complete (Brc "keep on toiling"; cf. Eph 6.13). Keep on working should not be rendered in such a way as to refer merely to physical toil. A more satisfactory equivalent may be "keep on striving," "give all your strength to," or "endeavor very much to."

Your salvation can hardly be taken in a personal sense. In Greek both the verb "work out" and the reflexive pronoun "yourselves" are plural. It is not an exhortation to the Philippian Christians to accomplish the personal salvation of the individual members. Paul is rather concerned about the well-being of their common life together as a community (cf. 1.28; 2.4). Paul often uses salvation to refer to the ultimate saving act of God which will reach its completion at the end of the world. For him it is primarily a future reality, an attainment of final blessedness (cf. 1 Cor 5.5), and a deliverance from approaching wrath (Rom 5.9; 1 Cor 3.15; 1 Thes 5.10). In the present context, however, the word can be taken in the broader sense of the restoration of the health and the spiritual well-being of the community (Mark 3.4; Acts 4.9; 14.9; 27.34).

A literal rendering of to complete your salvation could be understood to mean that individuals had complete responsibility for their personal salvation, but Paul always speaks of personal salvation as the act of God. This expression is better interpreted in the present context as "cause your well-being to be complete," "cause nothing to be lacking in your well-being," or "...in your state of well-being."

The Philippian readers are encouraged to attain this goal with fear and trembling. This is a stereotyped Old Testament expression (see Psa 2.11; Isa 19.16) denoting humble reverence, dependence, and devotion to God. It does not appear in the New Testament apart from the Pauline writings. In every instance (here and in 1 Cor 2.3; Eph 6.5) it is used to describe the spirit of reverence and humility which should characterize mutual relationships within the Christian community. It is precisely with this spirit that Paul is urging the Philippian Christians to keep on working toward the restoration of the spiritual welfare of the community (see 2.2-4, 14; 4.2). A literal rendering of with fear and trembling might suggest that the Philippian Christians should be fearful of their enemies and tremble because of them. It may even be misleading to speak of "with fear and trembling before God," or "while you are fearing God and trembling before him." A more appropriate equivalent in a number of languages is "with complete devotion to God," or "with complete reverence for God."

2.13   because God is always at work in you to make you willing and able to obey his own purpose.

This verse gives the reason for Paul's injunction in the preceding verse. Here he is neither contradicting nor correcting himself. Rather, he is arguing that God's initiative in working should serve as an incentive for the Philippian Christians to participate actively in the fulfillment of God's own purpose. In other words, if they did not cooperate with God in bringing about the restoration of the spiritual welfare of their own community, they would be impeding his work. God's inward working in man is a recurrent thought in Paul's letters (1 Cor 12.6; 15.10; 2 Cor 3.5; 1 Thes 2.13). God is in an emphatic position in the Greek text. The force of the present participle "working" is continuous; thus TEV renders it explicitly always at work. The word usually carries the idea of effective working (Rom 7.5; Gal 5.6). In you can mean "in your hearts" (Gpd), but it seems better in the present context to take in you in the corporate sense of "among you," meaning the work of God in the life of the Christian community.

Again, it may be important to avoid an expression for work which suggests primarily physical activity. A more appropriate equivalent may be "because God is always in you trying hard to make you willing...," or "...is always in you causing you to be willing...."

To make you willing and able to obey his own purpose is literally "both to will and to work in behalf of the good pleasure." The TEV rendering makes explicit that it is God who makes the Philippian Christians "to will" and "to work." God is the primary agent, and the Philippian themselves are the secondary agents. Rather than rendering these two infinitive phrases as nouns (NEB "the will and the deed"; JB "the will and the action"), it is better to translate them dynamically as TEV does (Brc expands them to mean "the will to desire and the power to achieve"). Willing here is certainly more than mere "wishing"; it involves a purposive determination. To make you willing may be rendered as "cause you to want to," or even "cause you to be glad to."

The noun translated purpose is the same as the one used in 1.15 to express good will. When it is used in reference to God, it usually means "gracious will" or "loving purpose." It has been suggested that "to work in behalf of the good pleasure" should be taken to mean "to promote good will" among the members of the Christian community at Philippi. This is not necessarily incorrect, as the ultimate purpose of God is precisely this. Grammatically, however, the phrase is rather to be connected with the subject "God." The focus is on God; it is his good pleasure, and so TEV renders explicitly to obey his own purpose (Knox "to carry out his loving purpose"; Bruce "to act as He pleases"; Phps "to achieve his purpose"; Brc "to achieve what his purpose has planned for you"). In this context, God's ultimate purpose is no doubt the restoration of the spiritual welfare of the divided community. Only by regaining spiritual health will the Philippians be able to fulfill their mission as a witnessing community in the world (v. 15). To obey his own purpose may be expressed as "to obey what God has determined you should do," "to do what God has said you should do," or "... wants you to do."

2.14   Do everything without complaining or arguing,

In Greek verses 14-16 consist of one complex sentence, but for clarity of thought it is better to break it into several short sentences.

Paul continues his injunction by making specific applications to the Philippians' situation. They are to do all they have to do without complaining or arguing. Here the apostle appears to see his relation to his converts as parallel to that of Moses to the Israelites (e.g. Exo 15.24; 16.2; Num 14; 1 Cor 10.10). It is not likely, however, that the complaining or arguing of the Philippians is against God. These terms point rather to mutual disagreements and disputes among the Philippians themselves. Both nouns are plural in Greek, but it is more natural to render them as singular in the imperative statement as most translators do.

The preposition without involves a negation, and this must be made explicit in some languages. For example, in rendering verse 14 one must sometimes translate the relation between doing and complaining as "whenever you do anything you must not complain," "do not complain when you do something," or "do not complain when you have something you must do." Since the complaining or arguing probably refers to the relationship between believers in Philippi, it may be best to translate "you should not complain to one another or argue with one another."

2.15   so that you may be innocent and pure as God's perfect children, who live in a world of corrupt and sinful people. You must shine among them like stars lighting up the sky,

By avoiding complaining and arguing within the community, the Philippian Christians may become innocent and pure. The adjective innocent is often used to characterize someone who is flawless in the sight of other people, while pure means literally "unmixed" or "unadulterated." The latter term is used of wine not mixed with water and of metal that contains no alloy. It is often used to describe inward purity and sincerity (e.g. Matt 10.16; Rom 16.19).

The phrase so that introduces purpose. If, however, verse 14 is so restructured as to make complaining or arguing the principal verbs, it may

[69]

not be easy to indicate clearly the purpose involved in verse 15. It may be necessary to refer back to the contents of verse 14 by saying "you should refrain from complaining and arguing so that you may be innocent and pure."

In many languages the closest equivalent of innocent is "not guilty." It is also possible to use a phrase such as "you will have nothing to be blamed for." In some languages the closest equivalent is an idiomatic expression, for example, "there will be no mark against you," or "there will be nothing weighed against you."

It is possible in some instances to translate pure as "nothing wrong in you," or "no badness in your heart."

As God's perfect children, who live in a world of corrupt and sinful people represents a more natural restructuring of the literal "children of God without blemish in the midst of a crooked and perverse generation" (ASV). These words are adapted from the "Song of Moses" (Deut 32.5 LXX). The adjective rendered perfect (NEB "faultless") is generally used in connection with sacrifices. Only a "spotless" and thus "perfect" sacrifice is fit to be offered to God. In the New Testament, the adjective is usually employed to portray what a Christian is and should be in the sight of God (Eph 1.4; Col 1.22; Jude 24; Rev 14.4-5). God's perfect children may be rendered as "God's completely good children." The same sense may be expressed negatively as "God's children in whom there is nothing bad."

In the original setting in Deuteronomy, corrupt and sinful people refers to the erring Israelites; but Paul applies it to the hostile world, not to the Christian community at Philippi. The word rendered sinful means literally "twisted" or "distorted," denoting an abnormal moral condition. It can also be rendered "perverted" (Gpd Brc), or "depraved" (NAB). A world of corrupt and sinful people may be expressed as "a world filled with corrupt and sinful people," or "a world in which corrupt and sinful people live." The closest equivalent of corrupt may be in some languages "very bad," and sinful may be rendered as "those who constantly sin," or "those who habitually do what is bad."

There are several possible ways of rendering the next clause, which is literally "among whom you appear (are seen) as luminaries in the world." Some of the older commentators insisted that the middle verb should be taken in the sense of "appear," "become visible," or "are seen." Most modern translators, however, render the verb as "shine," but they are divided as to whether it should be taken as indicative or imperative. The context appears to require the imperative, thus you must shine (TEV Brc). The Greek noun rendered "luminaries" is commonly used in the Septuagint to refer to the heavenly bodies, the sun, the moon, and the stars (Gen 1.14, 16 LXX). Rather than a generic term such as "lights" (KJV RSV), most modern translations use (on the basis of similar expressions in the LXX of Dan 12.3) a more specific term, "stars," to render this Greek word (NEB JB NAB TEV). Since the expression "like stars in the world" is somewhat awkward, some modern translators change it to "like stars in the dark world" (Gpd Mft NEB SpCL). Although the Greek word *kosmos* usually means "world," it can also mean "sky." Accordingly, one can render the expression as "like stars in the sky" (NAB FrCL GeCL), or, even more vividly, like stars lighting up the sky.

A literal rendering of you must shine among them like stars lighting up the sky may not be very meaningful in some languages, since good behavior is not normally regarded as "shining." Nevertheless, it is probably better to retain this figure of speech, since it can be comprehended, at least in some measure, and it is not likely to cause special problems of understanding.

2.16   as you offer them the message of life. If you do so, I shall have reason to be proud of you on the Day of Christ, because it will show that all my effort and work have not been wasted.

As you offer them the message of life should be connected to the preceding clause to form a complete sentence (the verb offer is a participle in Greek). The participial phrase can be expressed in two ways, depending on how one interprets verse 15. Some scholars claim that Paul is there simply speaking of the contrast between the church and the world, and they generally take the participle to mean "holding fast" or "adhering to" (Mft RSV NAB). However, it is more likely that Paul is thinking about the missionary influence of the Philippian church upon the surrounding evil world, as implied in the TEV rendering. It is therefore better to take the participle in the sense of "holding forth" or "offering" (Gpd JB NEB). In order to be more explicit, it is desirable to make the message of life the direct object and supply an indirect object, them, hence as you offer them the message of life.

This is the only instance in which Paul uses the phrase the message of life, literally, "the word of life." There seems to be no need to take this expression in the Johannine sense of "as the very principle of its life" (John 1.1-5), as suggested in the NEB footnote. The genitive construction here is better taken in the sense of "the message that brings life," not "the message concerning life." Thus "the word of life" is here used synonymously with "the gospel." Paul calls upon his readers to shine like stars by making their lives a constant demonstration of the Christian gospel.

If one assumes that the message of life is to be understood as "the message that brings life," one may use a causative expression, for example, "the message that causes people to really live." Such a causative relation, however, is rather difficult in some languages because it would involve a human agent. Therefore it may be preferable to translate the message of life as "the message that shows people how they can really live." It may be necessary to use some type of qualification for the term life, for the good news is not merely an explanation about how human existence is to be continued. The life spoken of in the New Testament is characterized as "real life," in contrast with mere human existence.

The Greek prepositional phrase rendered in RSV as "so that in the Day of Christ I may be proud" appears to carry a conditional force. Thus Gpd has "then I will have reason to boast of you" (with an "if" clause implied; cf. GeCL). One can go a step further, as TEV does, and render it explicitly as If you do so, I shall have reason to be proud of you (Brc "for, if you do, . . . I will be able proudly to claim . . ."). Obviously, Paul is not speaking about the pride he now has in his readers, but he is suggesting a reason for such pride as he expects to have in the future, namely, on the Day of Christ. As in 1.6 and 1.10, the Day of Christ refers to the Parousia, the second coming of Christ (Brc "on the day when Christ comes"; cf. GeCL).

The pronoun it in the expression because it will show must refer to the behavior of the Christians in Philippi. It may be important to make this rather specific, for example, "because what you have done will show," or "because what you are like will show."

Paul now proceeds to explain the basis for his pride by picturing himself as looking back on his life from the time of the Day of Christ. He does this by using two aorist tense verbs, literally, "that I did not run in vain neither labor in vain" (ASV). "That" is an added explanation of the preceding clause, thus because it will show that (NEB "proof that").

The verb "run" is a favorite Pauline metaphor. It is taken from the life of an athlete and depicts a runner in the stadium dashing toward the finish line (Acts 13.25; 20.24; 1 Cor 9.24, 26; Gal 2.2). The phrase "in vain" (used in the New Testament only by Paul) is found in the papyri as describing water running to waste. The metaphor can be kept in the translation, thus "I did not run the race in vain" (NAB), "I did not run a loser's race" (Brc), or "I had not run in the race . . . for nothing" (JB). For some languages, it may be best to substitute a nonmetaphor, as TEV does, all my effort and work have not been wasted.

It is possible that the second verb work is a continuation of the metaphor picturing the hard work of the athlete's training for the race. It means "to work to the point of exhaustion" (JB "exhausted myself for nothing").

One may find it difficult to speak of effort and work being wasted. It may be easy enough to speak of wasting a substance, but not of wasting an activity. One may therefore need to restructure the final part of this verse as "what you are like will show that when I engaged in all my hard work I did not do it for nothing," or ". . . this was not useless." In some languages it is important to combine effort and work in a single expression indicating the exhausting nature of the work, for example, "when I worked so hard that I became exhausted," or "when I worked to the point where I hardly had any more strength."

2.17   Perhaps my life's blood is to be poured out like an offering on the sacrifice that your faith offers to God. If that is so, I am glad and share my joy with you all.

The scene shifts here from the athletic stadium to the altar and sacrificial rites.

The verse begins with a series of particles, literally, "but if also." "But" functions here as an introductory particle, not as an adversative. "If also" is not an improbable supposition as the rendering "even if" (RSV) appears to suggest; the possibility of martyrdom is apparently in Paul's mind (cf. 2 Tim 4.6). TEV expresses this possibility by perhaps . . . if that is so. In some languages perhaps may be expressed as "it is possible that" or "it may happen that."

My life's blood is to be poured out like an offering translates a single Greek verb, which means literally "I am poured out" (that is, as a libation or drink offering). The drink offering was usually a cup of wine poured out on the ground to honor a deity. When used of a person, the verb denotes a violent or bloody death. This kind of offering was common in both pagan and Jewish worship (cf. Num 15.3-10). In talking about the possibility of his martyrdom, Paul likens his life's blood to a drink offering poured out to honor God (cf. Rom 15.16; 2 Tim 4.6).

My life's blood is in some languages equivalent to "the blood which causes me to live," but my life's blood is to be poured out may not indicate in some languages the meaning of "death." It may be necessary to change the idiom or to employ a nonidiomatic expression, for example, "it is possible that I will be killed like a sacrifice," "perhaps I will be sacrificed," or ". . . caused to die, as it were, like a sacrifice." The difficulty with this type of expression, however, is that Paul's death would be regarded as a kind of sacrifice, but the faith of the Philippians is itself regarded as a sacrifice offered to God. It may, therefore, be preferable to translate the beginning of verse 17 as "Perhaps I will be killed and in this way be like an offering of blood which is poured out on the sacrifice that your own faith offers to God."

Literally, the offering is poured out "upon the sacrifice and service

[73]

of your faith" (KJV). The exact meaning of this phrase is much debated. The difficulty involves first the precise meaning of the preposition "upon" (*epi*); secondly, the relation of the coordinate construction "sacrifice and service"; and, thirdly, the sense of the genitive construction "service of your faith."

The meaning of the preposition "upon" is conditioned by Paul's allusion to the sacrificial system. If the allusion is to Jewish usage, the meaning is "in addition to," since the Jews poured the drink offering, not over the sacrifice, but beside or around the altar. NEB favors this view by rendering "to crown that sacrifice." On the other hand, if the allusion is to pagan ritual, the meaning is "upon" or "on," since the pagans poured the drink offering on the sacrifice that was on the altar. This interpretation is adopted by the majority of translations, including TEV, on the sacrifice. In view of the fact that most of the Philippian Christians were converts from paganism, it is more likely that Paul would draw his illustration from the pagan sacrificial system (cf. 2 Cor 2.14 ff.).

The noun rendered "service" in KJV is the Greek word from which the English word "liturgy" is derived. In secular usage, it meant a service to the public or the state. In both the Septuagint and the New Testament, it is sometimes used in the general sense of service rendered to men, but more frequently in reference to priestly functions. Here the noun is used metaphorically in the latter sense, denoting the offering up of the sacrifice. "Service" in this context is thus best understood in the sense of "offering." Since in Greek two nouns often share one article, this coordinate construction is probably to be taken, not as referring to two things, but as forming one event. The "sacrifice" is the semantic goal of the "offering," and God is the implied recipient of the "sacrifice." Now, by making this information explicit and restructuring the construction into a verbal phrase, we have the TEV rendering the sacrifice that . . . offers to God.

The identification of the subject of the offering depends on the analysis of the genitive construction "offering of your faith." The ambiguity of this construction is reflected in the various translations. It is interpreted by some as "the offering is your faith"; thus JB has "offering—which is your faith" (cf. NEB "that sacrifice which is the offering up of your faith"). Mft provides a variation of this interpretation by identifying the agent as "you," thus "the sacred sacrifice of faith you are offering to God." These renderings regard "faith" as the thing offered. Another possibility, adopted by TEV, is to take the construction in the sense of "your faith offers something (sacrifice)." The context makes it clear that it is not Paul who is offering the sacrifice, but the Philippians. Furthermore, what the Philippians offer is not their faith; rather their new-found faith is the source or the impulse for that offering. The sacrifice which their faith offers is probably their gifts to Paul, for these constitute a sacrifice on their part (cf. 2.30 and especially 4.18).

It may be difficult to speak of the sacrifice that your faith offers to God, since in many languages the event implied in faith cannot be regarded as an agent which would offer a sacrifice. It is much simpler to speak of "your faith" as being a "sacrifice" or "an offering." But even this interpretation may be difficult to express in a receptor language in which faith must be regarded as a verb, not as a noun. If one assumes the interpretation that "the offering is your faith," it may be possible to say "that which you offer to God is the fact that you trust him," or ". . . is your trusting him." On the other hand, if one understands faith as being the motivation or impulse for an offering to God, one may speak of "the sacrifice that you offer to God as the result of your trusting him," or ". . . which your trusting him causes you to offer."

The possibility of death is for Paul not a cause for grief, but of joy. This joy is based on the confidence that death will be a gain, because by it Christ will be glorified and the gospel proclaimed. Here again we have the characteristic refrain of this letter, "joy" and "you all." In this verse and the following, Paul employs the verb "to rejoice" twice, and also its compound "to rejoice with" twice. Here he says I am glad and share my joy with you all.

If that is so refers, not to the sacrifice that your faith offers to God, but to the possibility of Paul's death. Therefore if that is so may be rendered as "if that turns out to be the case," or "if I die."

2.18   In the same way, you too must be glad and share your joy with me.

In this verse the Philippian Christians are called upon to be happy about their sacrifice and to share their joy with the apostle. As there is a correspondence in sacrifice, so also there must be a correspondence in joy. Thus you too must be glad and share your joy with me. A perfect Christian comradeship!

In some languages one may be compelled to indicate the basis for gladness. And so it may be necessary to translate you too must be glad as "you, too, must be glad because of what is likely to happen," or ". . . because of what will happen." Similarly, share your joy with me must parallel the expression in verse 17, share my joy with you all. Accordingly, one may translate share your joy with me as "cause me to have joy as you do," or "cause me to join with you in being happy."

It may be difficult to speak of "sharing one's joy" with others. The only way in which joy may be "shared" in some languages is to "cause others to be joyful." Therefore, <u>share my joy with you all</u> must be rendered as "cause you all to have the same kind of joy that I have," or "cause all of you to rejoice in some measure as I rejoice."

TEV	RSV
Timothy and Epaphroditus	
19 If it is the Lord's will, I hope that I will be able to send Timothy to you soon, so that I may be encouraged by news about you. 20 He is the only one who shares my feelings and who really cares about you. 21 Everyone else is concerned only with his own affairs, not with the cause of Jesus Christ. 22 And you yourselves know how he has proved his worth, how he and I, like a son and his father, have worked together for the sake of the gospel. 23 So I hope to send him to you as soon as I know how things are going to turn out for me. 24 And I trust in the Lord that I myself will be able to come to you soon.	19 I hope in the Lord Jesus to send Timothy to you soon, so that I may be cheered by news of you. 20 I have no one like him, who will be genuinely anxious for your welfare. 21 They all look after their own interests, not those of Jesus Christ. 22 But Timothy's worth you know, how as a son with a father he has served with me in the gospel. 23 I hope therefore to send him just as soon as I see how it will go with me; 24 and I trust in the Lord that shortly I myself shall come also.
25 I have thought it necessary to send to you our brother Epaphroditus, who has worked and fought by my side and who has served as your messenger in helping me. 26 He is anxious to see you all and is very upset because you had heard that he was sick. 27 Indeed he was sick and almost died. But God had pity on him, and not only on him but on me, too, and spared me an even greater sorrow. 28 I am all the more eager, then, to send him to you, so that you will be glad again when you see him, and my own sorrow will disappear. 29 Receive him, then, with joy, as a brother in the Lord. Show respect to all such people as he, 30 because he risked his life and nearly died for the sake of the work of Christ, in order to give me the help that you yourselves could not give.	25 I have thought it necessary to send to you Epaphroditus my brother and fellow worker and fellow soldier, and your messenger and minister to my need, 26 for he has been longing for you all, and has been distressed because you heard that he was ill. 27 Indeed he was ill, near to death. But God had mercy on him, and not only on him, but on me also, lest I should have sorrow upon sorrow. 28 I am the more eager to send him, therefore, that you may rejoice at seeing him again, and that I may be less anxious. 29 So receive him in the Lord with all joy; and honor such men, 30 for he nearly died for the work of Christ, risking his life to complete your service to me.
	(2.19-30)

(2.19-30)

In most languages a section heading such as <u>Timothy and Epaphroditus</u> is quite satisfactory. But in certain languages a phrase involving two proper names connected by a conjunction such as "and" may be misleading, for it would suggest that the two individuals engaged in some kind of joint activity. To avoid this implication, it is possible to say "Paul writes about Timothy and Epaphroditus," or "Paul writes about Timothy and also about Epaphroditus." One may also make the reference to these men more specific by a section heading such as "The proposed visits of Timothy and Epaphroditus to Philippi," or "Timothy and Epaphroditus will visit Philippi."

At this point Paul introduces a new subject. He expresses his hopes for the future and his intention to send his most trusted associate, Timothy, on a goodwill mission to Philippi (vv. 19-24). But since Paul is quite uncertain as to when Timothy or he may be able to visit the Philippians, he has to send their messenger Epaphroditus back to them at once (vv. 25-30).

2.19   If it is the Lord's will, I hope that I will be able to send Timothy to you soon, so that I may be encouraged by news about you.

Paul's hope for sending Timothy is governed by the Lord's will (literally, "I hope in the Lord Jesus"). He apparently has a confident expectation that the Lord will favor his plans. The word hope here has the components of "expectation" and "confidence," and may often be rendered as "I look forward with trust," or "I want to and think it will happen." If it is the Lord's will may be rendered as "if the Lord wishes it to be so," or "if that is what the Lord wants."

In selecting an equivalent for send, one must make certain that the proper components of meaning are present. For example, in some languages a verb meaning "send" may suggest that Paul wishes to get rid of Timothy. Other terms may suggest sending Timothy back home permanently. The meaning in this context is that Paul wishes to send Timothy to be of some help to the people in Philippi, but not on a permanent basis.

The purpose of Timothy's mission is stated as that I may be encouraged by news about you. The verb be encouraged (literally, "be well in the soul") is found only here in the New Testament. Its imperative form is very common in gravestone inscriptions, representing a pious wish for the dead: "Farewell!" or "Be it well with your soul!" The meaning in this context is "to be encouraged" or "to be cheered up." The subject I in this purpose clause is emphatic and is preceded by a coordinating conjunction used adverbially in the sense of "also." This particle is often left untranslated, but its implication is that the Philippians will be heartened by the visit of Timothy.

The passive expression of purpose, so that I may be encouraged by news about you, may be expressed in an active form as "so that informa-

[77]

tion about how you are will encourage me." In this type of context encouragement may be expressed in a negative manner, for example, "take
away my anxieties," or "remove my worries about you."

By news about you represents a participial phrase in Greek which
means literally "knowing the things concerning you."

2.20　　He is the only one who shares my feelings and who really cares
　　　　about you.

He is the only one who shares my feelings represents a positive statement corresponding to the negative one in the original (KJV "for I have
no man like-minded"). Who shares my feelings translates a very rare Greek
adjective meaning "like-souled." This word means not so much a sharing
of the same disposition as a sharing of intimate feelings, a genuine concern
and care, as Paul goes on to say. Obviously, Paul is not talking about someone who shares Timothy's feelings, as some translations seem to suggest
(Mft "I have no one like him"; so also RSV JB NAB). Rather, he is comparing Timothy with himself, indicating that Timothy is the person he can
rely on to share his own concerns for the Philippian Christians (TEV NEB).
In some languages who shares my feelings is best rendered "who shares one
heart with me." In other languages one may say "he has my heart and
mind," "he thinks the same in his heart as I do," or "my thoughts are his
thoughts."

Paul wants his friends in Philippi to know that Timothy is the one
who, like himself, really cares about you. The adverb rendered really is a
word suggesting kinship (literally, "legitimately born"). It is often used in
the sense of "genuinely" or "sincerely" or "truly." The adjectival form is
used in 1 Tim 1.2, where Paul speaks of Timothy as "my *true* son in the
faith." The verb "to care" in this clause is the same verb as that used in
4.6, where the readers are advised "Don't *worry* about anything." In the
present context the verb does not have the negative sense of "to be anxious for" but the positive sense of "to take genuine interest in" (NEB
NAB), or "to really care about" the well-being of others. In some languages "to care for someone else" may be most effectively expressed as
"help," for example, "he really wants to help you."

2.21　　Everyone else is concerned only with his own affairs, not with
　　　　the cause of Jesus Christ.

It is difficult to tell whether Paul is here making a parenthetical statement as to the general state of the world around him, or is making a harsh
and sweeping indictment of his associates. It is, of course, clear that apart
from Timothy there was no one he could count on at the moment. Every-

one else is concerned only with his own affairs is literally "that all seek after their own thing." The verb rendered is concerned is literally "seek" or "look after"; the meaning is that everyone is pursuing his own interests. In some languages one may translate this statement as "everyone else thinks only about helping himself," "...thinks just about how he can make everything turn out to his own advantage," or "...thinks only about how he can advance himself."

The cause of Jesus Christ (literally, "the things of Jesus Christ"), refers probably to the work that is to be done for Jesus Christ in restoring the harmony of the Christian community at Philippi. Not with the cause of Jesus Christ may be expressed by "not thinking about how he can help Jesus Christ," or "not concerned about how he can do what Jesus Christ would want."

2.22   And you yourselves know how he has proved his worth, how he and I, like a son and his father, have worked together for the sake of the gospel.

Not only does Timothy have Paul's fullest confidence; he also has proved his worth to the Philippians. This verbal phrase is the translation of a Greek noun meaning literally "proof." It is related to the verb used in 1.10, where TEV renders "to choose." It is used of gold or silver which has been tested and found genuine. Paul is not just saying that "Timothy's record is known to you" (NEB), but that "you know how he has stood the test" (Mft). The Philippians know that Tomothy is not a mediocre substitute, for he cooperated with Paul when the apostle first brought the gospel to their city (Acts 16). The verb "you know" should not be taken as an imperative but as an indicative; Timothy's worth was something the Philippians already knew.

You yourselves know may be expressed in some languages as "you yourselves already know," or "you yourselves surely know."

It may be difficult to speak of Paul's estimation of Timothy by using literally a term such as worth, for this might suggest in some languages a kind of commercial value rather than Timothy's inherent qualities. How he has proved his worth may be rendered, therefore, as "how good he has proved to be," or "how valuable he has been."

What Paul goes on to say is somewhat cryptic; it is literally "how, as a child a father, he served with me ...." The focus is not on the manner in which Timothy served Paul (like a son to his father), but on the very intimate relationship in which the two worked together for the advancement of the gospel. Accordingly, TEV renders explicitly how he and I, like a son and his father, have worked together. The original meaning of the verb rendered <u>worked</u> is "to serve, or work, as a slave" (Gpd "he worked like a slave with me." See also the discussion under 1.1).

<u>How he and I, like a son and his father, have worked together for the sake of the gospel</u> is an amplification of the first part of the verse, and it may be understood as an explanation of how Timothy <u>proved his worth</u>. However, in a number of languages it may be necessary to repeat here the verb "know," for example, "You yourselves know how valuable he has proved to be, and how Timothy and I, like a son and his father, have worked...." In some languages it may even be necessary to show clearly that <u>like a son and his father</u> is to be understood in a figurative sense, for example, "he has worked with me just like a son would work with his own father," or "...just like a man's son would help his father."

The phrase <u>for the sake of the gospel</u> can also be taken as meaning "for the advancement of the gospel" (Brc). In several languages the most effective way of speaking about "the advancement of the gospel" would be to say "in order that more and more people would hear the good news," or "...believe the good news."

2.23   So I hope to send him to you as soon as I know how things are going to turn out for me.

The pronoun <u>him</u> is emphatic in Greek (literally, "this one, then, I hope to send").

<u>I know</u> is rendered "I see" in some translations. It means literally "to look away," that is, to exclude everything else and to concentrate on one thing. It can also be used in the sense of seeing the issue of events, or of knowing the outcome of a situation. The last sense appears to be the one most suitable in the present context. In this type of context <u>I know</u> may be best rendered in some languages as "I learn," "I found out about," or "the news has come to me."

<u>How things are going to turn out for me</u> refers apparently to the verdict of the trial, which Paul expected would shortly be handed down. This clause may be rendered as "what will happen to me," "whether I will be convicted or not," or "whether or not I will be released."

2.24   And I trust in the Lord that I myself will be able to come to you soon.

<u>I trust</u> can also be rendered "I am confident" (NEB NAB). The verb used is a strong one, carrying the components of confidence, reliance, and hope. The ground of this confidence and hope is <u>in the Lord</u>. Every mood of Paul's life is regulated by the will of the Lord. <u>I trust</u> has here the force of "if the Lord wills it" (Brc; cf. 1 Cor 4.19). It is only <u>in the Lord</u> that

the apostle can look ahead with confidence, and with this confidence he says I myself will be able to come to you soon, that is, to follow soon after Timothy.

For the translation of I trust in the Lord, see the similar phrase in verse 19. In this context, in the Lord may suggest either the agency of the confidence, for example, "the Lord has given me confidence that"; or the condition for the content of what is believed or hoped, for example, "I trust that, if it is the Lord's will, I myself will be able to come to you soon."

Languages differ rather radically in the so-called "locative viewpoint" for the use of verbs such as "come" and "go." In this context Paul is speaking as though from the standpoint of the people at Philippi, that is, their viewpoint when they hear Paul's letter, and so he can appropriately use "come." However, in some languages it is necessary to maintain the viewpoint of the writer, and therefore it is necessary to say "to go to you soon."

2.25   I have thought it necessary to send to you our brother Epaphroditus, who has worked and fought by my side and who has served as your messenger in helping me.

Paul now turns to speak about Epaphroditus, commending him and explaining his situation. It is difficult to be certain whether Epaphroditus is still with Paul as this letter is being written or has already begun his journey back to Philippi. If he is still with Paul, he will be the bearer of this letter. The verb I have thought, which is in the aorist tense, is then taken as a so-called "epistolary" aorist; that is, the writer puts himself in the position of the reader for whom, when the letter arrives, the writer's present thoughts and actions would be matters of the past. In English, however, one would normally render the verb in the present or the perfect tense. This view is favored by most modern translators, thus "I feel" (NEB), "I think" (Mft JB), or I have thought ("I have decided" NAB).

Since Epaphroditus is obviously a member of the Philippian community, both NEB and TEV render our brother (inclusive our) rather than the exclusive "my brother" (RSV NAB). The expression means "our fellow-Christian" (Brc). Our brother may be expressed in some languages as "our fellow believer." But such an expression must be extended even further in some languages as "one who believes in Jesus even as we do."

Who has worked and fought by my side translates two Greek compound nouns, literally "my fellow-worker and fellow-soldier." These terms refer to Epaphroditus as Paul's partner in his labor and fight for the cause of Christ and the gospel (Brc "who has done Christ's work and fought

[81]

Christ's battle with me"). The expression "fellow-soldier," occurring elsewhere only in Philemon 2, reminds us that Christian work is a battle (cf.
1.27 ff.).

A rendering of the verb <u>has worked</u> should not suggest mere physical
activity — "tent making," for example. What is important here is that Epaphroditus had "worked for the gospel." Also, it may be misleading to use the
military figure of speech suggested by <u>fought by my side.</u> This could suggest to some readers that Paul and Epaphroditus were actually soldiers, or
that they had fought together against lions in some arena where Christians
were being persecuted. One can, however, preserve something of the concept of a struggle by rendering fought by my side as "joined me in defending the good news."

Epaphroditus is further described as "your apostle and minister of my
need." In the New Testament "apostle" is often used in the technical
sense of "the Twelve," that is, the apostles chosen by Jesus, and "minister" is understood as "one who performs priestly functions." It is not likely
that the special sense of either of these terms is intended here. Furthermore, the coordinate construction "apostle and minister" is best taken as
forming one event, the latter being the semantic goal of the former. Thus
one can render "your messenger to serve my need" (cf. NEB JB NAB).
By transforming this phrase into a relative clause parallel to the preceding
clause, we have the TEV rendering, <u>who has served as your messenger in
helping me.</u> This may be rendered in some languages as "who has been
your messenger in coming to help me," or "he has been your messenger
who has come and helped me."

2.26   He is anxious to see you all and is very upset because you had
        heard that he was sick.

Paul now gives his reason for sending Epaphroditus back to Philippi.
Since the context makes it clear that what Paul goes on to say is explanatory, it may be necessary to indicate clearly the meaning of the Greek
conjunction rendered often as "since," "because," or "for."

<u>He is anxious to see you all</u> is literally "he was longing for you all."
Some Greek manuscripts read "he was longing to see you all," but there
is really no difference in meaning. In Greek, this construction of connecting a participle with an imperfect predicate verb indicates a continued or
constant state. The verb rendered <u>anxious to see</u> is a very strong term, denoting a strong feeling of homesickness (Brc "he was homesick to see you
all"). It is used in 1.8 of Paul's <u>deep feeling</u> towards the Philippians. Ob-
serve the recurring <u>you all</u>; the feeling of Epaphroditus for all the believers
in Philippi is emphasized. <u>He is anxious to see you all</u> may be rendered as

"he wants very much to see you all," sometimes expressed idiomatically as "his heart is telling him how much he wants to see you all," or "his heart is reaching out to you all."

In Greek is very upset is a participle which goes with the imperfect predicate verb in the preceding clause. This is another strong verb, denoting great mental distress and agitation. It is used in Mark 14.33 to describe Jesus' agony in Gethsemane. Such mental distress may be expressed idiomatically as "his heart is jumping" or "his insides are moving." It may be necessary to introduce one element which is lacking in the second part of this verse. Epaphroditus' distress involved the fact that he had learned that the believers in Philippi had heard about his sickness. Therefore it may be necessary to say "he was very distressed because he learned that you had heard about his sickness," or ". . . that he was sick."

2.27   Indeed he was sick and almost died. But God had pity on him, and not only on him but on me, too, and spared me an even greater sorrow.

Epaphroditus' sickness must have been grave, for he almost died. The serious nature of the sickness is emphasized again in verse 30, he . . . nearly died. To indicate the seriousness of Epaphroditus' illness, it may be advisable to translate the first part of this verse as "indeed he was very sick," or "it is certainly true that he was very sick." He . . . almost died may be expressed as "he was about to die," "he was just close to dying," or "we thought he would die."

God had pity on him may be expressed in some languages as "God was very good to him," or "God showed great kindness to him."

God's mercy not only saved the life of Epaphroditus; it also affected Paul personally. It spared me an even greater sorrow, literally, "lest I should have sorrow upon sorrow" (RSV). An even greater sorrow probably means the sorrow that would have resulted from the death of Epaphroditus in addition to the sorrow caused by his grave illness.

The verb spared in this type of context suggests both negation and causation, for example, "God caused me not to have even greater sorrow," or "God caused me not to sorrow even more." In some languages sorrow may itself be translated as a causative, for example, "a cause for weeping." Therefore, in some instances one may say "God caused me not to experience a cause for weeping."

2.28   I am all the more eager, then, to send him to you, so that you will be glad again when you see him, and my own sorrow will disappear.

I am all the more eager, then, to send him is literally "I sent him, therefore, the more eagerly." Here "I sent" is probably to be taken as an epistolary aorist (cf. 2.25). The Greek comparative adverb rendered all the more eager should not be taken in the sense of "more hastily." It is used, rather, in the sense of "more eagerly," referring to the spirit in which Paul dispatches his fellow-worker, not to outward haste. Paul's eagerness may be expressed as a type of desire, for example, "I want all the more, therefore, to send him to you," or "that is why I want so much to send him to you."

The Greek word order seems to suggest that the adverb again is best taken with glad, as in TEV (cf. NAB), rather than with see, as in RSV and NEB. The Philippians' cheerfulness had been clouded by Epaphroditus' sickness; they would certainly regain their cheerfulness at his safe return.

The apostle identifies himself so closely with his readers that their sorrow and anxiety are his own. If Epaphroditus' safe return will mean the restoration of their happiness, then, he says, my own sorrow will disappear (literally, "I might be the less sorrowful"). The adjective "less sorrowful" appears only here in the New Testament. It means "to be free from sorrow" or "to be relieved of anxiety." My own sorrow will disappear is part of the purpose introduced by the conjunctive phrase so that. It may be necessary to repeat the expression of purpose, for example, "so that you will be glad again when you see him, and so that my own sorrow will disappear," or ". . . so that I will not have sorrow any longer."

2.29   Receive him, then, with joy, as a brother in the Lord. Show
          respect to all such people as he,

Paul now appeals to the Philippians to give Epaphroditus a cordial welcome. With joy (literally, "with all joy") is best understood in the sense of "hearts full of joy" (Mft) or "most hearty welcome" (JB). As a brother in the Lord is literally "in the Lord." It is possible to take the phrase with receive him. If so, it could mean "receive him as the Lord would receive him." It is also possible to take it as qualifying with joy. The sense would then be to give Epaphroditus a most hearty Christian welcome, that is, "welcome him the way Christians should welcome fellow believers." If this phrase is to be understood as an attributive to joy, it may be necessary to expand it in such a way as to indicate more precisely what the relation would be, for example, "with all joy, as would be characteristic of those who are in union with the Lord," "with all joy, such as being in union with the Lord would produce," or "with all joy, as believers in the Lord should." Another possibility is to take the phrase as referring to the mutual relationship of the Philippians and Epaphroditus. If so, it can mean as a brother in the Lord, or "as a fellow believer who is in union with the Lord," or even "because you are fellow believers in the Lord."

The clause show respect to all such people as he is rendered in NEB as "you should honor men like him." The expression translated respect has the components of honor and value (Mft "value men like that"). Since the honor and respect due to people who are like Epaphroditus must be based upon what they have done, rather than upon some personal characteristic or outward features, it may be useful to translate show respect to all such people as he as "give honor to all people who have done what he has done."

2.30   because he risked his life and nearly died for the sake of the work of Christ, in order to give me the help that you yourselves could not give.

He risked his life translates a Greek participial phrase which occurs nowhere else in the New Testament. The word rendered risked may be used in reference to a gambler's staking everything on a throw of the dice. While these are rather strong words in the present context, they probably refer to nothing more than the risk of ill-health involved in Epaphroditus' devoted service to the people. In a number of languages he risked his life can best be rendered as "he came near to dying," or "he exposed himself to the possibility of dying." The final phrase in this clause, and nearly died, must be rendered in a way that will indicate, not only the risk that was involved, but even the great likelihood that Epaphroditus would actually die.

Even though some old manuscripts have the reading "the work of the Lord" (ASV margin), instead of the work of Christ adopted in the UBS text, it is not favored by modern translators. The reading "the Lord" was probably substituted for "Christ" by certain copyists who were influenced by the expression "the work of the Lord" in 1 Cor 15.58 and 16.10. The work of Christ must be understood in the sense of "working for Christ"; not what Christ did, but the work which Christ wants to have done. The phrase for the sake of the work of Christ may then be rendered as "in order to help in working for Christ," or "in order to help in doing what Christ would want people to do."

In order to give me the help that you yourselves could not give is literally "in order that he might supply your lack of service to me." The TEV rendering makes clear that Paul is not complaining about the deficiency of the Philippians' service to him, as a literal rendering might suggest. The only "deficiency" is that they were not able to be with the apostle to help

[85]

him. Their messenger Epaphroditus made up this deficiency, even to the extent of risking his life.

Since the phrase for the sake of the work of Christ has already introduced a kind of purpose involved in the activity of Epaphroditus, it may be necessary to separate the final purpose clause from what precedes by reintroducing an expression of Epaphroditus' activity, for example, "He did all this in order to help me in the way in which you yourselves were not able to help."

CHAPTER 3

TEV

The True Righteousness

1 In conclusion, my brothers, be joyful in your union with the Lord. I don't mind repeating what I have written before, and you will be safer if I do so. 2 Watch out for those who do evil things, those dogs, those men who insist on cutting the body. 3 It is we, not they, who have received the true circumcision, for we worship God by means of his Spirit and rejoice in our life in union with Christ Jesus. We do not put any trust in external ceremonies. 4 I could, of course, put my trust in such things. If anyone thinks he can trust in external ceremonies, I have even more reason to feel that way. 5 I was circumcised when I was a week old. I am an Israelite by birth, of the tribe of Benjamin, a pure-blooded Hebrew. As far as keeping the Jewish Law is concerned, I was a Pharisee, 6 and I was so zealous that I persecuted the church. As far a person can be righteous by obeying the commands of the Law, I was without fault. 7 But all those things that I might count as profit I now reckon as loss for Christ's sake. 8 Not only those things; I reckon everything as complete loss for the sake of what is so much more valuable, the knowledge of Christ Jesus my Lord. For his sake I have thrown everything away; I consider it all as mere garbage, so that I may gain Christ 9 and be completely united with him. I no longer have a righteousness of my own, the kind that is gained by obeying the Law. I now have the righteousness that is given through faith in Christ, the righteousness that comes from God and is based on faith. 10 All I want is to know Christ and to experience the power of his resurrection, to share in his sufferings and become like him in his death, 11 in the hope that I myself will be raised from death to life.

(3.1-11)

RSV

1 Finally, my brethren, rejoice in the Lord. To write the same things to you is not irksome to me, and is safe for you. 2 Look out for the dogs, look out for those who mutilate the flesh. 3 For we are the true circumcision, who worship God in spirit,[e] and glory in Christ Jesus, and put no confidence in the flesh. 4 Though I myself have reason for confidence in the flesh also. If any other man thinks he has reason for confidence in the flesh, I have more: 5 circumcised on the eighth day, of the people of Israel, of the tribe of Benjamin, a Hebrew born of Hebrews; as to the law a Pharisee, 6 as to zeal a persecutor of the church, as to righteousness under the law blameless. 7 But whatever gain I had, I counted as loss for the sake of Christ. 8 Indeed I count everything as loss because of the surpassing worth of knowing Christ Jesus my Lord. For his sake I have suffered the loss of all things, and count them as refuse, in order that I may gain Christ 9 and be found in him, not having a righteousness of my own, based on law, but that which is through faith in Christ, the righteousness from God that depends on faith; 10 that I may know him and the power of his resurrection, and may share his sufferings, becoming like him in his death, 11 that if possible I may attain the resurrection from the dead.

[e]Other ancient authorities read *worship by the Spirit of God*

(3.1-11)

Instead of The True Righteousness, one may use as a section heading
an expression such as "The righteousness which is through faith in Christ,"
"The righteousness which comes from God," or "The righteousness which
is based on faith." Such nominal expressions may require a verbal form in
certain languages, for example, "How people can truly be put right with
God," "How people are put right through believing in Christ," or "God
puts us right with himself through our trusting him."

At this point of the letter, Paul appears to be about to conclude his
usual farewell message, but suddenly he breaks in with what could be considered a long postscript. This kind of digression and abrupt change in
mood are not entirely unknown in the Pauline letters (see, for example,
Gal 3.1). As the apostle is about to conclude his letter, he feels constrained
to add a few words of warning against his opponents from outside (vv. 1b-
3). This leads him into a moving statement of his personal religious experience (vv. 4-11). He recounts his religious activity under the Law and as-
sesses the results of his conversion to Christ. To him, the true righteousness
comes from God, is given through Christ, and is based on faith (v. 9).

3.1   In conclusion, my brothers, be joyful in your union with the
        Lord. I don't mind repeating what I have written before, and
        you will be safer if I do so.

That there is a break in the flow of thought in this verse is recognized
by practically all interpreters and is reflected in various translations, but
scholars cannot agree as to whether the break is in the middle of the verse
or at the end of it. NEB JB GeCL have the break in the middle of the
verse, while Phps and NAB have it at the end. While the context seems to
indicate a break in the middle of the verse, it is not necessary to consider
the first part of verse 1 as the conclusion of the preceding paragraph, as
the Greek phrase rendered in conclusion is sometimes loosely used as a
marker of transition to a new section or fresh subject matter (cf. 1 Thes
4.1; 2 Thes 3.1). Here Paul is no doubt introducing new subject matter,
most likely a concluding remark, and so renderings like "finally" (RSV JB)
or in conclusion (Phps TEV) are quite adequate. This may be expressed in
some languages as "now I want to end my letter by saying," "finally, this
is what I say," or "before stopping my writing I want to say."

As in other contexts, my brothers may be rendered as "my fellow believers." Such expressions of direct address must be placed at the beginning
of a discourse in some languages, and therefore one may wish to modify
the order by saying "My fellow believers, in finishing this statement I still
want to say...."

The exhortation be joyful in your union with the Lord, rendered in most translations as "rejoice in the Lord," may express a wish (Brc "... to wish you the joy that comes from being united with the Lord"). Christians are to be joyful, and their joy springs from Christ. In sounding this note Paul picks up the thought of 2.18, and the same phrase is repeated in 4.4.

The phrase "in the Lord" may be understood in the sense of the condition which leads to joy, for example, "be happy because of your union with the Lord" (cf. GeCL). It can also be taken as an indication of the agent which causes the joy, for example, "may the Lord give you much joy," or "may the Lord cause you to be very happy." With expressions such as these, it may be necessary to suggest that this is a kind of prayer addressed to the Lord. In this type of interpretation it cannot be understood as an imperative, and therefore one may translate "I pray that the Lord will cause you to be very happy."

The verb rendered "rejoice" is also the Greek word for "farewell." For this reason NEB, for example, includes both meanings in the translation, "... farewell; I wish you joy in the Lord" (cf. TNT). However, except in 2 Cor 13.11, the word is generally not used in the sense of "farewell" in the New Testament.

I don't mind repeating what I have written before is literally "to write the same things to you is not irksome to me" (RSV). There are several possible interpretations of "the same things." It is possible to regard the phrase as referring to the repeated call of "rejoicing" in this letter (Mft "I am repeating this word 'rejoice' in my letter"). But such an exhortation appears to have no direct bearing on the safety of the Philippians. It is also suggested that the words refer to the repeated warnings against disasters within the church mentioned in 4.1 ff. Verses 2-21 of chapter 3 are then of necessity taken as a long digression. The most likely explanation, however, is to take the words as an introduction to what follows in 3.2 ff., that is, a repetition of the warnings against false teachers which the apostle has sent in previous letters. Repeated warnings are necessary for the safety or spiritual well-being of the Philippians.

To avoid the implication that this sentence is merely a reference to the preceding admonition or prayer, it may be important to translate before as "on another occasion." I don't mind may be rendered in some instances as "I do not hesitate at all," or, perhaps, "it doesn't bother me."

The word rendered safer means primarily "stable," and is used of something to be relied on as profitable. Safer may be expressed in some languages as being "in less danger." Therefore one may say "you will be in less danger if I do so," or "... if I repeat what I have said."

[89]

3.2   Watch out for those wo do evil things, those dogs, those men
         who insist on cutting the body.

In Greek the imperative <u>watch out for</u> is repeated three times in this
verse. Thus the earnestness and seriousness of the warning is quite apparent. This warning is not against three different groups of people, but
against the same group described in three ways. For this reason a number of
translations, including SpCL and TEV, retain only one imperative and restructure the verse into one sentence with a series of appositional clauses.
A literal rendering of <u>watch out for</u> can suggest merely "looking around in
order to see." It is important, therefore, to employ a rendering which will
clearly mean "beware of" or "be on your guard against."

Most probably Paul's opponents were gnostic Jewish Christians who
insisted on combining the gospel with the Law. These people are characterized by extremely derogatory terms. <u>Those who do evil things</u>, literally,
"evil workers" or "malicious workers," is reminiscent of the "deceitful
workmen" mentioned in 2 Cor 11.13. It is possible that there is a play on
words here, a censure against those Judaizers who teach a salvation by
"works," not by faith. The focus, however, seems to be on their works
rather than their teachings, so a more generic statement like that of TEV
seems desirable. Those wo do evil things may be rendered simply as
"those who do what is bad" or "those who do what is wrong." This should
not be merely an expression meaning "sinners."

<u>Dogs</u> were regarded by the Jews as despicable and miserable creatures.
They are usually mentioned with contempt in the Old Testament (1 Sam
24.14; Psa 22.16, 20). In Rev 22.15 the word "dogs" stands for those who
are so impure that they are barred from the Holy City (cf. Matt 7.6; 15.26).
This is the most insulting term of abuse applied by orthodox Jews to Gentiles. Here Paul turns it around and applies it to those Jewish Christians
who misrepresent the gospel and subvert the faith.

In English the translation <u>those dogs</u>, in apposition with the clause
<u>who do evil things</u>, is very effective. But in some languages it would be
understood only as a kind of appositional explanation of "evil things."
Therefore one must often make the phrase <u>those dogs</u> into a complete sentence or into another relative clause, for example, "they are like dogs" or
"who are dogs." In some languages, a word for "dogs" does not carry the
bad connotations associated with it in Greek and, to a somewhat lesser
extent, in English. It may, therefore, be necessary to qualify the term as
"bad dogs" or "foul dogs."

<u>Those men who insist on cutting the body</u> translates a noun in Greek
which means literally "the cutting" (JB "the cutters," NEB "mutilation").
This word puns on another Greek word meaning "circumcision." NEB adds

explicitly "mutilation—'circumcision' I will not call it" (cf. Brc). The "circumcision" is for the Jews a proud title, used to refer to the community set apart as God's people. But Paul denies those erring Jewish Christians this honored title, instead, he calls them mockingly "the cutters," comparing them to the self-inflicted mutilations of the prophets of Baal (1 Kgs 18.28). Self-mutilation, which was practiced in pagan cults, is explicitly forbidden in the Law (Lev 21.5).

In some languages the appositional phrase those men who insist on cutting the body may need to be rendered as a separate sentence, for example, "They are men who insist on cutting the body." Since a literal rendering of cutting the body could suggest "cutting up the body," it may be necessary to say "make cuts on the body," or "cut off a part of the body."

3.3   It is we, not they, who have received the true circumcision, for we worship God by means of his Spirit and rejoice in our life in union with Christ Jesus. We do not put any trust in external ceremonies.

Paul now explains why the Judaizers have no right to claim the title of "the true circumcision." The pronoun we is emphatic, stressing the contrast between the true Christians and the Judaizers. TEV, accordingly, makes it explicit, it is we, not they (so also FrCL). In this context we must be inclusive in those languages which make a distinction between inclusive and exclusive first person plural, for Paul includes, not only himself and Timothy, but also the believers in Philippi. The phrase not they should be understood as a reference to those who do evil things; it could be rendered as "not those other men," or "not those other people."

Who have received the true circumcision represents a restructuring of a single noun in Greek, meaning "the circumcision." True is supplied to emphasize the contrast (JB "the real people of the circumcision"; Brc "it is we who are really circumcised"). The reference is obviously to the church's consciousness of being the new people of God. The true significance of circumcision does not lie in an outward mark on the body, but in the inward consecration of the heart (Rom 2.28-29).

The verb received, in the clause who have received the true circumcision, may be regarded as a kind of pseudopassive for the subject who (that is, we) are the ones who undergo the process of being circumcised. Therefore one may translate who have received the true circumcision as "who have been truly circumcised," or "who have been circumcised in the way one really should be circumcised."

The claim to the title of true circumcision is based on three reasons, which in the Greek text are given in three participial phrases. TEV connects these explanations to the main clause with for.

First, we worship God by means of his Spirit. This is a difficult statement; and the several Greek textual variants are reflected in different translations. The earliest extant reading is "who worship in spirit," without reference to God, but the omission of "God" is probably due to a scribal oversight. NEB understands this statement in the sense of "whose worship is spiritual." Some translations (for example, Mft RSV Bruce) support the reading "who worship God in spirit," which makes "God" the object of worship. The translators who adopt either of the above readings understand Paul to mean that the worship of the true Christian is offered in the domain of the spirit, not in the realm of external ceremonies. While it is true that Paul is here emphasizing the "spiritual" aspect of circumcision, there is a serious problem in taking "spirit" as a reference to the human spirit. In the Greek New Testament the term "spirit" without a qualifier usually means the Holy Spirit, so it is more likely that "spirit" here is not the human spirit but the Holy Spirit. This interpretation is supported by the fact that "spirit" appears side by side with "God." For this reason, a number of translations prefer a third reading which is supported by some important early manuscripts. It reads "who worship by the Spirit of God." The Holy Spirit is the dynamic source of Christian life, and he alone can inspire us to worship God. In many languages it is obligatory to identify the object of worship; thus we can restructure this statement into we worship God by means of his Spirit (so also Gpd cf. Phps Brc). By means of his Spirit represents an instrumental dative, indicating that the worship is under the impulse and direction of the Holy Spirit.

The verb rendered worship originally meant "to serve for hire." It is usually used of a service rendered willingly; thus it came to be used in the technical sense of religious service. In biblical Greek it always refers to service rendered either to God or to pagan deities. Whenever God is the object of service, the verb is usually rendered worship.

In many languages a term for worship develops from a more specific meaning such as "to pray to," since prayer seems to be such an essential element of worship. An expression of means indicated by the phrase by means of his Spirit is rendered in some languages as "by the help of his Spirit," "with his Spirit helping us," or even "his Spirit helps us to do this."

The second reason given in support of the claim that Christians are "the true circumcision" is that we rejoice in our life in union with Christ Jesus, literally, "boasting in Christ Jesus." The verb in this clause, "boast," is one of Paul's favorite words, used some thirty-five times in his letters. It is sometimes used in the sense of proud self-confidence (Rom 2.23; 1 Cor

4.7; Gal 6.13) and sometimes of humble submission to God's grace as shown in the death of Jesus and in what he has done (Rom 5.2, 11; 1 Cor 1.31; Gal 6.14). The latter sense is used in this context, with the focus on the triumphant joy of the Christians. The clause may mean either that Christ Jesus is the object of the pride (NEB Brc), or that our life in union with Christ Jesus is the source of our joy (TEV).

In order to indicate clearly that to rejoice in our life in union with Christ Jesus is also a reason for knowing that the believers had received the true circumcision, it may be important to repeat a conjunction indicating cause, for example, "and it is also because we rejoice in our life in union with Christ Jesus."

Rejoice in our life in union with Christ Jesus may be expressed by saying "are very happy because of our life which is in union with Christ Jesus," since the goal of rejoicing is also the cause for rejoicing. In those languages in which a noun such as life must be expressed as a verb, one may say "we are happy because we live in union with Christ Jesus," "...live joined to Christ Jesus," or "...live as though we are one with Christ Jesus."

The third reason that Christians are "the true circumcision" is that we do not put any trust in external ceremonies (literally, "having no confidence in the flesh"). This clause represents a rather negative restatement of the preceding clause. For this reason some translations link the two statements together, using, for example, "without" (JB), "rather than" (NAB), "instead of" (Knox), etc. (cf. GeCL "not...but..."). To indicate clearly that this is an added reason for knowing that Christian believers have received the true circumcision, one may say "and it is because we do not put any trust in ceremonies involving our bodies," "...in religious ritual involving our bodies," "...in what happens to our bodies," or "...in what we do to our bodies."

The word "flesh" can mean various things in biblical Greek, depending on the context. It can mean physical "flesh" (Luke 24.39), "race" (Rom 11.14), "human beings" (Acts 2.17), "human nature" (Rom 8.3), "human standard" (1 Cor 1.26), etc. In the present context, the rendering "anything external" (NEB) appears to be rather vague. What Paul means by the term is explained in the following verses, namely, the ceremonial observances of the Law, with circumcision as the most typical example. It is therefore best to render "flesh" more specifically as external ceremonies.

3.4   I could, of course, put my trust in such things. If anyone thinks he can trust in external ceremonies, I have even more reason to feel that way.

Paul now takes great pains in giving a brief account of his past religious life. The purpose is to let his readers understand why he has warned them in such blunt terms, and to refute the claims of his opponents. For the purpose of argument he deliberately places himself in the position of an authentic Jew.

I is emphatic. The shift from "we" to "I" and the frequent use of "I" show that what Paul has to say here is personal. The tone of the argument makes it clear that he does not rely on outward privileges and ceremonies, thus I could, of course.... The phrase put my trust in such things is literally "having confidence even in the flesh," and "in the flesh" is used three times in succession. To avoid redundancy, TEV renders the second occurrence in such things, the context making it perfectly clear what is referred to (NEB "that kind"). The third occurrence is again rendered as in external ceremonies. For the meaning of trust, see 2.24.

The phrase of course may be rendered in some languages as "there is every reason for me to...," or "I would be fully justified in...."

Put my trust in such things may be expressed as "put my confidence in such ceremonies," or "believe that such things as would happen to my body would be valuable." The reference here is not merely to circumcision as an outward ceremony; it involves much more, a matter of total ritual observance. One may even say "put my trust in being the kind of person I am."

I have even more reason to feel that way adequately brings out the sense and force of a terse expression in Greek which means literally "I more" (cf. Brc "I have an even stronger claim").

3.5   I was circumcised when I was a week old, I am an Israelite by birth, of the tribe of Benjamin, a pure-blooded Hebrew. As far as keeping the Jewish Law is concerned, I was a Pharisee.

Paul now gives a list of qualifications which make him truly a Jew. I was circumcised when I was a week old (literally, "as to the circumcision, on the eighth day"). This is in accordance with the provision of the Law (Gen 17.9-14; Lev 12.3) and indicates that he was from a family which was meticulous in its fulfillment of all prescribed duties. He was not a proselyte, a convert whose circumcision occurred after his conversion as an adult. In Jewish reckoning the day of one's birth was counted as a full day; thus when I was a week old means "seven days after my birth."

In languages in which the passive expression I was circumcised cannot

[94]

3.5

be employed, it is often possible to use an indefinite third person plural subject, for example, "they circumcised me." In some languages it is possible to translate circumcised in this kind of context as "cut off the foreskin." If such vocabulary is regarded as vulgar or in bad taste, it may be better to say "made a cut upon me." In some languages translators simply borrow an expression meaning "cut around" without indicating specifically what part of the body is involved. A precise explanation can be given in a glossary, thus avoiding in the text terms which might be offensive, especially in the public reading of the Scriptures.

I am an Israelite by birth (literally, "out of the race of Israel") indicates that Paul possessed by birth all the privileges of the chosen people. Israel is the covenant name of the people of God (Rom 9.4; 11.1; 2 Cor 11.22). I am an Israelite by birth may be expressed as "I have been an Israelite from the time I was born," but it would be more natural in many languages to say "both my parents were Israelites."

Paul claims adherence to the tribe of Benjamin, a tribe regarded with particular esteem (Judges 5.14; Hos 5.8). The Benjamites had given the nation its first lawful king, whose name was Saul, the same as the apostle's original Hebrew name. Except for David's own tribe of Judah, the tribe of Benjamin alone remained loyal to the house of David after the disruption of the monarchy (1 Kgs 12.21). It also had the unique privilege of having within its borders the Holy City of Jerusalem and the Temple (Judges 1.21). Although of the tribe of Benjamin is a reference specifically to Paul, in many languages it would be more natural to speak of the parents of Paul as belonging to the tribe of Benjamin. This would assure Paul's membership in the same tribe.

A pure-blooded Hebrew is literally "a Hebrew of Hebrews" (JB "a Hebrew born of Hebrew parents"). There was no heathen blood in him. In the Old Testament the word "Hebrew" is a distinctive national term; while in the New Testament it usually designates the Jew who retained his national language and way of life, in contrast to the "Hellenist," a Jew who generally spoke Greek and conformed to Gentile customs and cultures (Acts 6.1; 22.2). Thus the "Hebrew" regarded himself as belonging to the elite of his race. A pure-blooded Hebrew can be best expressed in some languages as "my forefathers were all Hebrews," or "my lineage has always been Hebrew."

Thus far Paul has listed his inherited privileges. Now he proceeds to mention his personal attainments.

He says, literally, "with reference to the Law, a Pharisee." The Pharisees were the strictest sect in Judaism, taking upon themselves the sacred duty of keeping and defending both the Mosaic Law and the tradition of the fathers. Paul's statement can be rendered more explicitly as far as

[95]

keeping the Jewish Law is concerned, I was a Pharisee. Notice that, instead of the more restricted term "Mosaic Law," TEV has Jewish Law (so also Brc). This term is more inclusive, since it covers the twofold duties of keeping the Mosaic Law and the interpretive traditions of the scribes. In saying I was a Pharisee, Paul claims faithfulness and sincerity in fulfilling the duties prescribed in the Jewish Law. For him Pharisee is not a name for reproach, but a title of honor (Acts 23.6; 26.5).

As far as keeping the Jewish Law is concerned may be expressed as "in my keeping the Jewish Law." Or one can shift the relation between the clauses in the final sentence and say "I kept the Jewish Law as a Pharisee." In a number of languages, however, one cannot speak of "keeping the Law" except in the sense of preserving a book of the Law in one's house. What is meant here, of course, is that Paul faithfully obeyed all the commandments in the Law. Therefore one may translate as "I did everything that the Jewish Law said I should do." The phrase the Jewish Law may be translated as "the Law which the Jews followed," or "the laws which the Jews obeyed," or "... were supposed to obey."

3.6   and I was so zealous that I persecuted the church. As far as a person can be righteous by obeying the commands of the Law, I was without fault.

The apostle continues with an ironical statement, literally "with reference to zeal, persecuting the church." This is the second in a series of three "with reference to" statements. In order to provide freshness in style and to bring out the ironical force better, the statement is best rephrased I was so zealous that I persecuted the church (cf. NAB Brc). To a Jew "zeal" for God was the greatest quality in religious life. Paul's zeal reached to the extent that he tried to wipe out those whom he considered the opponents of Judaism (Acts 8.3; 22.4; 26.9-11). The term church here embraces not primarily various local Christian congregations, but the universal body of Christ.

In some languages it may be necessary to specify the goal of Paul's zeal, or that which prompted the zeal. Therefore one may translate I was so zealous as "I was so anxious to serve God," or "I was very desirous to do what I thought God wanted me to do."

I persecuted the church may be rendered as "I caused the people in the church to suffer," or "I made it very difficult for the people who belonged to the church." In this type of context church may be rendered as "those who believed in Jesus," or "those who gathered together to worship Jesus."

Paul goes on to list one final personal achievement, that is, legal uprightness. He says, literally, "with reference to righteousness which is in the Law, having become faultless." Here "which is the Law" is best taken in the sense of "which consists of strict observance of the commandments prescribed by the Law." Thus TEV rephrases the clause explicitly as <u>as far as a person can be righteous by obeying the commands of the Law</u>. It may be very difficult in some languages to express the degree indicated by the phrase <u>as far as</u>. The closest natural equivalent may be a conditional expression, for example, "if you are thinking about how a man can be righteous by obeying the commands of the Law." <u>The commands of the Law</u> may be expressed in some languages as "what the Law commands," or "what a man is commanded to do in the Law."

The Greek noun rendered "righteousness" by most translators is a key term in Pauline thought. It is a difficult word with various shades of meaning. Depending on contexts, it can mean "religious duties," "the requirements of God," "that which is right," "righteousness," "uprightness," "justice," "right relationship with God," etc. In the present instance, the JB rendering "perfection" appears to lean too strongly on the moral aspect (so also "goodness" in Brc). "Legal rectitude" (NEB) is a good rendering, but it is too difficult for the average reader. Most translations retain the conventional rendering here. One can be more specific in rendering "so far as a man can stand in a right relationship with God by obeying the commands of the Law...."

The adjective rendered <u>without fault</u> is the same word translated <u>innocent</u> in 2.15. This word is often used to characterize someone who is faultless in the sight of other people. Paul is claiming that, as a devout Pharisee, there was no demand of the Law which he did not fulfill. He met all the standards of righteousness prescribed by the Law. <u>I was without fault</u> may be rendered as "there was nothing which I had not done," or "I had done everything," referring to his obeying all the commands of the Law. <u>I was without fault</u> may also be expressed as "no one could say I had failed in anything," or "it could not be said that I was in any way guilty."

3.7   **But all those things that I might count as profit I now reckon as loss for Christ's sake.**

Having stated his qualifications and achievements, Paul now reassesses his spiritual life after his conversion. With the conjunction <u>but</u> he marks the dramatic change of perspective.

<u>I might count as profit</u> is literally "were gains to me." This clause can also be taken in the sense of "were once gains to me" (NAB "I used to consider gain"). The tense of the verb rendered <u>reckon</u> is significant. It is the perfect tense ("have counted"), denoting an action in past time which con-

tinues to be effective in the present. The full force of the meaning would be something like "I counted those things as a loss, and I still reckon them as such." Since the focus is on the present effect, TEV renders the verb in the present tense (cf. 3.8, where Paul uses the same verb again, this time in the present tense). TEV supplies <u>now</u> to strengthen the force of contrast.

Paul here uses the figure of a balance sheet, showing assets and liabilities, <u>profit</u> and <u>loss</u>. All his advantages of birth and upbringing and his personal achievements as a zealous Pharisee, he had formerly set down in the "profit" column; now he has transferred them to the "loss" column. <u>For Christ's sake</u> supplies the motive for this dramatic revaluation and drastic change.

<u>All those things</u> can best be rendered in some languages as "all that I was and all that I did," or ". . . all that I did in obeying the Law."

It may be necessary in some languages to shift the figurative expressions of "profit and loss" and to speak of "advantage and disadvantage," for example, "all that I used to do which I might have counted as an advantage to myself I now realize is a disadvantage," ". . . has no value," or ". . . is of no advantage."

It is not easy to indicate clearly the relation of the phrase <u>for Christ's sake</u> to what has preceded. In some instances one may interpret this in the sense of "because of what Christ has done for me." Or one may render <u>for Christ's sake</u> as "because of what I want to do for Christ."

3.8   Not only those things; I reckon everything as complete loss for the sake of what is so much more valuable, the knowledge of Christ Jesus my Lord. For his sake I have thrown everything away; I consider it all as mere garbage, so that I may gain Christ

Verses 8-11 are a complicated long sentence in Greek. This sentence needs to be restructured into shorter sentences in order to preserve clarity of thought.

Paul uses a series of particles ("yes rather even") as a forceful introduction for an important statement. The combined force of these particles indicates that his statement in verse 7 is inadequate, and he feels constrained to reinforce it. The force of these particles has been expressed in various ways: JB "not only that"; NEB "I would say more"; Brc "yes, and more than that"; TEV <u>not only those things.</u> The TEV translation makes explicit the fact that the things which Paul counts as loss are not limited to those already mentioned. "Nothing" can compete with the supreme gain of knowing Christ. The contrast between verses 7 and 8 is clearly brought out in the TEV rendering: <u>those things</u> vs. <u>everything,</u> and <u>loss</u> vs. <u>complete loss.</u>

With the phrase not only those things, it may be necessary to add some verbal expression such as "I consider as a loss," or "I consider as no advantage at all," for example, "not only do I consider all these matters as no advantage at all, but I consider everything as nothing for the sake of what is so much more valuable."

TEV takes the preposition rendered "for" in both KJV and ASV to mean for the sake of, as in 3.7 above. It can also mean "because of" (RSV), signifying that the supreme worth of knowing Christ surpasses all other gains. Since the idea of comparison is already implicit in the neuter participle (used as a noun) rendered what is so much more valuable, there seems to be no need to give the preposition the unusual meaning of "compared to" (Mft Gpd). The basic meaning of this neuter participle is "surpassing" (Gpd JB; "supreme advantage"; Mft "supreme value").

It may be necessary in some languages to make more specific the expression I reckon everything as complete loss, for example, "I count everything I used to do as a complete loss," or "whatever I used to do is now completely valueless in my reckoning."

If for the sake of is understood as cause, one may translate this phrase as "because of what is so much more valuable." It is also possible to interpret for the sake of as introducing a type of goal, for example, "in order to gain what is so much more valuable," "in order to have what is so much more valuable," or "... what is worth so much more."

Paul further defines this "supreme advantage" as The knowledge of Christ Jesus my Lord. The noun translated knowledge is a difficult word. It was one of the key words in the pagan religions in Paul's time, often used of a revealed knowledge of the mystery of salvation — a mystical knowledge, a communion with the deity. It is possible that this sense is used here also, but more likely Paul's use of this word is rooted in an Old Testament concept of knowledge — God's knowledge of his people in election and grace (Exo 33.12, 17; Amos 3.2) and his people's knowledge of him in love and obedience (Jer 31.34; Hos 6.3; 8.2). Primarily, this knowledge is not intellectual but experiential. In this context, the knowledge of Christ is personal and intimate, as the expression my Lord shows, certainly more than an intellectual apprehension of truth about Christ. Rather, it is a personal appropriation of and communion with Christ himself. The knowledge of Christ Jesus no doubt does involve one's thoughts, but in its distinctive biblical usage it may be said to involve primarily one's heart. The knowledge of Christ Jesus means, not the knowledge Christ has, but my knowing Christ, and so one may restructure the phrase as "to know Christ Jesus as my Lord" (cf. GeCL). In some languages the order of Christ Jesus my Lord has to be reversed, that is, "my Lord Christ Jesus."

The knowledge of Christ Jesus my Lord is in apposition to the pre-

ceding clause, what is so much more valuable, and this appositional relation may need to be made more specific, for example, "namely, the knowledge of Christ Jesus my Lord," or "that is to say, the knowledge of Christ
Jesus my Lord."

Since in this context knowledge is not a matter merely of "knowing
about," it may be essential in some languages to employ a rendering such
as "experiencing Christ Jesus my Lord with me," or "becoming associated
with Christ Jesus my Lord."

I have thrown everything away is literally "I suffered the loss of all
things" (ASV). The verb is related to the word rendered loss in both the
previous and the present verses. The aorist tense looks back to a definite
occasion, presumably at Paul's conversion, when this great renunciation
took place. It is obvious in the present context (and especially in what
follows) that the act of renunciation is voluntary. Thus TEV renders the
passive verb as active, have thrown . . . away (NAB "have forfeited"; Brc
"have abandoned").

For his sake may be rendered as "because of him" or, as in some languages, "in order to serve him." I have thrown everything away should not
be understood in merely a physical sense. One can translate this expression
as "everything I used to do has become a complete loss," or ". . . has become useless." Or one may shift the figure somewhat by saying "I have
abandoned everything I used to do."

For the third time in this section Paul uses the same verb rendered
consistently as "count" in RSV. In the two previous occurrences TEV renders it as reckon, but in this last instance as consider. The intention is no
doubt to declare Paul's considered decision to do away with his old life.
In the light of this new valuation, he now sees everything as mere garbage.
The Greek word rendered garbage can mean either "excrement" (KJV
"dung") or "that which is thrown to the dogs," that is, "rubbish" (JB
NAB), "refuse" (RSV), or "garbage" (NEB). In any case, the idea is that
of utter worthlessness and disgust. I consider it all as mere garbage may be
rendered as "I count all this as fit for the refuse heap," or, expressed
somewhat more idiomatically, "I throw all of it into the street."

The motive of Paul's revaluation is to gain Christ. The verb used here
is a cognate of the noun rendered profit in verse 7. To gain Christ is best
understood in the sense of gaining a profit by personal appropriation of
Christ. It may be impossible in some languages to translate literally so that
I may gain Christ, for that might imply that Christ was an object which
could be acquired by purchase. In certain instances the metaphor gain
Christ may be modified into the form of a simile, for example, "I may, so
to speak, gain Christ." But this rendering could impair the significance of
the phrase as a whole. It may be better in some cases to translate "so that

I may have the advantage of being related to Christ," or "so that I may have the value of belonging to Christ."

3.9   and be completely united with him. I no longer have a righteous-
       ness of my own, the kind that is gained by obeying the Law. I
       now have the righteousness that is given through faith in Christ,
       the righteousness that comes from God and is based on faith.

Be completely united with him is literally "be found in him." Some commentators take this phrase as a reference to the final judgment ("the Day of Christ") or specifically to the time of the apostle's death (Mft "be found at death in him"). There seems to be no indication, however, that Paul is thinking of any particular moment in his life. More likely he has in mind the whole course of his Christian life. As the punctuation of TEV suggests, the phrase is to be taken closely with the preceding phrase, of which it is an expanded explanation. To gain Christ means to be complete-ly united with him.

The formula "in him" (along with "in Christ," "in me," and "in you") is one of the most characteristic Pauline phrases. It points to the closest possible union between Christ and the believer (see the discussion under 1.1). This close bond is best expressed in the apostle's own words: For what is life? To me, it is Christ (1.21). It is no longer I who live, but it is Christ who lives in me (Gal 2.20). The sense of this intimate relationship is brought out in various ways: NEB "incorporate in him"; Brc "to make my life one with his"; TEV completely united with him (so also SpCL FrCL).

And be completely united with him should be rendered in substantial-ly the same way as other expressions involving the phrase "in Christ" or "in the Lord," for example, "becoming completely one with him," or "being bound closely to him."

Paul moves on to define "complete union" by means of his under-standing of what is generally known as the doctrine of justification by faith, which is the main subject of his letter to the Romans (especially chapters 1–8), and to a large extent also of his letter to the Galatians. In effect, he is claiming that to be in Christ is nothing else than having the righteous-ness which comes from God through faith in Christ.

In Greek there is a chiastic structure (or "chiasmus"—from the Greek letter *chi*, which has the form X) in the following clauses:

(a) righteousness of my own   (b) from the Law

(b*) through faith in Christ   (a*) righteousness from God

In this construction (a) is in contrast with (a*) and (b) with (b*).

Obviously the apostle is now speaking as a converted Christian with a new perspective. The focus is on his present experience, and TEV makes this explicit: I no longer have . . . I now have . . . . The phrase righteousness of my own refers to righteousness acquired by Paul's own efforts, further defined as "which is from the Law." The preposition "from" is sometimes taken in the sense of "based on" (NAB "which is based on observance of the Law"; cf. RSV Bruce). It can also have the sense of "by means of," as is reflected in the TEV rendering the kind that is gained by obeying the Law.

In a number of languages it is quite impossible to speak of "having righteousness." It is often possible to say "to be right," "to be in a right relationship with God," or "to be rightly related to God." But frequently "righteousness" is not something one may possess. Accordingly, I no longer have a righteousness of my own may be rendered as "no longer am I rightly related to God because of what I myself have done," or "no longer am I right in God's eyes just because of what I have done." The following appositional and explanatory phrase, the kind that is gained by obeying the Law, may then be rendered as "that is, being right because I have obeyed the Law," or ". . . have done what the Law said I should do."

Paul makes clear that the principle of law is not the means by which he received true righteousness. He insists, literally, "but which is through faith of Christ." It is the principle of faith that really works. The relative pronoun "which" refers to righteousness, and TEV makes this explicit, I now have the righteousness. As is evident from the next clause, the initiative is with God; and it is best to make this fact explicit, that is given, with "God" as the implied subject. The genitive construction "faith of Christ" is formally ambiguous, but most commentators agree that we have here an objective genitive with "Christ" as the object of "faith." "Faith" is an event word, and "Paul" is the implied subject of the event. The unambiguous meaning of this construction, then, is faith in Christ (Knox "believing in Christ"). In biblical understanding, faith is basically, not a matter of intellectual assent, but of personal trust. It is an attitude of constant and total dependence on God, a response to the trustworthiness of God.

In some respects the clause I now have the righteousness that is given through faith in Christ is even more complicated than the preceding statement. One may translate I now have the righteousness as "I am now rightly related to God," or "I am now right before God." The qualifying clause, that is given through faith in Christ, indicates essentially the means by which one is right with God, and this may be expressed in some languages as a causative, for example, "because of my trust in Christ." The emphasis upon the source of righteousness as something that is granted by God is more fully expressed in the following clause, the righteousness that comes from God.

[102]

The apostle further defines the new righteousness by describing more precisely its source and its basis. This is <u>the righteousness that comes from God and is based on faith</u> (literally, "the righteousness from God upon the faith"). It is not advisable to take the preposition rendered <u>based on</u> as equivalent to the preceding preposition rendered <u>through</u> (Gpd "through faith ... through faith"), since "faith" is explained in one instance as the means and in the other as the basis for receiving the true righteousness. It has been suggested that the preposition here carries the sense of "on the condition of" (Knox), but Paul stresses the essential character of the new righteousness, rather than the conditions on which it is received. Furthermore, for Paul faith is primarily a response, not a condition (NEB "given by God in response to faith").

According to the Pharisaic concept of piety, <u>righteousness</u> for man consists in the minute and precise fulfillment of all the requirements of the Law. This was thought to be the only way to communion with God, the only guarantee of man's right relationship with God. According to Paul as a Christian, faith alone is able to insure for him such a relation. It is clear, then, that <u>righteousness</u> as used in the present context is not understood as ethical. It is not a result of one's moral attainment or quality. The significance is basically relational, that is, denoting a right relationship with God.

Since the <u>righteousness that comes from God</u> is an amplification and qualification of <u>the righteousness that is given through faith in Christ</u>, it may be preferable in some languages to begin a new sentence here and to make God the agent of the relationship of righteousness, for example, "God is the one who causes me to be put right with himself," "God is the one who puts me right with himself," or "God is the one who causes me to be right." The final phrase of this verse, <u>is based on faith</u>, serves to reinforce what has already been said about <u>the righteousness that is given through faith in Christ</u>. In a number of languages, <u>faith</u> must be understood in this context as the reason, or cause, for this righteousness. Therefore, one may translate "I am thus put right with God because of my trust," or "... by means of my trusting in Christ."

3.10   All I want is to know Christ and to experience the power of his resurrection, to share in his sufferings and become like him in his death,

In verses 10 and 11 there is another instance of the rhetorical device called "chiasmus":

(a) resurrection   (b) suffering

(b*) death   (a*) resurrection

Here (a) corresponds to (a*) and (b) to (b*). In these two verses Paul further explains what is involved in gaining Christ.

Paul uses here an infinitive phrase construction rendered in the RSV as "that I may know him." The force of this grammatical construction can be interpreted as consecutive, expressing the result of the previous conditions. When it is taken in this sense, the clause means "so that I may know him." Most commentators, however, take it in the sense of expressing purpose and motive. The resultant rendering may be "in order that I may know him"; that is, "my one aim is to know Christ" (NEB "all I care for is to know Christ"), or all I want is to know Christ (TEV JB). The "him" in the original Greek refers to Christ, not to God; and it is best to make this explicit in translation. The use of the aorist infinitive to know indicates that knowing Christ is a decisive act, not a process. The emphasis appears to be placed on the point of final attainment.

A literal rendering of to know Christ is liable to be misunderstood as merely "knowing about Christ" (the same problem encountered in verse 8). Accordingly, in some languages it may be preferable to translate this phrase as "to experience Christ with me," or even as "to be associated with Christ."

And to experience the power of his resurrection is literally "and the power of his resurrection." Obviously, this phrase is connected with the verb to know. As already pointed out (v. 8), to know in the biblical sense is to have intimate personal knowledge involving experience and appropriation. For this reason several translations include the component of experience (NEB Brc cf. SpCL). The rendering and to experience... may suggest that knowing Christ and experiencing the power of his resurrection are two distinctive events, but the latter (and also the sharing of his sufferings) is really a part of the former. Accordingly, both Mft and Gpd connect the two clauses by rendering "know him in the power of ...." The conjunction and is here more than a simple connective; it introduces the fuller explanation, to know Christ, and thus has the force of "namely" or "that is." The power of his resurrection does not mean the power by which Christ was raised from the dead, or the power of Christ by which Paul would be raised from the dead. Rather, it refers to the power of the resurrected Christ which is at work in the life of the believer, raising him from death in sin to the new life in Christ (Rom 6.4 ff.; Eph 1.19 ff.).

If one understands the resurrection in the sense of Christ as a resurrected person, then the expression to experience the power of his resurrection may be rendered as "to experience the power of Christ who was resurrected." However, it may be impossible in some languages to speak of "experiencing power." The closest equivalent may be "to be able to do what Christ, who was resurrected, was able to do." For languages in which "resurrection" or "resurrected" must be rendered by an active verb, it is possible to say "whom God raised from death."

To share in his sufferings translates a noun phrase, literally "fellowship of his sufferings." This phrase is to be taken closely with the preceding clause, since it is linked with a connective "and" (left untranslated in TEV and NEB), and the noun "fellowship" shares the same definite article with the power. This indicates that experiencing the power of the resurrected Christ and participating in his sufferings are not two separate experiences, but two aspects of the same experience. To share in his sufferings refers most probably to an inward experience, not to outward hardships and persecutions, just as the experience of the power of the risen Christ is an inward experience. This understanding is confirmed by the next clause.

If one assumes that to share in his sufferings and become like him in his death are basically aspects of experiencing the power of his resurrection, this relation may be indicated clearly by translating to share in his sufferings as "that is, by suffering as he suffered and by becoming like him in the way in which he died," or ". . . even to the point of dying." In a sense, it is impossible to "share sufferings," for sufferings are intensely personal. However, it is possible "to have the same kind of sufferings," or "to suffer in the same way he suffered."

Become like him in his death translates a participial phrase which means literally "becoming conformed to his death." Grammatically, the participle is attributive to the subject of the infinitive to know. The verb translated "conformed" is found nowhere else in the New Testament, but the related adjective is used in 3.21 and Rom 8.29. The root noun, from which the compound verb is derived, is rendered nature in 2.6, 7. Commentators who interpret the preceding clause in the sense of outward sufferings generally see in the present clause a reference to physical death. The present clause can then mean "by reproducing the pattern of his death" (JB cf. Knox "moulded into the pattern of his death"), thus focusing on the manner of death. It can also mean "even to death," that is suffering to the extent of death. While not denying the possibility that the reference can be to physical death, the context appears to demand an interpretation which speaks of an inward transformation of one's nature (Mft "with my nature transformed, to . . ."). As such it would refer primarily to Paul's wish to become so completely united with Christ that he continually strives to put his old self (his sinful nature) to death. That is why the rendering of TEV (so also RSV), which does not specify physical death, is preferable. The present participle "becoming" suggests a continual striving—a linear action (in contrast to a punctiliar action, to know).

[105]

3.11   in the hope that I myself will be raised from death to life.

What Paul now says is literally "if in some way I may attain the resurrection from the dead." The chiastic structure of verses 10 and 11 shows that this clause is to be taken with the clause immediately preceding. The expression "if in some way" appears to suggest some doubt or uncertainty in the apostle's mind, but in reality what he expresses here is his sense of expectation and hope with humility. TEV accordingly renders the expression as in the hope that (Gpd "in the hope of"; JB "that is the way I can hope to"; NAB "thus do I hope that"; Phps "so that I may somehow").

The noun translated "resurrection" is an unusual double compound word used only here in the New Testament. It has the preposition *ek* (meaning "from" or "out of") added to the ordinary word for resurrection. There is no indication, however, that one should attach special meaning to this rare word. Paul is probably not thinking of a "general resurrection" of all the dead, but of the resurrection of the faithful believers which will take place at the Parousia, that is at Christ's second coming (1 Thes 4.16). Here the focus shifts from the participation in the life of the risen Christ here and now to the final and ultimate rising of the dead, when the believers will enter the promised state of eternal blessedness. In biblical thinking, resurrection is always an act of God. He is the agent who causes life and return to life. It is, therefore, best to restructure the final clause as I myself will be raised from death to life, implying that God is the author of this event. The passive construction will be raised from death to life may be made active by saying "God will raise me from death to life." In a number of languages, however, death and life must be translated as verbs, thus requiring certain restructuring, for example, "that God himself will cause me no longer to be dead but to live."

Based on the analysis given above, one can restructure verses 10-11 into two sentences: "All I want is to know Christ, namely to experience the power of his resurrection and share in his sufferings. I want to know Christ by becoming like him in his death, in the hope that I myself will be raised from death to life." It may, however, be necessary to make verse 11 into a complete sentence which could begin "In this way I can hope," or "In view of this, I hope."

TEV	RSV
Running toward the Goal	
12 I do not claim that I have already succeeded or have already become perfect. I keep striving to win the prize for which Christ Jesus has already won me to himself. 13 Of course, my brothers, I really do	12 Not that I have already obtained this or am already perfect; but I press on to make it my own, because Christ Jesus has made me his own. 13 Brethren, I do

not*e* think that I have already won it; the one thing I do, however, is to forget what lies behind me and do my best to reach what is ahead. 14 So I run straight toward the goal in order to win the prize, which is God's call through Christ Jesus to the life above.

15 All of us who are spiritually mature should have this same attitude. But if some of you have a different attitude, God will make this clear to you. 16 However that may be, let us go forward according to the same rules we have followed until now.

17 Keep on imitating me, my brothers. Pay attention to those who follow the right example that we have set for you. 18 I have told you this many times before, and now I repeat it with tears: there are many whose lives make them enemies of Christ's death on the cross. 19 They are going to end up in hell, because their god is their bodily desires. They are proud of what they should be ashamed of, and they think only of things that belong to this world. 20 We, however, are citizens of heaven, and we eagerly wait for our Savior, the Lord Jesus Christ, to come from heaven. 21 He will change our weak mortal bodies and make them like his own glorious body, using that power by which he is able to bring all things under his rule.

*e*not; *some manuscripts have* not yet.
(3.12-21)

not consider that I have made it my own; but one thing I do, forgetting what lies behind and straining forward to what lies ahead, 14 I press on toward the goal for the prize of the upward call of God in Christ Jesus. 15 Let those of us who are mature be thus minded; and if in anything you are otherwise minded, God will reveal that also to you. 16 Only let us hold true to what we have obtained.

17 Brethren, join in imitating me, and mark those who so live as you have an example in us. 18 For many, of whom I have often told you and now tell you even with tears, live as enemies of the cross of Christ. 19 Their end is destruction, their god is the belly, and they glory in their shame, with minds set on earthly things. 20 But our commonwealth is in heaven, and from it we await a Savior, the Lord Jesus Christ, 21 who will change our lowly body to be like his glorious body, by the power which enables him even to subject all things to himself.

(3.12-21)

The section heading <u>Running Toward the Goal</u> is an effective way of presenting in English the theme of the following three paragraphs. In some languages, however, such a metaphor does not lend itself readily to this type of passage. Even the form of a complete sentence (for example, "I am running toward the goal") could be misleading. It may be more appropriate in some languages to choose another phrase from the text of this section as being indicative of the theme, for example, "God's call through Christ Jesus," "Winning the prize," or "Citizens of heaven."

Paul now states the tension between "having" and "not having," between his present attainment and his aspiration for the future. He wants to make clear that his goal has not yet been reached. The Christian life is for him a constant and persistent running toward the goal. His words reveal his desire, on the one hand, to prevent a possible misunderstanding of what he has just said in the previous verses and, on the other hand, to refute the claim that perfection is already a present reality. He concludes the section with a call to follow his example and a warning against false teachers.

3.12   I do not claim that I have already succeeded or have already become perfect. I keep striving to win the prize for which Christ Jesus has already won me for himself.

The apostle begins with an elliptical expression, literally "not that." What is understood here can be made explicit in various ways: "it is not to be thought that" (NEB), "I do not mean that" (Bruce GeCL SpCL), I do not claim that (TEV Brc).

I do not claim may be rendered simply as "I do not say." It is also possible to transform this into a negative imperative, for example, "Do not think that."

The Greek verb rendered I have . . . succeeded (literally, "received") is without an object, but some translations supply "this" as the object of the verb. Commentators are divided as to what its object is. Some suggest that it is all that is included in verses 8-11, while others believe that Paul is referring to his resurrection from the dead in verse 11; still others interpret the object as the prize referred to in verse 14 (cf. 1 Cor 9.24-25). Another possibility is to render the verb in such a way as to leave the object open, somewhat parallel to have already become perfect. These suggestions are really not mutually exclusive, as the TEV rendering of verse 14 indicates.

The prize is identified as God's call through Christ Jesus to the life above (v. 14), which appears to correspond to the hope of being raised from death to life (v. 11). The verb rendered have . . . succeeded means "to receive," "to obtain," "to get hold of," but in the present context (and especially in the environment of its compounded verb, which appears twice in this verse) it acquires the sense of "to achieve" (NEB), "to reach" (NAB), or even more explicitly "to win the prize" (Seg). The aorist tense here is to be taken in the sense of summing up the whole course of events. Its force is best brought out by the perfect tense in English, thus "I have reached" (NAB), "I have achieved" (NEB), and I have already succeeded.

It may be essential in some languages to make explicit the goal of succeeded. Sometimes this may be done by translating "that I have accomplished all I should have accomplished," "that I have done all that I should have done," or "that I have become all that I should become." This last expression is more in accord with the phrase which follows.

Several witnesses, including an early third century papyrus, add "or have already been justified" after I have already succeeded. This is probably a secondary addition, reflecting a pious copyist's desire to emphasize the divine initiative in Christian life.

The clause or have already become perfect (literally, "or have already been perfected") further defines the preceding clause, I have already succeeded. It is obvious that the conjunction or connects two similar, not two contrastive, events. In view of this evident meaning of or, it may be preferable to use a conjunction such as "and." In this way one may avoid giving the impression that succeeding and becoming perfect are two distinct and alternative processes. The verb translated have . . . become perfect appears nowhere else in Paul's writings, but it appears frequently in the Letter to the Hebrews. It is one of the key words of the mystery religions which promised "perfection" to their initiates by means of sacramental rituals and secret knowledge. "Perfection" is the highest state of religious attainment. It is possible that Paul borrows this word from the mystery religions in order to deny the possibility of a Christian's being admitted to the highest state of the Christian life in the present world. The verb means "to attain the aim," "to bring to completion," "to be full grown," "to be mature." In verse 15 the cognate adjective is rendered spiritually mature. The word denotes primarily not a moral but a functional perfection. A glance back at the preceding verse suggests that what Paul has in mind is that "perfection" which will be his only when he is raised from death to life. Most likely this "state of perfection" is a reference to, and a description of, the state of the resurrected life (v. 11), namely, the life above (v. 14).

Have already become perfect may be rendered as "have already become the kind of person I should be," or "have already become all that I should be." In some languages it may be necessary to explain this in a negative manner, for example, "have become the kind of person for whom there is nothing lacking."

I keep striving to win the prize is literally "but I pursue if I may also grasp." The force of "if also" is not that of doubt, but of expectation, thus "in hope of" (Knox), "hoping to" (NEB), "to try to" (Brc), or striving to (TEV). The first verb is a term used in hunting, meaning "to pursue"; it can be used of foot racing in the sense of "to press on." The present tense signifies a repeated action, thus I keep striving. This verb is sometimes paired with the next compound verb (which means "to grasp") in the sense of "seek and find," "pursue and overtake," "chase and capture," etc. (cf. Rom 9.30; also Exo 15.9 LXX). This compound expression signifies a strenuous attempt to reach the set goal which is not yet within one's grasp. Very likely the metaphor of a race is in Paul's mind. If this is the case, one can render the second verb explicitly as "to grasp the prize" (NAB), "to capture the prize" (JB), "to seize the prize" (FrCL), or to win the prize (TEV).

To show the contrast between the expression I keep striving to win and the immediately preceding phrases, it may be important to introduce at this point a contrastive particle such as "rather" or "but," for example, "rather, I keep going on to try to win."

A verb expression such as striving helps to indicate strenuous activity and suggests a basis for the figurative usage of run in verse 14. The phrase can also be translated, to give this same emphasis, as "I keep trying very hard to win," or "I keep using all my strength to try to win."

What Paul goes on to say is literally "upon which also I was grasped by Christ Jesus." The expression "upon which" can be taken in two different ways. It can be rendered "because," making Christ's "capture" of Paul the reason for Paul's effort to win the prize (Mft Gpd RSV). Or it can be taken in the sense of "for which," meaning that Paul's effort to win the prize is to fulfill the purpose for which Christ won him on the Damascus Road (NEB JB TEV). The second interpretation appears to be preferable. TEV, along with other recent translations, changes the passive "I was grasped by Christ Jesus" to an active construction, Christ Jesus has already won me to himself.

The clause for which Christ Jesus has already won me to himself may be misunderstood if translated literally, especially since the relative pronoun which might refer merely to the prize, in which case the implication would be that Christ Jesus himself had also been interested in winning this particular prize. The relative pronoun which, however, refers to the entire preceding clause. Therefore it may be better to translate this final clause of verse 12 as "It was for this reason that Christ Jesus has already won me to himself," "This was the purpose Christ Jesus had in mind when he won me to himself," or "This is what Christ Jesus purposed in winning me to himself."

It seems easy enough in many languages to speak of "winning a prize," but "to win a person" may be so unusual as to be meaningless or even misleading. One may therefore translate won me to himself as "caused me to be his," or "caused me to follow him."

3.13   Of course, my brothers, I really do note think that I have already won it; the one thing I do, however, is to forget what is behind me and do my best to reach what is ahead.

     enot; *some manuscripts have* not yet.

In this verse Paul repeats and expands what he has said in the preceding verse. He says literally "Brothers, I do not count myself to have grasped." "I myself" is emphatic in Greek, with the force of "I on my part" or, as TEV renders it, of course, . . . I really. The phrase of course may be rendered in some instances as "you may be sure," while <u>my brothers</u>, or "my fellow believers," must in some languages be placed at the beginning of the verse.

The verb rendered <u>think</u> often occurs in a commercial context, meaning essentially "to calculate." It is a favorite Pauline term and is often used in the sense of carefully weighing the point under consideration; thus it can mean "reckon" (NEB) or "consider" (RSV Phps). The compound verb discussed under verse 12, where it is used twice, is here used for the third time. The perfect infinitive form, which appears here without an object, is translated as <u>I have already won it</u>. The object <u>it</u>, supplied translationally, obviously refers to <u>the prize</u> (FrCL "have won the prize").

Paul proceeds with an elliptical but forceful statement, literally "but one thing." Several attempts have been made to bring out the exact force of this expression. Some supply the idea of thinking (Mft "my one thought is"); others of speaking (NEB "all I can say is this"; cf. JB). However, the context seems to indicate that <u>one thing</u> refers to what follows, which is a matter of doing. Accordingly, the force and sense of this expression is perhaps best rendered as "but one thing I do" (ASV), or, more forcefully, <u>the one thing I do, however</u> (TEV).

Paul uses the pictorial images of a race to describe the single-mindedness of his purpose. <u>Is to forget what is behind me</u> is in Greek a present participial phrase. The present participle signifies that his forgetting is a continuous action: "keep forgetting." <u>What is behind me</u> could be a reference to his life in Judaism, but more probably it includes his achievements as a Christian. The runner has lost when he turns back to see what is behind him. To translate <u>to forget what is behind me</u> in a strictly literal fashion is to risk the introduction of a wrong connotation, since this might imply that Paul wished to forget even the mistakes he had made. In this context it may be preferable to translate <u>to forget</u> as "to pay no attention to" or "to refuse to be concerned about." In reality Paul was not trying to forget; he simply refused to be concerned about what was behind him.

<u>Do my best to reach what is ahead</u> translates another participial phrase, literally "stretching forward to the things that are before." The participle is a double prepositional compound which pictures the runner with his eyes fixed on the goal, his hand stretching out to it, and his body bent toward it. It is a graphic description of the runner's intense desire and utmost effort to reach the goal (Brc "to strain every nerve to reach"). It may be difficult to speak of <u>what is ahead</u> without being more specific, for example, "the goal which is ahead," or "the end of the race which is ahead." Thus the figurative expression of running introduced in verse 14 is anticipated. It is also possible to use a more general expression, for example, "to accomplish what I must do in the future."

3.14   So I run straight toward the goal in order to win the prize, which is God's call through Christ Jesus to the life above.

The verb rendered <u>I run straight</u> is the same verb translated <u>I keep striving</u> in verse 12. The word translated <u>goal</u>, found only here in the New Testament, is basically the mark on which one fixes his attention. In shooting, this is the target; in racing, it is the <u>goal</u>. If one finds it difficult to introduce the metaphor of "running straight toward the goal," one may change this into a simile, for example, "So, as it were, I run straight toward the place where the race ends."

The prepositional phrase "unto the prize" (ASV) is best taken in the sense of "so that I may win the prize" (Bruce) or <u>in order to win the prize</u>. The <u>prize</u> in classical Greek refers to an award in games or contests. In the New Testament the word occurs only here and in 1 Cor 9.24; it is used to denote the reward for an achievement.

What Paul proceeds to say is literally "of the upward calling of God in Christ Jesus." This "upward calling of God" is to be understood as "God doing the calling." The sense of the other genitive construction, "the prize of the upward calling," is conditioned by the meaning of "the upward calling." Some translations (including KJV ASV Mft Seg) take the adverb "upward" to mean "high" or "heavenly," describing the quality of the calling (Heb 3.1). It is also possible that the reference is to God's call to faith as a summons "upwards." It appears, therefore, that the renderings of NEB and TEV make better sense, that is, <u>God's call . . . to the life above</u> (cf. 1 Thes 2.12). The phrase "the prize of the upward calling" is best taken as a genitive of apposition, meaning "the prize consists of" or <u>the prize, which is . . . .</u> One can be more explicit about the content of the prize by rendering "which is the life above to which God calls me . . ." (cf. GeCL "This prize is new life, to which God has called me through Christ Jesus"). <u>Life above</u> is equivalent to "eternal life." <u>Through Christ Jesus</u> makes it clear that "in Christ Jesus" is to be understood in an instrumental sense. God is the caller, and Christ is his agent.

In order to indicate clearly the nature of "the prize," it may be necessary to make the final relative clause in this verse into a completely new sentence, for example, "The prize is God calling me through Christ Jesus."

A literal translation of <u>the life above</u> might suggest merely "life in heaven." But since it is more likely that a quality of life is intended, it may be better to use such a phrase as "eternal life," "new life," or "real life."

3.15   All of us who are spiritually mature should have the same attitude. But if some of you have a different attitude, God will make this clear to you.

All of us who are spiritually mature is literally "therefore as many of us as are perfect." The "us" here is inclusive; Paul includes himself and his audience among the "perfect." The Greek term translated "perfect" is cognate with the verb used in verse 12, where Paul says that he does not claim to have . . . become perfect. Some commentators maintain that the two cognate words appearing in the same context should be interpreted in the same sense. If so, the apostle's words in verse 15 would be ironical. JB adopts this sense with its rendering "we who are called 'perfect.' " It is more likely, however, that Paul is referring to "spiritual maturity" (cf. 1 Cor 2.6; 14.20). One can accordingly render the phrase as "all of us who are spiritually adult" (Phps cf. FrCL), "all of us who are mature Christians" (Brc), or all of us who are spiritually mature (TEV cf. NAB Bruce).

The rendering spiritually mature certainly has many advantages over the literal translation "perfect," but it may be difficult to speak of spiritual maturity. Some translators try to use such a phrase as "all of us who have become adults in our lives as believers," but such an expression may have little or no figurative meaning. It may be possible to say "all of us who have advanced somewhat in our lives as believers," or "all of us who really know by experience what it means to follow Jesus Christ."

This same attitude refers to what is said in verses 12-14. The word attitude carries the components of "feeling" (Brc) and "thinking." (NEB). It denotes the total inner disposition of man (see the discussion under 2.2 and 2.5). Should have this same attitude may be rendered as "should think in this same way," or "should have these same intentions." In Greek, the force of if some of you have a different attitude indicates that this supposition is possible.

Paul is tolerant of some who cannot see eye to eye with him. He goes on to say, literally, "this also God will reveal to you." The particle "also" is most often used as a conjunction meaning "and," but here it is used adverbially. "This also" is to be preferred to "even this" (KJV). The verb rendered "reveal" is best taken in the general sense of "clarify" (NAB), "make plain" (NEB), or make . . . clear (TEV, so also Gpd; cf. JB Brc). This (in make this clear) seems to refer to the entire content of 15a. God will make this clear to you may be rendered as "God will cause you to understand clearly," or "God will make you understand this matter as you should."

3.16   However that may be, let us go forward according to the same rules we have followed until now.

A number of translations render the conjunction used here as "only" (Gpd Mft RSV NEB etc.). Such a rendering suggests that there must be a condition which needs to be satisfied, but it is not likely that Paul is introducing a parenthetical thought. Rather, he is making a kind of concluding statement, and one can best bring out the meaning by rendering the conjunction as "this one thing I say" (Brc), "it is important that" (Phps NAB), or however that may be (TEV).

What the apostle says next is somewhat elliptical, literally "whereunto we have reached, by the same to walk." Reflecting what appears to be the effort of some ancient copyist to remedy this obscurity, some inferior Greek texts (those which underlie the Textus Receptus on which KJV is based) include the word "rule" after "the same" and an appended clause "think the same thing." These interpolations seem to have been made on the basis of Phil 2.2 and Gal 6.16.

The infinitive "to walk" is used in an imperative sense. It means basically "to stand in a row" or "to walk in line." Even without inserting the word "rule," some kind of "rule" or "standard" may be understood as implied in the verb, and is demanded by the context. For this reason TEV renders the clause explicitly as let us go forward according to the same rules. One can also translate "we must live up to the standard" (Brc "Let us never fall below the standard of conduct"). Or one may keep the metaphor of the race by rendering "we must continue the course in accordance with the same rules." Let us go forward may be rendered in some instances as "let us continue to live," or "let us continue to act." It may, however, be important to restructure the relation of activity to rules by saying "let the same rules tell us what we should do," or "let us continue to do what the same rules say."

The verb rendered we have followed originally meant "to come before" or "to anticipate," but in the New Testament it is generally used in the sense of "to come," "to arrive at," or "to reach." The clause can be translated as we have followed until now or "we have obeyed thus far."

3.17   Keep on imitating me, my brothers. Pay attention to those who follow the right example that we have set for you.

Keep on imitating me is literally "become fellow-imitators of me." The noun "fellow-imitators" appears only here in the New Testament, but a similar expression is found in 1 Cor 4.16. Paul is not saying "join with me in imitating Christ," as some persons have thought. This injunction can also be rendered "follow my example, all of you," bringing out the "fellow" idea in the Greek (Mft "copy me, one and all of you"). One may render this injunction as "do just as I do," or "do whatever you see me doing."

Pay attention to those who follow the right example is literally "mark those who so walk." The verb rendered pay attention is the same used in 2.4, where it is translated look out for. Basically the verb means "to look attentively," that is, to fix one's attention on something with keen interest. It is certainly more than mere "watch." NAB gives this verb a strong sense, "take as your guide"; so also JB, "take as your models." In rendering the phrase pay attention to, it is important to suggest a positive aspect, that is, carefully watching in order to imitate or emulate. This means, essentially, watching carefully in order to be able to imitate the actions of those who give the right example.

The verb follow translates a Greek participle which means literally "walking." This reflects a Hebrew word which also means "to walk," used frequently in the ethical sense of "walking before God." Paul in particular often uses this word in the moral sense of the walk of life.

The right example that we have set for you represents a restructuring of what is literally "you have us as an example." Notice the shifts from me to we, probably now including Timothy and Epaphroditus. The word rendered right example means generally "image" or "mark," and in the moral sense "model" (Seg NEB) or "pattern" (Gpd Knox Brc etc.). The right example that we have set for you may be rendered as "we have shown you the right way in which you should act," or "we have made it clear to you by what we have done what you should do."

3.18   I have told you this many times before, and now I repeat it with tears: there are many whose lives make them enemies of Christ's death on the cross.

There seems to be no need to regard verses 18 and 19 as a digression (cf. KJV), since they are an integral part of the section. In these two verses Paul gives his reason for the injunctions in verse 17, and his tone is sarcastic, as in 3.2.

Notice the contrast between before (implicit in the context) and now, and the word play on many times and many (people).

This (in I have told you this) and it (in I repeat it) both refer to the contrast in what Paul proceeds to say with tears. The phrase with tears translates a Greek participle, commonly used of loud expression of sorrow and pain. It signifies intense grief. It is essential to render this phrase in such a way as to indicate clearly that Paul is extremely sorry to have to say what he does. It may, therefore, be necessary to render with tears as "I am so sorry about this that I could cry," or "this makes me so sorry that I am crying." Note, however, that the pronouns this and it must refer to what follows in verses 18 and 19. Therefore it may be necessary to translate the first part of verse 18 as "What I am going to tell you I have already told you many times before, and now I am going to repeat it, but it makes me so sorry that I cry."

[115]

The noun lives renders the same Greek word translated follow in verse 17. It is generally used in Paul's letters in the sense of one's practical conduct (NEB "way of life"; Brc "conduct"). In some languages whose lives is best expressed in more concrete terms, while preserving the original component in Greek, for example, "whose walkings and doings." It may be necessary in certain other languages to translate whose lives by means of a verb, for example, "there are many who live in such a way as to cause them to become enemies of Christ's death on the cross," or "... by means of the way in which they live they make themselves enemies...."

Enemies of Christ's death on the cross is literally "the enemies of the cross of Christ." The cross is not simply an abstract symbol, it points to Christ's death. As a Christian symbol the cross would have no meaning without the death of Christ. TEV makes this fact explicit (cf. Gal 3.13). It is not entirely clear who these enemies were. They could have been the Judaizers referred to in 3.2 ff., who held fast to the Law as an agent of salvation. More likely, however, there were Gentile Christians who were guilty of a relaxation of the moral law. In either case, the persons referred to were professed Christians whose lives disavowed the significance of Christ's death.

It may be quite difficult to render effectively the expression enemies of Christ's death on the cross. It would be easy enough to speak of being "an enemy of Christ," but to be "an enemy of Christ's death" is much more complex. One should, of course, avoid a translation which would merely imply "they are against the idea of Christ's having died on the cross." One may, however, say "There are many who, by the way in which they live, tend to destroy the meaning of Christ's death on the cross."

3.19   They are going to end up in hell, because their god is their bodily desires. They are proud of what they should be ashamed of, and they think only of things that belong to this world.

Paul now describes the fate and character of these enemies. They are going to end up in hell is literally "whose end is destruction" (RSV). Here the "end" is more than a mere point of termination; it means the inevitable outcome (Gpd Brc "they are doomed to destruction"). The noun "destruction" is Paul's usual word to express the opposite of "salvation" (Phil 1.28; cf. 1 Cor 1.18; 2 Cor 2.15); it is equivalent to eternal punishment. They are going to end up in hell may, of course, be translated simply as "they will finally be destroyed," or "... suffer destruction." One may also say "they will finally go to hell," or "... will be sent to hell." In this type of context hell may be rendered in some languages as "the place of punishment" or "the place of suffering."

Their god is their bodily desires is literally "whose god is the belly" (ASV). The expression bodily desires is used also in Rom 16.18, where most translations, including TEV, render it as "appetites." Some commentators understand it in the sense of unnecessary concern with laws about clean and unclean foods. Taken in this sense, the reference is to the Judaizers. Others take it to mean "greediness," referring to those Christians who were excessively greedy for food (JB "they make foods into their god"). But is is probably best to interpret it, along with TEV and some commentators, in the general and wider sense of bodily desires. In some languages a literal rendering of "belly" may be able to convey the right meaning. In this clause the focus is on their god, and in some languages this focus can best be brought out be reversing the clause order, thus "their bodily desires are their god" (GeCL).

It may not be possible to translate literally their god is their bodily desires or even to say "what they desire for their body is their god," because such a rendering might be taken to refer to an idol or fetish. One can, however, make very good sense of this clause by saying in some languages "the only thing they worship is what they themselves want for their bodies," or "their only real concern is for what their own bodies desire."

These enemies are further described as "whose glory is in their shame" (KJV). The noun "glory" here is equivalent to "pride" (Knox) or "boast." The somewhat abstract noun phrase "their shame" really means conduct which should be considered shameful. TEV rephrases the statement as they are proud of what they should be ashamed of. It is possible to take "shame" as an allusion to the nakedness involved in the act of circumcision (3.2), but the immediate context appears to indicate that Paul is thinking of immoral conduct in general (see the expressions bodily desires and things that belong to this world). They are proud of what they should be ashamed of may be expressed as "they are proud of doing certain things, but these things are what they should be ashamed of," or "they are proud of what they do, but they should be ashamed of what they do."

The last element in the description of these enemies of Christ's death prepares the way for the sharp contrast which follows in verses 20-21. They think only of things that belong to this world translates a Greek participial phrase, literally "who think earthly things." Some commentators interpret the sudden change in the Greek construction as a return to the primary construction in verse 18, thus summing up what has just been said (NAB "I am talking about those who are set upon the things of this world"). This is grammatically possible. The majority, however, regard this as a kind of apposition with the preceding clauses. The word "think," which appears twice in verse 15, means more than mere intellectual perception; it denotes one's inward disposition, state of mind, or attitude (see the discussion under 3.15).

[117]

In some languages the clause is best rendered as "their hearts are set on the things of this world." Things that belong to this world means things that are not of divine origin, that have no eternal quality or value (cf. Rom 6.5-6). This statement is a damaging indictment of certain people who are considered to be citizens of heaven (v. 20).

The phrase things that belong to this world can be easily misunderstood as a reference to objects which are simply here in this world. Paul, however, is not thinking particularly of material things; in fact, the object of the thinking of the persons he is speaking about is not an assortment of things, but a series of activities. One may, therefore, translate the final clause of this verse as "they are only thinking about doing what people of this world do," "they only think like people who are typical people in this world," or "... like most people think." In this way the contrast with citizens of heaven (v. 20) may be clearly marked.

3.20   We, however, are citizens of heaven, and we eagerly wait for our Savior, the Lord Jesus Christ, to come from heaven.

Over against the enemies of Christ's death on the cross (v. 18), Paul sets the citizens of heaven. Notice the twofold contrast, they / we and world / heaven, in verses 19-20.

We, however, are citizens of heaven is literally "for our citizenship is in heaven." The possessive pronoun "our" is in an emphatic position in Greek. The Greek particle often translated "for" has here an adversative force and introduces a contrast. "For" is not a natural connective with the previous verse. It is therefore best rendered as however, "by contrast" (NEB cf. GeCL), or "but" (Gpd RSV Seg).

The noun "citizenship" appears nowhere else in the New Testament, although its corresponding verb is used in 1.27 and in Acts 23.1. One possible meaning would be "our manner of life is in harmony with heaven," but the majority of translators favor another meaning, for example, "commonwealth" (Gpd RSV), "citizenship" (NEB), "homeland" (JB). However, since the focus in the context is on people, some modern translations employ the term "citizens," thus we ... are citizens of heaven (TEV Phps NEB). It seems clear that Paul uses this political imagery to describe the fact that true Christians are temporary resident aliens here on the earth, but that they have their citizenship in the heavenly commonwealth (Eph 2.6, 19: Heb 12.22). It may be added that biblical writers often use heaven as a way of talking about God (Matt 3.2; 21.25; 22.2; Luke 15.18, 21, etc.). Consequently, we ... are citizens of heaven can mean that "our citizenship is of divine origin."

In order to show clearly the distinction between being citizens of heaven and doing those things which belong to this world, it is possible to translate we ... are citizens of heaven as "we belong to heaven," "our homeland is heaven," "heaven is our native country," or even "heaven is the place where we really belong."

And we eagerly wait for our Savior, the Lord Jesus Christ, to come from heaven translates a Greek relative clause, literally "out of which also we await a Savior, the Lord Jesus Christ." Since the relative pronoun traditionally rendered as "which" is singular, while heaven in Greek is plural, some commentators insist that the pronoun can refer only to "commonwealth." This interpretation seems unnecessary, however, in view of the fact that the use of the plural number for heaven is a Semitism. Furthermore, "out of which" can be taken adverbially in the sense of "whence." For this reason the majority of modern translators render explicitly from heaven (Phps NEB JB etc.).

The word rendered "wait" in a number of translations is a strong compound verb suggesting earnest expectation; it is often used in connection with the second coming of Christ (Rom 8.19, 23; 1 Cor 1.7; cf. Gal 5.5). This sense is reflected in several translations: eagerly wait (TEV Phps Brc cf. Gpd NAB), "expect" (Bruce NEB).

Several aspects of the word Savior should be noted. First, it is in an emphatic position in the Greek text. Secondly, it is without a definite article, and therefore is to be understood in a descriptive sense, not a title of reference. The emphasis is thus on the role or capacity of the Savior (NEB "deliverer") in his final return. Thirdly, it is a term rarely used as a title for Jesus in the New Testament. This infrequent use is probably due to the popular use of the same term in reference to the gods of the Greek religion and in emperor worship. It is quite possible that Paul deliberately uses Savior here to counter the claim of heathen emperor worshipers.

Since the focus here is on Jesus' rule as Savior, the designation Lord Jesus Christ appears to serve only as a kind of proper name. But underlying this designation is an early Christological confession, "Jesus Christ is Lord" (see the discussion under 2.11).

3.21   He will change our weak mortal bodies and make them like his own glorious body, using that power by which he is able to bring all things under his rule.

In this verse Paul explains the purpose of the Savior's coming. Most probably the reason for mentioning the subject of the transformation of the body is to introduce a contrast to what is said in verse 19.

There is a close parallel in the words and thoughts of this verse with those of 2.5-11. The verb rendered will change (NEB JB "will transfigure";

Brc "will change the form"; NAB "will give a new form") is related to the noun translated likeness in 2.7. This compound verb focuses on the unstable outward shape and appearance, as against the inner stable nature (see the discussion under 2.5-11).

There is nothing in our weak mortal bodies (literally, "the body of our humiliation") to suggest that our bodies are inherently evil. It simply means that they are subject to change, weakness, death, and decay. In the Greek text the term rendered as bodies is singular (see RSV; NEB "body"), but in English the plural forms seems more natural. The attributives weak and mortal must be expressed in some languages as restrictive relative clauses, for example, "he will change our bodies which are weak and which will die." In some cases it may be best to render change our... bodies as "cause us to have different bodies."

Make them like translates a Greek adjective (literally, "conformed") whose cognate noun is rendered nature in 2.6. It suggests that the conformity is not simply a superficial and outward change of form, but a complete change of inward nature and quality.

His own glorious body (literally, "the body of his glory" ASV) obviously refers to Christ's resurrected and glorified body, in contrast to our weak mortal bodies. At Christ's coming, according to Paul, true Christians will enter into a new state of existence, and their bodies will be similar in quality and nature to the body of the exalted Christ. The word "glory" is often used to express the active and radiant presence of God, and in Pauline usage it often refers to the resurrection life. The body, as Paul uses it here, signifies not the outward form, but the whole person. Salvation is not considered in terms of the immortality of the soul apart from the body, but of the total person. For a clearer picture of Paul's idea about the transformation of human existence, see 1 Cor 15.42-57 and 2 Cor 5.1-5.

In some languages glorious body is rendered as "shining body." In this way a reference is introduced to the type of body which Jesus had at the transfiguration. However, the focus in this particular passage seems to be, not upon the shining appearance of Christ's body, but upon its wonderful qualities as a resurrected body, and therefore it is somewhat better to translate glorious body as "wonderful body."

The process of transformation is accomplished by using that power by which he is able to bring all things under his rule (literally, "according to the working of his being able even to subdue all things to himself"). The word for power is used only of suprahuman power in the New Testament. In 2 Thes 2.9-11 it refers to the power of the Wicked One, but in all other occurrences it refers to divine power (Eph 1.19-20; 3.7; 4.16; Col 1.29; 2.12). This transforming power is inherent in the Lordship of Christ, which is conferred on him by God at the time of his resurrection (see 2.10-11; cf. 1 Cor 15.20-28).

In this context power is not a reference to "authority," but rather it suggests personal ability or capacity. This final clause may be rendered as "he will use that ability by which he is able to bring all things under his rule." In some cases the term "strength" may suggest such personal power, for example, "he will use his strength so as to be able to...."

The expression all things appears also in 3.8, where it is rendered everything, meaning the sum total of what one did, has, or could have. The same expression is sometimes used in Paul's letters to mean the entire universe (Rom 11.36; Eph 1.10; 3.9; Col 1.15-20; etc.). Since it is this latter sense which occurs in the present context, one can render the clause as "he is able to bring the whole universe under his rule" (JB "he can subdue the whole universe"; GeCL "has the power to subject all things to his Lordship"). The thoughts here correspond closely with those in 2.10-11, where all beings in the universe are brought under Jesus' rule with an open confession of his Lordship. There God takes the initiative, but here Christ is the originator of this power. To bring all things under his rule may be rendered as "to cause all things to be controlled by him," "to extend his control over all things," "to have everything under his control," or "to cause everything to happen as he determines it should happen."

CHAPTER 4

TEV	RSV
Instructions	
1 So then, my brothers, how dear you are to me and how I miss you! How happy you make me, and how proud I am of you!—this, dear brothers, is how you should stand firm in your life in the Lord.	1 Therefore, my brethren, whom I love and long for, my joy and crown, stand firm thus in the Lord, my beloved.
2 Euodia and Syntyche, please, I beg you, try to agree as sisters in the Lord. 3 And you too, my faithful partner, I want you to help these women; for they have worked hard with me to spread the gospel, together with Clement and all my other fellow workers, whose names are in God's book of the living.	2 I entreat Euodia and I entreat Syntyche to agree in the Lord. 3 And I ask you also, true yokefellow, help these women, for they have labored side by side with me in the gospel together with Clement and the rest of my fellow workers, whose names are in the book of life.
4 May you always be joyful in your union with the Lord. I say it again: rejoice!	4 Rejoice in the Lord always; again I say, Rejoice. 5 Let all men know your forbearance. The Lord is at hand. 6 Have no anxiety about anything, but in everything by prayer and supplication with thanksgiving let your requests be made known to God. 7 And the peace of God, which passes all understanding, will keep your hearts and your minds in Christ Jesus.
5 Show a gentle attitude toward everyone. The Lord is coming soon. 6 Don't worry about anything, but in all your prayers ask God for what you need, always asking him with a thankful heart. 7 And God's peace, which is far beyond human understanding, will keep your hearts and minds safe in union with Christ Jesus.	
8 In conclusion, my brothers, fill your minds with those things that are good and that deserve praise: things that are true, noble, right, pure, lovely, and honorable. 9 Put into practice what you learned and received from me, both from my words and from my actions. And the God who gives us peace will be with you.	8 Finally, brethren, whatever is true, whatever is honorable, whatever is just, whatever is pure, whatever is lovely, whatever is gracious, if there is any excellence, if there is anything worthy of praise, think about these things. 9 What you have learned and received and heard and seen in me, do; and the God of peace will be with you.
(4.1-9)	(4.1-9)

In place of a noun such as <u>Instructions</u> as a section heading, it may be important in some languages to use an entire sentence such as "Paul tells the believers in Philippi what they should do." It may also be possible to use a phrase from the first verse of this section, namely, "Stand firm in your life in the Lord." Or an equally useful phrase from verse 9, "Put into practice what you learned," may be employed.

Paul customarily closes each letter with a section made up of practical instructions, personal notices, and greetings. The letter to the Philippians is no exception, even though it is very personal throughout. Paul begins with an exhortation to stand firm (v. 1), then brings in the theme of unity, which is one of the underlying motives of this letter. Paul emphasizes unity in the form of an appeal to two women to reconcile their differences (vv. 2-3). In verse 4 he returns to the theme of joy, and after giving encouragement to gentleness, prayer, and noblemindedness, he ends the instructions with a promise of God's peace (vv. 5-9).

4.1   So then, my brothers, how dear you are to me and how I miss you! How happy you make me, and how proud I am of you! — this, dear brothers, is how you should stand firm in your life in the Lord.

This verse is introduced in Greek by a conjunction meaning "so then," "therefore," or "accordingly"; possible equivalents may be "as the result of what I have said" or "the purpose of what I have already said is that . . . ." It is possible to regard this verse as forming the conclusion of the previous paragraph (Phps Seg JB TOB UBS Greek text), but is is equally possible to make the verse as an introduction to what follows. The transition is made by referring back to the thoughts presented in the previous paragraph and using them as a basis for the exhortations that follow.

Paul addresses his Philippian brothers with a series of endearing terms, showing his deep affection for them. To capture this feeling TEV transforms the adjectives and nouns into a series of exclamatory clauses, an effective way in English of indicating intense feeling. In some languages, however, such a series of exclamations would be disconcerting to the reader. It would be best, therefore, in certain instances to translate verse 1 as "My dear fellow believers, you are very dear to me, and I miss you greatly. You make me so happy, and I am very proud of you. In view of all that I have said to you, this is how you should stand firm in your life in the Lord . . . ," or ". . . what I am going to say to you now is how you should stand firm in your life in the Lord . . . ." Note that in this restructuring of verse 1 brothers ("fellow believers") is rendered only once since a repetition of the term might seem unnecessarily redundant. Note also that the exclamatory forms are altered so as to make them positive indicative statements.

How dear you are to me, an adjective in the Greek meaning "beloved," is one of Paul's favorite words used in reference to his friends. The same adjective, rendered dear brothers, is used again later in the verse to emphasize the deep affection he has toward his friends. How dear you are to me may be rendered as "I love you very much" or "I care about you greatly."

How I miss you translates another adjective, which means literally "longed for" (KJV). The word occurs only here in the New Testament, but

[123]

its cognate verb and nouns appear elsewhere in Paul's letters. It signifies an intense emotion, what might be called a "homesick tenderness." In 1.8 its verbal form is rendered deep feeling . . . comes. How I miss you may be rendered as "how sorrowfully I feel when I am not with you." In a number of languages a closer equivalent may be "I desire very much to be with you."

How happy you make me renders another favorite word of Paul in this letter, literally "joy." How happy you make me may be restructured as "you cause me to be very happy."

How proud I am of you is literally "you are my crown." This is not the word generally used for the crown (diadem) worn by a king or queen. It refers, rather, to the crown awarded to a victor in Greek athletic games or to the wreath placed on the head of a guest at a feast. It is a symbol of victory, pride, happiness, and honor (see GeCL "my crown of victory"). These words recall Paul's tribute to the church at Thessalonica (cf. 1 Thes 2.19, 20). In some languages one may be able to preserve the figurative usage of "my crown" in a statement such as "you are like a crown for my head." But this type of rendering has, in some instances, resulted in wrong interpretations; for example, it has been understood in the sense of "you are a weight upon my head," and thus a mental burden. In some instances, how proud I am of you! may be rendered as "I am always glad to tell people about you," or "I am always boasting about you."

The adverb rendered this . . . is how should be taken closely with the opening conjunction so, then. It carries the force of "in view of all that I have said to you" (Brc).

The imperative rendered you should stand firm is the same word used in 1.27. With this word one can visualize a soldier standing firmly amidst the horrors of a battle. The idea is to remain faithful without giving way (JB), or to demonstrate unswerving loyalty (Brc) amidst attacks from without and false teachings within. As in other instances in which the metaphor stand firm is employed, one can sometimes express it better in negative terms, for example, "you should never run away," "you should never give in," or "you must never collapse."

In your life in the Lord is literally "in the Lord." There can be no closer relation possible than for one to be in another person's life, "living in another person's blood stream," as some languages would phrase it. This thought is vividly expressed in 1.21 (see the discussion there). In your life in the Lord may be rendered in some instances as "as you live in the Lord." In some instances a literal rendering of "in the Lord" may be rather meaningless, and so it may be better to say "as you live joined in the Lord," or "as you live like one person together with the Lord."

In order to reproduce the proper force and to make it easier to follow the train of thought, this verse may have to be restructured in some languages. Thus "So then, my brothers, in view of all that I have said to you, you should stand firm in your life in the Lord, dear brothers! How dear you are to me, and how I miss you! how happy you make me, and how proud I am of you!" (cf. GeCL).

4.2   Euodia and Syntyche, please, I beg you, try to agree as sisters in the Lord.

Euodia and Syntyche were presumably members of the church at Philippi. Evidently there was some disagreement between them. These women in verse 3 obviously refers back to them.

In his appeal to them Paul repeats the verb "I urge," indicating his eagerness in trying to resolve their disagreement. TEV tries to capture this sense by rendering "I urge" as please, I beg you.

Try to agree as sisters in the Lord is literally "to think the same thing ..." or "to have the same mind in the Lord." The expression try to agree as sisters (rendered having the same thoughts in 2.2) means much more than to agree in thought or opinion; it means rather to strive after a unity and harmony in life which is possible because of their common bond in the Lord. No sisterhood is possible without the lordship of Christ. In this context the familiar phrase in the Lord may have the meaning of "in submission to the Lord." A literal rendering of try to agree as sisters might suggest to some readers that Euodia and Syntyche were, in fact, close kin. It may be better in some languages to render sisters in a manner parallel to the way in which brothers is translated, namely, "as fellow believers." In this type of context in the Lord may be made more specific by rendering this phrase as "by obeying the Lord."

4.3   And you, too, my faithful partner, I want you to help these women; for they have worked hard with me to spread the gospel, together with Clement and all my other fellow workers, whose names are in God's book of the living.

In addition to the direct appeal to these two women, a third person is requested to help them work out a reconciliation. Paul addresses this person as my faithful partner, literally "true yokefellow" (RSV). A number of commentators suggest that it is possible to take the word partner as a proper name, Syzygos, and the accompanying adjective to mean "true to his name" or "rightly so called." On the basis of this interpretation Paul would be playing on the meaning of the name. In effect he would be saying: "I ask you, Syzygos, as your name suggests, a faithful partner,..." (JB "I ask you, Syzygos, to be truly a 'companion' "). It is better, however, to follow the majority of modern translations, including TEV, and to take this expres-

[125]

sion as a description of an unidentified Christian colleague of Paul (NEB "loyal comrade," Gpd "true comrade," NAB "dependable fellow worker"). My faithful partner may be rendered as "you who have joined with me so constantly in the work," "you who have worked with me so well," or "you on whom I depend so much to help me."

To help these women (literally, "to help them") obviously means to assist Euodia and Syntyche to reconcile their differences, and it may be useful (perhaps even necessary) to indicate clearly the expected result of what this faithful partner would do to help these women, for example, "to help these women to agree," ". . . to throw away their contrary words," or ". . . to forget their arguments."

For they have worked hard with me to spread the gospel translates a Greek relative clause, literally "inasmuch as they labored with me in the gospel," giving the reason why they deserve help. The compound verb rendered have worked hard appears elsewhere in the New Testament only in 1.27, where it is translated fighting together. It is a word normally used of fighting in war or of a contest in an athletic arena. This metaphorical sense is reflected in several translations, for example, "was fighting to defend" (JB), "shared my contests" (Bruce). In any case, the basic connotation is hard and strenuous work. The phrase "in the gospel" should be taken in the sense of "for the gospel" (Phps), "in the cause of the Gospel" (NEB), "in promoting the gospel" (NAB), or, more explicitly, to spread the gospel (TEV Gpd GeCL). It may be impossible in some languages to speak of "spreading the gospel." It is, however, almost always possible to say "telling more and more people about the good news."

Clement, otherwise unknown in the New Testament, is evidently another of Paul's fellow workers at Philippi (as also Epaphroditus; see 2.25). Together with Clement and all my other fellow workers must be expressed in some languages as a complete sentence, to show clearly that Clement and the other fellow workers were also engaged in spreading the gospel. This sentence may take the form of "Clement and all the other persons who worked with me also told many people about the good news."

The relative pronoun whose should refer to all those who have been mentioned in verse 3, including the two women (Euodia and Syntyche), Clement, and the other fellow workers. To make this quite clear it may be useful to render this final relative clause as a separate sentence, for example, "The names of all these persons who helped me are in God's book of the living." If one does not add the phrase "those who helped me," a reader might assume that the reference is to those who heard the good news rather than to those who were so faithful in telling others about the good news.

God's book of the living is literally "book of life." The figure may be taken from the ancient practice by which cities kept an official register in which names of its citizens were recorded. It is a common Old Testament symbol for God's record of the covenant people (cf. Exo 32.32; Psa 69.28; Isa 4.3; Ezek 13.9; Dan 12.1), and so TEV renders explicitly that it is God's book. In later Judaism and in the New Testament, the expression is used predominantly of the book of the life to come, that is, eternal life, as can be seen in Aramaic phrases of the Hebrew Bible on Isa 4.3 and Ezek 13.9 (see also Rev 3.5; 13.8; 17.8; 20.12, 15; etc.). The same idea is expressed in Luke 10.20 in different words. The word "life" here is not a reference to the abstract principle of life but to the living. The reference may or may not imply that Clement and other fellow workers of Paul are already dead. In either case, the translation is not affected.

A literal rendering of whose names are in God's book of the living might suggest that this is merely a book of those Christians who were alive at the time since book of the living would be literally translated in many languages as "book concerning those who are alive," or "book in which the names of those who are living are written down." In some languages a more satisfactory wording would be "book of those who possess real life," "book with the names of those who really have life" or ". . . have true life." The use of a phrase such as "to have true life" would help to suggest the quality of life which is characteristic of those having so-called "eternal life." This particular quality of life is expressed in some languages as "have life from God," "who have been made alive by God," or "who have come to have a new life through Christ."

4.4   May you always be joyful in your union with the Lord. I say it again: rejoice!

With this verse Paul returns to his favorite theme in this letter. The exhortation in 3.1 is repeated (see the discussion there), but now the adverb always is added. The addition of this adverb and the repetition of the injunction makes it almost impossible to render the verb as "farewell." It is not likely that the apostle would say "farewell always in the Lord. I say it again: farewell."

In this context, as in many other contexts in this letter, to be joyful is essentially to "be completely happy."

The phrase in your union with the Lord (literally, "in the Lord") is the governing factor in the exhortation. The Lord is the inexhaustible source of joy, and it is only by maintaining the closest possible union with him that the Christians will be able to experience uninterrupted joy. In your union with the Lord should not be interpreted as the cause of joy but the circumstance in which one is completely happy. One may, therefore, render in your union with the Lord as "as you live joined with the Lord."

[127]

The force of this verse can be brought out in several ways, depending on how one interprets the two imperative verbs meaning "rejoice." Both can be taken as having an optative force, thus "may you always be joyful in the Lord. I say it again: may you be joyful" (cf. Knox "Joy to you in the Lord at all times; once again I wish you joy"). A second possibility is to take the first verb with an imperative force, and the second with an optative, with the resultant rendering, "Rejoice always in the Lord. I say it again: may you be joyful." A third possibility is to understand the first with an optative force and the second with an imperative, resulting in the TEV rendering, <u>May you always be joyful in your union with the Lord. I say it again: rejoice!</u> A final possibility is to take both verbs in the normal imperative sense: "Rejoice always in the Lord. I say it again: rejoice." This last possibility appears to be favored by most translators. One can also render this last possibility as a negative command: "Never lose your joy in the Lord. I say it again: never lose your joy" (cf. Brc).

4.5   Show a gentle attitude toward everyone. The Lord is coming soon.

<u>Show a gentle attitude toward everyone</u> is literally "let your forbearance be known to all men." In many languages this third person imperative construction must be restructured as in TEV (cf. Knox "give proof to all of your courtesy"). The word rendered <u>gentle attitude</u> (an adjective used as a noun) stands for the spirit or attitude that does not seek to retaliate. It denotes one's willingness to give and take instead of always standing rigidly on one's rights (cf. Brc "never insist on the letter of the law"). In a number of languages <u>show a gentle attitude</u> toward everyone can best be expressed negatively, for example, "do not always insist that you are right," or "do not be demanding in your attitude toward everyone."

<u>The Lord is coming soon</u> (literally, "the Lord is near") can be interpreted in two different ways. When taken closely with what follows, the clause is usually regarded as having a local sense (near in space), that is, "the Lord is nearby"; in other words, he is near to all who call upon him (cf. Psa 119.151). NEB appears to favor this interpretation. If, however, one connects the clause with the preceding sentence, it is generally interpreted in a temporal sense (near in time), or <u>soon</u>, as the TEV rendering indicates (also Mft GeCL). On the basis of this interpretation, the imminent coming of the Lord is the ground for the exhortation to show an attitude of gentleness. On the whole, this is the more probable interpretation. It echoes the prayer of the early church which expected the Lord's early return (1 Cor 16.22; Heb 10.37; James 5.8-9).

[128]

4.6   Don't worry about anything, but in all your prayers ask God for
           what you need, always asking him with a thankful heart.

The Philippians had more than enough reason for worry and anxiety
in the hostility of their neighbors and the threat of persecution (1.28; 3.1;
4.1). To them Paul offered the following words of comfort and hope.
Don't worry about anything is literally "in nothing be anxious." The
verb rendered worry here is the same verb used in 2.20. There it has the
positive sense of "to care" (for someone), but here it has the negative sense
of anxiety, a lack of trust in God's care (Matt 6.25-34; cf. 1 Peter 5.7).
Don't worry about anything is often expressed idiomatically, for example,
"Do not eat up your own heart," "Don't let your thoughts kill you," or
"Don't let your thoughts take away your strength."
What Paul goes on to say involves a rather long and complex clause.
It is advisable to restructure this clause in order to bring out the meaning
more clearly. The clause may be translated literally as "but in everything
by prayer and supplication with thanksgiving let your requests be made
known to God" (RSV). There is an obvious contrast between the phrase
"in everything" here and "in nothing" in the preceding clause. "In everything" is sometimes taken in the sense of "always," denoting time (Mft),
and sometimes in the meaning of "in every situation" or "in every circumstance of life" (Bruce cf. FrCL GeCL). The majority of translations, however, take it in the sense of "all things," that is, all one's interests.
There is still another possibility. "In everything" may be connected
with the two following nouns, and so have the meaning "in all prayer and
supplication" (Vulgate). This combination is more in line with modern
speech, and is apparently the one favored by TEV. However, TEV does not
regard these two nouns as representing two distinct forms of prayer. It is
true that the word generally rendered "prayer" is commonly used in the
general sense of man's approach to God, and the word rendered "supplication" is normally employed in the more restricted sense of making request
for one's own needs or the needs of others, but in Paul's letters the two
words are often used interchangeably. Consequently, there seems to be no
need to press for a precise difference between the two terms; they are
linked together to convey inclusiveness, and so TEV renders in all your
prayers. The phrase in all your prayers may, of course, be rendered as
"whenever you pray." In some languages this would be expressed as "whenever you talk to God."
The literal "let your requests be made known to God" is a third person imperative construction which must be restructured in many languages.
One can rephrase it as "make your requests known to God" (Mft NEB), or,
even better, a straightforward "present your needs to God" (NAB), "tell

[129]

God about the things you want to ask him for" (Brc), or simply ask God for what you need. The word "requests" usually denotes things asked for rather than the specific act or form of prayer. What you need may be expressed doubly in some languages as "what you should have but do not have," or "what is important for you, but which you still do not have."

Always asking him with a thankful heart (literally, "with thanksgiving") is the accompanying attitude which should go with every act of prayer, an attitude arising from a remembrance of God's goodness in the past and a realization of his blessings in the present. In Paul's view, a thankful heart is an important element in prayer; this is evident in his fondness for pairing "prayer" and "thanksgiving" together (Col 4.2; 1 Thes 5.17-18; 1 Tim 2.1; cf. 1 Thes 3.9-10). Asking him with a thankful heart may be expressed as a combination of two verb phrases, for example, "always express your thanks to him, when you ask him for something," "whenever you pray to him, be sure to express thanks," or ". . . to say that you are thankful to him."

4.7   And God's peace, which is far beyond human understanding,
            will keep your hearts and minds safe in union with Christ Jesus.

And God's peace is literally "and the peace of God." The conjunction and indicates that what follows is the consequence of what precedes; thus it can be rendered "and so" or "then" (Gpd NEB NAB). The phrase "the peace of God" appears only here in the New Testament; elsewhere we often find the expression "the God of peace" (4.9; Rom 15.33; 16.20; 1 Thes 5.23; Heb 13.20). The difference in meaning in these two expressions is a matter of focus. Here the focus is on the "peace" which originates in and comes from God, while in verse 9 it is "God" who causes or gives peace. Peace in the Bible is never merely the absence of strife and trouble. Rather, this term stands for a total well-being associated with the state of salvation (Isa 52.7). It follows from the right relationship with God made possible through Jesus Christ (Rom 5.1) and the resultant friendly relationship with one's fellow man (Eph 2.14). As such it is a gift from God. In this type of context peace may be rendered in some languages as "sitting down in one's heart," or "not running around in one's mind." The relation of God to "peace" may be expressed as "this has been caused by God," or "God causes us to sit down in our hearts."

The Greek of the next clause (literally, "which rises above all mind") can be interpreted in two different ways. It can mean that God's peace can produce far better results than human cleverness and devices can accomplish (NEB alternative rendering "of far more worth than human reasoning"). Or the clause can mean that God's peace is completely beyond all power of human comprehension. Accordingly, TEV renders which is far beyond human understanding (cf. JB "which is so much greater than we can understand"). There is an implicit contrast between God's peace and human understanding, and TEV makes this information explicit (so also Phps). In this particular instance, the context offers little help as to which interpretation is correct, since neither seems to fit well; but on linguistic grounds the second meaning appears to be preferable. Basically, the verb rendered is far beyond means "to rise above," "to surpass," or "to excel." The focus is on the idea of uniqueness rather than relative superiority. Paul is not interested in making a comparison between God's peace and human ingenuities; rather he is explaining the nature of God's peace. Furthermore, the basic meaning of the noun translated understanding is "the mind" as the faculty of thinking and reflection, not "cleverness" or "inventiveness." Which is far beyond human understanding may be rendered as "because we are only people, we are not able to understand how God can do this," or "people are not able to understand this kind of peace."

The verb rendered will keep . . . safe is a military term. It pictures a garrison or a military sentinel "keeping guard over" a city or a fort to maintain peace and to protect against attacks. The city of Philippi in Paul's time was guarded by a Roman garrison, so the metaphor would probably appeal to his readers. What Paul says to his friends is this: as the result of your prayers God's peace will stand like a guard to keep your hearts and minds safe from attacks of worries and anxieties.

In biblical understanding the "heart" is not merely the center of feeling (1.7; Rom 9.2; 2 Cor 2.4), but also of willing (Mark 3.5; 1 Cor 7.37; 2 Cor 9.7), and of thinking (Matt 12.34; Rom 1.21; Eph 1.18). In Greek, the form of the word rendered minds indicates that its primary meaning is "thoughts" (NEB JB), yet the thinking faculty, the mind, seems to be meant here. What God's peace is keeping guard over is the mind rather than the thoughts, which are the product of the mind (2 Cor 3.14; 4.4; 11.3). Most likely Paul brings hearts and minds together to emphasize the whole inner being of the Christian, consisting of his faculties of feeling, willing, and thinking.

It is relatively simple to speak of "God keeping your hearts and minds safe," but it may be more difficult to introduce peace as the means by which the hearts and minds are kept safe. This relation may be expressed most satisfactorily in some instances as a type of condition. Accordingly, God's peace . . . will keep your hearts and minds safe may be rendered as "if you experience the kind of peace that God can cause for you, then your hearts and minds will be kept safe," ". . . then there will

[131]

be no danger to your hearts and minds," or "... then in all you feel and think there will be no reason for being anxious."

Paul introduces the important phrase <u>in union with Christ Jesus</u> (literally, "in Christ Jesus") to close the sentence. It is a solemn reminder to his readers that outside of their closest possible union with Christ there is no protection, no safekeeping by <u>God's peace</u>. In many languages the phrase may have to be rendered as "through your union with the life of Christ Jesus." In some instances one may relate the phrase to what precedes it by saying "because of the fact that you are united with Christ Jesus" (cf. GeCL), or "this is true because you are united with Christ Jesus."

4.8   In conclusion, my brothers, fill your minds with those things that are good and that deserve praise: things that are true, noble, right, pure, lovely, and honorable.

Apparently Paul is here making use of some ethical terms which are found in lists of virtues. The teaching device of reciting such a list is typically that of moral philosophers. But there seems to be no need for suggesting that Paul's purpose is to urge his readers to learn from pagan society. He is simply interested in seeing that his Philippian friends develop certain good qualities. These apparently reflect the apostle's own conduct and are the qualities which help to bring God's presence (v. 9). Even though some of the terms used here are not found elsewhere in Paul's letters or in the entire New Testament, all except one (<u>honorable</u>) are found in the Septuagint.

As the phrase <u>in conclusion</u> shows, the apostle once again prepares to bring his letter to a close. This adverbial expression is literally "for the rest" or "for what remains," meaning "as to what remains to be said." Most likely this is the meaning intended here, and so a number of translators render it as "finally" (Mft RSV JB NAB). In some instances <u>in conclusion</u> may be rendered as "and now to end what I am going to say," "and now my final words are," or "what follows is all that I am going to say."

Paul lists eight good qualities. These are introduced by a series of six phrases, each beginning with "as many things as" and summed up by two phrases, each beginning with "if there is." The first six ethical terms are adjectives and all have plural forms, and the last two are nouns and have singular forms. This rather stately and symmetrical construction can be arranged in pairs (cf. NEB JB). But since the last two "if there is" phrases, being more generic, serve to sum up the preceding "as many things as" phrases, TEV reorders the structure by moving the last two constructions to the front and punctuates them with a colon, thus . . . things that are good and that deserve praise: .

The present imperative verb rendered fill your minds with (literally, "consider" or "calculate") certainly means more than "keep in mind" (Mft) or "think about" (RSV). It is rather "take (them) into account" and reflect carefully upon them in order that they may shape your conduct. These good qualities are not merely things that are good for the head, but things that need to be transformed into action. The present imperative has the force of continual action (Brc "your thoughts must continually dwell on . . ."). The phrase fill your minds poses a number of problems if translated literally into other languages. It is often better, therefore, to employ such an expression as "think only about" or "consider only."

In this type of context the English word things refers not to particular concrete objects but primarily to actions and events. In many languages one can avoid a reference to "things" by translating simply "think only about what is good and deserves praise." In some cases, however, it is necessary to talk about "happenings" or "events" which have certain qualities. Therefore one can say "think only about those happenings that are good and ought to be praised," or ". . . what people do that is good and worthy of being praised by other people."

The noun rendered good appears nowhere else in Paul's letters, and elsewhere in the New Testament only in 1 Peter 2.9 and 2 Peter 1.3, 5. This word is one of the most important terms in Hellenistic moral philosophy. The difficulty in translating it is indicated by the many different renderings: "virtue" (KJV Knox cf. JB NAB), "excellence" (RSV Mft Brc cf. Gpd), "goodness" (Phps). In classical thought it is an inclusive term that can describe every kind of excellence. The English word "virtue" is by no means as inclusive in meaning as the original Greek word. "Excellence" in modern usage has very little to do with moral conduct. The only word which may have nearly all the force of the original is "goodness."

The word praise (Mft Knox "merit"; NEB "admirable") is used in 1.11 in reference to the praise of God. As a rule Paul thinks only of what God will praise, but in this context he is obviously speaking of the kind of conduct that wins the praise of men (Brc "wins men's praise").

In order to indicate clearly the relation between the clause those things that are good and that deserve praise and the clause things that are true, noble, right, pure, lovely, and honorable, it may be very useful to introduce the second clause by some such expression as "that is to say," "that includes," or "these actions are also."

Things that are true certainly refers to more than truthfulness in speech; it includes truthfulness and sincerity in thought, attitude, and action. In this type of context the meaning of <u>true</u> may often be conveyed more satisfactorily in a negative expression, for example, "in which there is nothing false."

It is difficult to find a good word for the adjective rendered <u>noble</u>. This fact is reflected in the diverse translations: "honest" (KJV), "honorable" (ASV Phps), "worthy" (Mft Gpd), "nobly serious" (Brc), and "deserve respect" (NAB). Another possibility is "dignified," since this adjective is often used in that sense. Sometimes the concept of <u>noble</u> may be expressed by an idiomatic phrase, for example, "that which causes people to look up," or "that which causes people's eyes to admire."

<u>Right</u> is a relational term. A man is "just" (RSV NEB etc.) and therefore <u>right</u> when he gives to God and to his fellow men what is their due. He accepts and performs his proper duty to God and man. Some of the implications of a term for <u>right</u> may be expressed as "right in the eyes of God and people." Something of the same meaning may be expressed in some languages as "fair for all people."

The word <u>pure</u>, when used of ceremonial activity, describes that which has been cleansed and is fit to offer to God. But it is used here in the ethical sense as a description of what is morally pure, undefiled, blameless. This meaning may often be expressed by a negative phrase, for example, "in which there is nothing to be blamed," "something which has no fault," or "something in which nothing bad has been added."

The word rendered <u>lovely</u> appears only here in the New Testament. It basically means "that which calls forth love," or "that which is love-inspiring." One may thus render <u>lovely</u> as "that which causes love," or "what people want to love." When it is used of man, it describes someone who has a winsome personality, is friendly and pleasant to be with. He is "attractive" (Mft), "amiable" (Gpd), "lovable" (NEB). In some languages "lovable" or "lovely" cannot apply to things, so "likable" or "pleasing" would be the term to use.

The rendering <u>honorable</u> represents another Greek term found only here in the New Testament. It means basically something that is "good sounding," that is, fit or pleasant to be heard, not likely to offend people (NAB "decent"; Bruce "reputable"; NEB alternative "of good repute"). <u>Honorable</u> may also be translated as "what men can always think good about." Or it may be expressed negatively as "something in which there is nothing bad to take away from the good."

4.9   Put into practice what you learned and received from me, both from my words and from my actions. And the God who gives us peace will be with you.

Not only must the Philippians take into account all that is generally considered good and worthy, they must put into practice what the apostle has exemplified in his words and deeds.

There are considerable differences of opinion as to the connection and arrangement of this verse. There are four verbs ("learned . . . received . . . heard . . . saw"), each preceded by the conjunction normally translated "and." We must decide first how to translate the conjunctions. Grammatically, they can be taken in two basic ways. First, the obvious one is to take them as a series of conjunctions. But since the first one cannot be taken as "and" (as it does not stand between grammatical elements of the same type), it can be left untranslated (RSV) or be rendered "also" (Mft). Secondly, it is possible to take the four conjunctions as forming two pairs of "both . . . and." Variation of this basic pattern can be seen in dropping either the first "both" (TEV Phps) or in dropping both of them (NAB Bruce). In either case the underlying meaning remains the same.

The second question, related to the first, has to do with understanding the relation of the four verbs. It is possible to leave the question open by stringing all the verbs together (KJV RSV). However, one can understand the first three verbs as referring specifically to Paul's teaching and the last to his example in life—thus Gpd: "Do the things that you learned, received, and heard from me, and that you saw me do" (cf. also Seg and Traduction Oecuménique de la Bible [TOB]). For translations that understand the conjunctions as consisting of "both . . . and" pairs, two possible renderings are possible. The first is to take the first pair as referring to Paul's teachings and the second pair to his example, thus: "You must keep putting into practice the lessons you have learned from me, the instruction you have received from me, and the example I have given you in speech and in action" (Brc). The second possibility is suggested by TEV, that is, to take what the Philippians heard and saw as the content of what they learned and received, thus <u>what you learned and received from me, both from my words and from my actions</u> (cf. also Phps Bruce NAB).

Notice again the word order. In Greek the order is "what you learned and received from me . . . these things put into practice." However, since the main verb and therefore the focus is on "put into practice," a number of translations, including TEV, restructure the order by beginning the sentence with the main verb.

The verb rendered <u>put into practice</u> is in the present imperative and indicates continuous action, so it can be rendered "you must keep putting into practice" (Brc).

The verb rendered <u>received</u> is a technical term used for receiving a tradition (1 Cor 11.23; 15.3). Before the writing of the New Testament books and their acceptance by the church as authoritative Scripture, the teachings were handed down from a teacher to his disciples. Christian tradition in the New Testament generally consists of certain facts about Christ, interpretations of them, and ascribed Christian conduct based on them (1 Cor 11.23; 15.3 ff.; Gal 1.9; 2 Thes 2.15).

Put into practice is often rendered simply as "do," and the verbal doublet learned and received may be best rendered in some languages simply as "learned," since in this type of context received can only refer to what was actually learned from Paul. It is possible to render received in such a way as to suggest an implied tradition, for example, "what you learned, that I passed on to you." In other languages it may be more natural to restructure the whole clause as "what I taught you and passed on to you" (cf. GeCL).

The words from me are not in the Greek, but are understood from the phrase "in me" in the following clause.

Both from my words and from my actions (literally, "you both heard and saw in me") is another way of saying "what you heard me say and what you saw me do" (Mft).

And the God who gives us peace will be with you is literally "and the God of peace will be with you." As in 4.7, the conjunction and again points to what follows, and can therefore be rendered "and so" or "as a result." "God of peace" obviously does not mean a peaceful God. In the Bible the emphasis is not upon the qualities of God but upon his acts. In this case, God is the one who gives us peace (cf. Rom 15.33; 16.20; 1 Thes 5.23). Us here is inclusive. The focus here is on "God who gives peace," not on "peace which comes from God" as in 4.7 (see the discussion there). In this context it would seem appropriate to understand this phrase in the sense of "the God who causes us to rest in our hearts," ". . . who frees us from anxieties," or ". . . erases our worries."

TEV	RSV
Thanks for the Gift	
10 In my life in union with the Lord it is a great joy to me that after so long a time you once more had the chance of showing that you care for me. I don't mean that you had stopped caring for me—you just had no chance to show it. 11 And I am not saying this because I feel neglected, for I have learned to be satisfied with what I have. 12 I know what it is to be in need and what it is to have more than enough. I have learned this secret, so that anywhere, at any time,	10 I rejoice in the Lord greatly that now at length you have revived your concern for me; you were indeed concerned for me, but you had no opportunity. 11 Not that I complain of want; for I have learned in whatever state I am, to be content. 12 I know how to be abased, and I know how to abound; in any and all circumstances I have learned the se-

I am content, whether I am full or hungry, whether I have too much or too little. 13 I have the strength to face all conditions by the power that Christ gives me.

But it was very good of you to help me in my troubles. 15 You Philippians know very well that when I left Macedonia in the early days of preaching the Good News, you were the only church to help me; you were the only ones who shared my profits and losses. 16 More than once when I needed help in Thessalonica, you sent it to me. 17 It is not that I just want to receive gifts; rather, I want to see profit added to your account. Here, then, is my receipt for everything you have given me—and it has been more than enough! I have all I need now that Epaphroditus has brought me all your gifts. They are like a sweet-smelling offering to God, a sacrifice which is acceptable and pleasing to him. 19 And with all his abundant wealth through Christ Jesus, my God will supply all your needs. 20 To our God and Father be the glory forever and ever! Amen.   (4.10-20)

cret of facing plenty and hunger, abundance and 'want. 13 I can do all things in him who strengthens me.

14 Yet it was kind of you to share my trouble. 15 And you Philippians yourselves know that in the beginning of the gospel, when I left Macedonia, no church entered into partnership with me in giving and receiving except you only; 16 for even in Thessalonica you sent me help*f* once and again. 17 Not that I seek the gift; but I seek the fruit which increases to your credit. 18 I have received full payment, and more; I am filled, having received from Epaphroditus the gifts you sent, a fragrant offering, a sacrifice acceptable and pleasing to God. 19 And my God will supply every need of yours according to his riches in glory in Christ Jesus. 20 To our God and Father be glory for ever and ever. Amen.

*f*Other ancient authorities read *money for my needs*

(4.10-20)

The section heading <u>Thanks for the Gift</u> may be expressed as "Paul thanks the Philippian believers for their gift," ". . . for what they have given to him," or ". . . for their help to him."

Paul now comes to one of his reasons for sending this letter. He wishes to express his thanks for the gift which his Philippian friends have sent him. He accepts it with gratitude, and yet he is anxious to show that he could have managed without the money, since with Christ's help he has learned the secret of independence (vv. 10-13). Nevertheless, the apostle wants his readers to know his genuine gratefulness, especially since they are the only community which supplied help when he needed it. He is certain that God will reward their generosity by fulfilling all their needs (vv. 14-20).

Assuming that the main purpose of this letter is to acknowledge the gift, some commentators find it difficult to understand why Paul leaves this "thank you note" till the very end of the letter. Accordingly, they would like to isolate this passage as part of yet another letter which the apostle sent to the Philippians. This conjecture, however, does not seem necessary. For one thing, the decision to send Epaphroditus back to Philippi is probably the main occasion for this letter (cf. 2.25 ff.). Needless to

[137]

4.10

say, Paul would not finish the letter without expressing thankfulness to his friends for their generous support. Furthermore, it is likely that Paul feels it desirable to deal first with the problems of internal divisions and false teachings which are threatening the unity of the church.

4.10   In my life in union with the Lord it is a great joy to me that after so long a time you once more had the chance of showing that you care for me. I don't mean that you had stopped caring for me—you just had no chance to show it.

In my life in union with the Lord it is a great joy to me is literally "but I rejoiced in the Lord greatly." Here the function of "but" is nothing more than to indicate a transition to new subject matter, and so it is left untranslated by most modern translators.

The aorist verb "I rejoiced" is sometimes taken to refer to the joy the apostle experienced when Epaphroditus met him with the gifts from his old friends at Philippi (Mft "it was a great joy to me"; Gpd "I was very glad"; NAB "it gave me a great joy"). A great number of translators, however, take the verb as a so-called "epistolary aorist." The apostle experiences the joy as he writes, but it will be something in the past by the time the letter is read by the believers in Philippi. In English such a verb is rendered in the present tense (NEB JB "it is a great joy to me"; Bruce "it gives me great joy"). The verb "I rejoice" and the adverb "greatly" occur in an emphatic position in the Greek text. To bring out the proper force of this clause, it is possible to restructure it as an exclamatory statement, "How great is the joy I have . . . ." Paul's joy is in keeping with or experienced in the light of his relation to his Lord: in my life in union with the Lord.

It is a great joy to me may be rendered simply as "I am very happy indeed." It may be possible at this point to use some idiomatic expression, for example, "my insides are sweet indeed."

As in many instances, in my life in union with the Lord may be rendered as "as I live my life joined with the Lord," or ". . . as one with the Lord."

In Greek the next clause is connected by a conjunction (that) which indicates that what follows is the basis for Paul's joy. Instead of translating it as that (Mft NEB JB GeCL), it is also possible to bring out the connection by a colon (FrCL). The basis of Paul's joy is not the gift he received from the Philippians; it is the fact that his readers finally had an opportunity to show their concern for him.

After so long a time (literally, "already at last" or "already once more") is an expression which appears elsewhere only in Rom 1.10, where TEV has at last. It is an extremely difficult expression to render adequately

[138]

into English. The basic idea is something like "now, after this waiting at last" (Brc "after so long an interval"). The expression seems to suggest that Paul is chiding the Philippians for their delay in sending the money to him. But this is not his intention, as can be seen in what he goes on to say next.

You once more had the chance of showing translates a single verb in Greek, rendered in a number of translations as "revived." This is a rare word, appearing only here in the New Testament. It suggests the picture of a bush or tree putting out fresh shoots or flowers in the springtime. This imagery is kept in some translations (NEB "has now blossomed afresh"; Brc "has flowered again"; NAB "bore fruit once more"). You once more had the chance may be appropriately expressed in a number of languages as "it was once more possible for you," "you once more had the opportunity," or even "you once more could."

That you care for me is an infinitive phrase in Greek. It can be taken as an accusative of reference, meaning "you revived regarding the thinking for me," but it is probably best taken as an accusative governed by the verb "you revived," meaning "you revived your thinking for me." The word care (literally, "think") is again (as in 1.7) to be taken in the positive sense of "concern" or "active interest" (Phps "interest in my welfare"). The chance of showing that you care for me may be expressed as "the possibility of showing me how much you care for me," "...how much you are concerned about me," or even "...how much you want to help me."

In order to avoid any hint of blame, Paul adds some words of explanation—literally, "on which indeed you were thinking." It is probably permissible to take "on which" to mean "for" with an explanatory force, but it is perhaps better to take it in the sense of "with regard to which." The antecedent would be the infinitive phrase immediately preceding, namely, "your thinking for me." The imperfect tense of the verb suggests that it has the force of "all along" or "all the time." The clause can be rendered as "you have indeed thought much about me all the time" (GeCL). Since this is an added explanation to avoid misunderstanding, one can bring the sense out explicitly as "I mean . . ." or "I know . . ." (cf. Bruce Brc). One can also turn the positive statement into a negative one, I don't mean that you had stopped caring for me (cf. Phps "I don't mean that you had forgotten me."). I don't mean may be appropriately rendered in some languages as "my words do not mean," or "do not let my words cause you to think."

That you had stopped caring for me may sometimes be expressed by an aspect of the verb which indicates cessation of an activity or state. In some languages, however, it may be better simply to say "that you no longer wanted to help me," or "...were caring for me."

Paul gives the real reason for the delay as <u>you just had no chance to show it</u>. This clause translates a single verb in Greek, which means literally "you were without opportunity," or "you were lacking opportunity." The verb refers to the circumstances which prevented the Philippians from sending their gift sooner. <u>You just had no chance to show it</u> may be best expressed in some languages as "it simply was not possible for you to show it," "...to show me that you cared for me," or "...wanted to help me."

4.11   And I am not saying this because I feel neglected, for I have learned to be satisfied with what I have.

Even though he appreciates the gift from his friends, Paul would like to make clear his attitude of independence and contentment. He does not deny that he was in need, but the supply of his need is not the motive of his joy. His statement is introduced by an elliptical expression, "not that ...I say," indicating that he does not want his readers to draw a wrong conclusion. One can render this expression explicitly as <u>and I am not saying this because</u> (Brc "don't think that I am saying this because").

<u>I feel neglected</u> is literally "according to want." The word rendered "want" is used elsewhere only in Mark 12.44, where it refers to the material poverty of a widow. In the present context where such thoughts as "care," "concern," and "active interest in one's welfare" are found, the TEV rendering is possible. Most translations, however, retain the original sense of poverty, for example, "not that I complain of want" (Mft RSV), "I am not saying this because I am in need of anything" (Translators' New Testament [TNT]), and "I am not talking about shortage of money" (JB).

In this verse there are two expressions of cause, one introduced by the conjunction <u>because</u> and the other by the conjunction <u>for</u>. The first is a more immediate type of cause and relates <u>I feel neglected</u> to the immediately preceding statement <u>I am not saying this</u>. The second expression of cause relates, not to the preceding clause, but to the entire concept combined in the first part of the verse.

Paul proceeds to explain a lesson he has learned. <u>I have learned</u> represents the rendering of a verb in the aorist tense, but the emphasis is on the result of an action (as opposed to the beginning), and so in English the perfect tense form is appropriate. The pronoun <u>I</u> is emphatic. Paul's sense of independence has been acquired, not through studies, but through the experiences and trials of life.

<u>To be satisfied with what I have</u> is literally "to be content in which things I am." The clause "in which things I am" can be taken as "in the circumstances in which I am," meaning "in my present circumstances."

But the context appears to favor the sense of "in whatever circumstances I find myself." This is the interpretation followed by most translators. Another possibility, however, is suggested in the TEV rendering <u>with what I have</u> (JB "on what I have"; cf. FrCL GeCL). What Paul goes on to say in the following verse seems to justify this third type of rendering.

The adjective rendered <u>satisfied</u> (literally "self-sufficient"), appearing only here in the New Testament, was an important word in Stoic ethics. It was used to describe a state of mind or attitude in which a man is absolutely independent of all things and of all people. It was a cultivated attitude of a wise man whose sufficiency was not dependent on circumstances and conditions. As used by Paul, however, this attitude is a gift from God, made possible through Christ (v. 13), not something achieved by an act of human will.

<u>For I have learned to be satisfied with what I have</u> may sometimes be expressed as "for I have learned how not to feel any lack, regardless of how little I have." It is also possible to translate this expression of cause as "for I have learned to be content even if I have very little."

4.12   I know what it is to be in need and what it is to have more than enough. I have learned this secret, so that anywhere, at any time, I am content, whether I am full or hungry, whether I have too much or too little.

Now follows an eloquent description of Paul's sense of self-sufficiency. This verse expands what is said in the second half of verse 11. The repetition of "I know" and the use of five infinitives in the Greek make this verse most impressive.

<u>I know</u> refers to what Paul has experienced (NAB "I am experienced"). <u>What it is to be in need</u> (literally, "to be abased"; see 2.8) does not mean "to live humbly," as some translations seem to suggest. The antithesis of what is said here is to be abundant or prosperous, as indicated in the next infinitive. This Greek word may be used of the dropping of water level in a river, and the reference here is to the needs in one's daily life (Brc "I know how to live with less than enough"). The idea is vividly brought out in Bruce's idiomatic rendering, "I know what it is to scrape the bottom of the barrel." In this context <u>I know</u> points clearly to experience, for example, "I know by experience." In fact, it may be better to translate the beginning of this verse as "I have experienced what it is to be in need," or ". . . to lack what is necessary."

As in Greek, <u>I know</u> may be repeated here for emphasis before <u>what it is to have more than enough</u>. This clause translates a Greek infinitive which means literally "to overflow." The idea is "to have enough and to

[141]

spare" in the needs of daily life. It may be rendered as "to have more than I need," or "to have more than what is necessary for me."

I have learned this secret renders a single Greek very which means literally "I have been initiated" or "I have been instructed." Used only here in the New Testament, it is a technical expression often used in the pagan mystery cults to denote the act of initiation into the secrets of those religions. Paul's initiation was not a secret affair; he learned from the hard experiences in life (NAB "I have learned to cope with"). This secret refers back to Paul's being satisfied with what he had (v. 11). This was really not a "secret" in the sense that it was hidden information. Hence one may translate I have learned this secret simply as "I have learned how to be satisfied," or ". . . to be content."

"In everything and in all things" (ASV) can be taken in the general sense of "in any and all circumstances" (RSV; cf. Mft "for all sorts and conditions of life," Gpd "in any and all conditions," NEB "whatever my circumstances"). But it is also possible to understand it in the sense of "anything anywhere" (JB), or anywhere, at any time (TEV), giving the preposition "in" both a local and a temporal sense. Thus, anywhere, at any time may be rendered as "regardless of where I am and regardless of when something happens." It is also possible to render these expressions as "wherever I happen to be, at any time," or "it makes no difference where I am, or when I experience such things."

Since the secret that Paul has learned is to be satisfied with whatever he has, TEV makes this information explicit: I am content.

The kind of life which Paul experienced is described in two pairs of infinitives, literally "both to be full and to be hungry, both to abound and to be in need." It appears that the focus is not on "how" but on "whether," not "how to eat well" (which may give a misleading meaning), but "whether I am full." So TEV renders explicitly whether I am full or hungry, whether I have too much or too little. The verb rendered I am full is often used of the feeding and fattening of animals, but the context makes clear that what is meant here is simply to have plenty of food. I have too much renders the same verb used in the phrase what it is to have more than enough. I have . . . too little renders a verb cognate with the word rendered I feel neglected in verse 11. The basic meaning of the term is "to fall behind"; here it is falling behind in the needs of daily life.

Whether I am full or hungry may be expressed as "if I have plenty to eat or if I am hungry, it makes no difference." Similarly, whether I have too much or too little may be rendered as "if I have too many things or if I do not have enough to fill my need, that makes no difference."

4.13   I have the strength to face all conditions by the power that
        Christ gives me.

Paul now gives the source of his strength to face all situations: literally, "I have strength for all things in him who strengthens me." The clause
"I have strength for all things" is generally taken to mean "I can do all
things" (so RSV NEB JB NAB). It is also possible, and, in view of the context (vv. 11-12), desirable, to interpret "all things" in the sense of all conditions (Brc "with any situation"). To face all conditions may be expressed
as "regardless of what happens," or "it makes no difference what happens."
    It is generally understood that "him" in the participial phrase "in him
who strengthens me" refers to Christ. It is best to make this meaning explicit, thus "through Christ who gives me power" or by the power that
Christ gives me. Verse 13 must sometimes be restructured so as to indicate
the causal relation between what Christ does and the strength which Paul
has, for example, "Christ causes me to be strong in every kind of circumstance," or "Christ causes me to have the power to face...."

4.14   But it was very good of you to help me in my troubles.

Paul now returns to the note of his sincere appreciation to the Philippians for their kindness. The particle but is the same one used in 3.16,
where TEV renders it as however that may be. It indicates that the apostle
is trying to keep his readers from drawing a wrong conclusion from what
he has said in the previous verses. The particle can also be translated "all
the same" (JB Brc) or "nevertheless" (Phps).
    It was very good of you is literally "you did well" or "you did no-
bly." In a number of translations it is rendered "it was kind of you."
    To help me in my troubles translates a participial phrase which means
literally "sharing my affliction." The participle "sharing" is a compound
and cognate of "partnership" in 1.5 and a cognate of "partakers" in 1.7.
The word "affliction" is often used in the technical sense of the disaster
that will come at the end of the age (Mark 13.19; 2 Thes 1.6), but in this
context it means "hardships" (JB NAB), "difficulties" (Gpd), or troubles
(TEV NAB). When Paul commends his readers for sharing his troubles, he
is probably thinking both of the material help they provided and of the
sympathy they showed in sending Epaphroditus to him. To help me in my
troubles is a more concrete way of saying "to share the burden of my
troubles" (NEB). The phrase suggests the closeness of the bond that held
the apostle and his readers together.
    In some languages there is danger in a literal translation of help me in
my troubles, since this can be interpreted as "add to my troubles." This
danger may be avoided by translating "to help me when I was in difficulty," or "to come to my aid when I was in trouble."

[143]

4.15   You Philippians know very well that when I left Macedonia in the early days of preaching the Good News, you were the only church to help me; you were the only ones who shared my profits and losses.

What Paul goes on to say is literally "And you yourselves also know, Philippians . . . ." The <u>you</u> is emphatic in Greek, and so one can render "you Philippians yourselves . . . ." "Also know" has the force of <u>know very well</u> (so also TNT; cf. JB Brc). Even though Paul does not often address his readers by name, there seems to be no need to suppose a tone of rebuke as sometimes has been suggested (see 2 Cor 6.11; Gal 3.1). Paul simply desires to express his affectionate feeling toward his friends (NAB "my dear Philippians"; Brc "my Philippian friends").

It is rather difficult to translate the next two temporal references: literally, "in the beginning of the gospel, when I departed from Macedonia." The relation of these clauses is appositional, but since the latter is more specific in mentioning a place name, it is probably better to reverse the clause order as in TEV (cf. Knox "when I left Macedonia in those early days of gospel preaching").

The clause <u>when I left Macedonia</u> can be understood in two different ways. Those who connect the gifts mentioned here with the ones referred to in 2 Cor 11.9 generally take the verb as a pluperfect, "when I had left Macedonia," meaning "after my departure from Macedonia" (Mft Gpd Brc). It is also possible, with the majority of modern translations, to take the clause to mean "at the time of my departure from Macedonia." According to this interpretation, the gifts are none other than those mentioned in verse 16, for Thessalonica was in the province of Macedonia. It is equally possible that the reference in verse 16 is to a still earlier instance. The translation is not affected in either case.

The clause "in the beginning of the gospel" does not seem to refer to the beginning of Paul's Christian life or to the beginning of his missionary work. Paul seems to say simply "when the gospel was first preached among you," that is, <u>in the early days of preaching the Good News among you</u>.

In some languages it may be awkward to have two temporal expressions, one following the other. Therefore one may translate the first part of verse 15 as "You Philippians know very well that when I left Macedonia you were the only church to help me; those were the early days of my preaching the Good News," or ". . . that was at the beginning of the time when I was preaching the Good News in that part of the world," or ". . . in that region."

What Paul says in the remainder of the verse is a negative statement in Greek, literally, "no church entered into partnership with me in the matter of giving and receiving, except you only." To bring out the proper emphasis of "except you only," one may restructure the sentence as TEV

does, you were the only church to help me; you were the only ones....
The church here is, of course, the local congregation (NEB "you were the
only congregation"). In some languages "congregation" may be rendered
as "group of believers."

The phrase "in the matter of giving and receiving," taken from commercial language, is equivalent to "on account of credit and debit." It can
be understood in various ways. (1) As a reference to financial transactions
in a general sense; for example, "no church but yours went into partnership and opened an account with me" (Gpd), or "no church but yourselves had any financial dealings with me" (Mft). (2) One can take "giving"
as the specific giving by the Philippians and "receiving" as the receiving by
Paul; thus "you were the only church by whom in partnership I was
offered, and from whom I accepted, any financial help" (Brc). (3) Since
Paul is obviously referring to the financial help he received from the Philippians, it is possible to take the phrase as alluding to the gifts of money,
for example, "no other church helped me with gifts of money" (JB).
(4) In view of the fact that the picture here is that of "sharing" or "partnership" in a business venture, it is possible to take the two terms in the
figurative sense of "profits" and "losses." as TEV does, you were the only
ones who shared my profits and losses.

In some languages a literal rendering of who shared my profits and
losses may be too specific, giving the impression that the church in Philippi was actually in some kind of business agreement with Paul—for example,
that when he made money at tentmaking, the church in Philippi received
profits, but when he lost money, they made up for his losses. Such an interpretation would go far beyond the implications of this text. Accordingly, most translators render the final clause of verse 15 as "the only ones
who made gifts of money to me."

4.16   More than once when I needed help in Thessalonica, you sent it
        to me.

In Greek this verse is introduced by a particle which is often not
translated. The particle can be understood in two ways: it can mean "that,"
introducing an object clause connected with you . . . know in verse 15; or
it can mean "for," introducing a justification for what the apostle has
said in the preceding verse. The latter alternative seems to be more natural
(cf. RSV NEB). This connection indicates that verses 15 and 16 refer to
the same gifts.

What Paul proceeds to say is literally "even in Thessalonica you sent
to my need both once and twice." The sentence can be rephrased as more
than once when I needed help in Thessalonica, you sent it to me, or

"even in Thessalonica you contributed to my needs more than once." The word "even" points to the fact that the Philippians had sent help soon after the apostle's departure from their city. Help refers probably to "money," as the renderings of Gpd and Mft show (cf. GeCL). One can, therefore, translate "when I needed money in Thessalonica."

The phrase "both once and twice," occurring also in 1 Thes 2.18, is sometimes taken to mean "not once but twice" (Phps NEB NAB) or, more specifically, "twice" (JB). But it probably means simply more than once (TEV Mft), with no indication of the exact number of times.

4.17   It is not that I just want to receive gifts; rather, I want to see profit added to your account.

I . . . want to receive (literally, "I seek") is in Greek an intensive verb with an active meaning of "I hunt for." It is repeated in Greek in order to emphasize a strong contrast . . . not that I . . . want to . . . rather, I want to. This may be rendered as "my interest is not to receive gifts," "my concern is not that I receive gifts," or "I am really not interested in receiving gifts."

Three key words now follow, all of them current business terms when this letter was written. (1) The word rendered profit is literally "fruit," but it can be used in the sense of "interest" gained in a business transaction (Mft). (2) The word added translates a participial form of a verb meaning "to increase," "to accumulate," "to multiply," suggesting compound interest. Paul welcomes the gifts, not so much for his personal benefit as for that of his friends. He considers their gifts a profitable investment in the service of God, for God will repay them rich dividends by adding interest to their account. (3) The third current business term appears in verse 18 , namely receipt.

In some languages it may be impossible to produce a satisfactory literal translation of I want to see profit added to your account, for many societies do not have the type of commercial structure which would provide the basis for such a rendering. In some instances the closest equivalent may be "I want to see even more good deeds added to the list of what you have done," or "I want you to have an even better record of the good that you have done."

4.18   Here, then, is my receipt for everything you have given me—and it has been more than enough! I have all I need now that Epaphroditus has brought me all your gifts. They are like a sweet-smelling offering to God, a sacrifice which is acceptable and pleasing to him.

In this verse Paul continues to use commercial language. Here, then, is my receipt for everything you have given me is literally the simple statement: "and I have everything." The particle "and" here is better taken as a connective then, rather than as an adversative "but" (RSV) or "however," (NEB).

The verb "I have" is often used in the sense of "I have received" as a technical expression for the drawing up of a receipt in financial transactions. This is the third of the three current business terms referred to under verse 17. It is therefore possible to render this phrase as "I have received full payment" (RSV), "here I give you my receipt for everything," or, even more explicitly, as in TEV, here, then, is my receipt for everything you have given me. In languages where commercial transaction involving bills and receipts is unknown, it may be necessary to modify my receipt for everything you have given me to read "my written statement acknowledging everything you have given me," or "these words which express thanks for everything you have given me."

Paul hastens to add and it has been more than enough! This clause translates a single verb which means literally "I abound." The same verb occurs twice in verse 12, where it is rendered to have more than enough and have too much. The clause may be rendered as "it has been more than I needed," or "I could have gotten along on less."

The clause I have all I need (Gpd "I am fully supplied") brings out the meaning of a single Greek verb in the perfect passive tense, but with a present meaning in English: "I am full." It is sometimes suggested that this verb is to be taken with what precedes, as the climax of a series of verbs describing the generosity of the Philippians. However, it is more natural to take it with the following clause, and hence introducing what follows.

Paul further explains what he means by I have all I need by using a participial phrase, literally "having received from Epaphroditus the things from you." Since the agent is specifically mentioned, it is best in many languages to change this pseudopassive construction into an active one as TEV does: now that Epaphroditus has brought me all your gifts. This clause states a type of causal condition, but it is rarely possible to introduce such a clause by a literal rendering of now that. In some languages the closest equivalent is "since Epaphroditus has now brought me all that you have given me," or "...all that you have sent me."

In the remainder of this verse Paul shifts from the language of commerce to that of sacrifice. The gifts of the Philippians are compared to an offering laid on the altar. Since the language is used metaphorically, TEV has the word like.

The gifts are <u>like a sweet-smelling offering to God</u>, literally "an odor of a sweet smell." The phrase is taken from the Greek Old Testament (LXX) and was originally used of burnt offerings. The idea is that God takes pleasure in the smell of the sacrifices offered by men (Gen 8.21; Exo 20.41; Ezek 20.41). It signifies the quality which a sacrificial offering should have in order to be acceptable to God. TEV explicitly indicates that the offering is <u>to God</u>.

In some languages it is not possible to speak of <u>a sweet-smelling offering</u> without indicating precisely who smells the offering. One can, of course, render this as "an offering to God which is sweet to his smell," or ". . . which he smells as being very sweet." However, in many languages the idea of smelling something which is "sweet" is very strange, since a term such as "sweet" would relate only to taste, not to smell. Because of the difficulties involved, some translators prefer to use such an expression as "agreeable to," "pleasing to," "acceptable to," or even "fine," for example, "these gifts are like a fine offering to God."

The focus in the word <u>sacrifice</u> is not on the act of sacrificing, but on the thing sacrificed. Notice that Paul compares the Philippians' gifts to him to <u>a sweet-smelling offering</u> and <u>sacrifice to God</u>, for the help rendered to God's servant is really help rendered to God. From this perspective we can understand why in verse 17b Paul wants to see <u>profit</u> added to the Philippians' account.

<u>A sacrifice which is acceptable and pleasing to him</u> can be rendered "the sort of sacrifice that he approves and welcomes" (Mft), "the sacrifice that he accepts and finds pleasing" (JB), "a sacrifice which he receives and which pleases him," or ". . . which he regards as good."

4.19   And with all his abundant wealth through Christ Jesus, my God will supply all your need.

The particle which connects this verse with the preceding can be rendered in two ways. (1) It can be taken as an adversative "but" (KJV) with focus on the loss incurred in helping the apostle. The implication is that God will not fail to repay their need. If so, the force can be brought out with "in return" (JB; "in turn" NAB). On the basis of this view, God's supply to the Philippians is seen as an act of compensation. (2) Most modern translators, however, take it as a copulative "and," with the possible meaning of "so" (Knox). In this case, God's supply to the Philippians is considered a natural consequence of their generosity.

The phrase <u>my God</u> suggests an intimate relationship that Paul has with God, but this relationship should not be understood as "the God whom I possess" but as "the God whom I serve" (Knox GeCL). It can also have the sense of "God on my behalf." Paul could not repay the debt, but God whom he serves would repay it on his behalf.

With all his abundant wealth through Christ Jesus is literally "according to his riches in glory in Christ Jesus" (ASV RSV). The preposition "according to" can be taken in several ways. (1) It can be understood in the sense of "in a worthy way of" (NAB), "according to the measure of," or "on the scale of," focusing on the extent to which God will supply his wealth (JB "as lavishly as only God can"). (2) It can have the force of "from" (Mft Phps NEB) ot "out of" (Brc), emphasizing God as the source of abundant wealth. (3) One can also render it as with (TEV), highlighting the nature and quality of God as the one who has abundant wealth. Or the whole, (3) and (2) appear to fit the context better than (1).

With all his abundant wealth through Christ Jesus is best treated as a clause of cause or attendant circumstance, for example, "since my God has so much wealth through Christ Jesus," or "in view of the fact that God is so very rich through Christ Jesus." There is a difficulty, however, in rendering the phrase through Christ Jesus, for this might imply that it is Christ Jesus who made God wealthy. The meaning, of course, is that God's wealth may be shared with others by means of Christ Jesus. In some languages it may be essential to combine the phrase through Christ Jesus with the expression will supply all your needs, or to make the phrase through Christ Jesus into a separate clause, for example, "wealth which God gives through Christ Jesus."

The phrase "in glory" is also open to different interpretations. One can hardly give it a local sense, "in the realm of the heavenly." Some persons want to give it a temporal sense, meaning "in the glorious life of the coming age." This suggestion seems equally unsatisfactory, as it is not likely that Paul had in mind only the future heavenly reward of the Philippian believers. Another possibility is to take the phrase adverbially as qualifying the verb "supply." The resultant meaning is "God will supply your needs in a glorious manner" (Gpd "gloriously supply"; cf. JB TOB). But is is probably best to join the phrase closely to the word "wealth," as the majority of modern translators do – thus abundant wealth, "magnificent riches" (NAB FrCL), "glorious wealth" (Bruce), "glorious resources" (Phps), etc.

The characteristic Pauline phrase "in Christ Jesus" should probably be taken with the verb supply. Accordingly, the preposition "in" would acquire an instrumental sense, thus through Christ Jesus (GeCL cf. Gpd), translated as "Jesus Christ caused this" or "Jesus Christ brought this about."

The clause will supply all your needs does not tell us whether Paul has in mind here material needs or spiritual needs. He probably means both. The verb will supply (identical with the one rendered I have all I

<u>need</u> in verse 18) can mean "will supply fully" (NAB), or "will fully meet every need" (Bruce).

4.20 To our God and Father be the glory forever and ever! Amen.

Paul closes his expression of thanks with a doxology, praising God for his greatness and goodness.

The wording of the first clause in Greek (literally, "to God and our Father") presents some problems. It is possible to take the conjunction "and" in the explanatory sense: thus "to God, that is, our Father," the latter term defining the former. The resultant rendering would be: "to God our Father" (JB FrCL TOB cf. GeCL). In view of the fact that both nouns share one article, the pronoun "our" should probably be taken with both nouns: <u>to our God and Father</u> (TEV RSV NEB NAB etc.). In some languages this coordinate construction must be rephrased as "to our God our Father," deleting the conjunction and repeating the possessive pronoun.

The word <u>glory</u> in this context has the components of "praise" and "honor." The expression <u>forever and ever</u> describes the duration in which men should praise God. In a number of languages this type of doxology can only be expressed as something which all people should do, for example, "All people should forever praise and honor our God, who is our Father." In other languages the doxology may be expressed as "We should praise our God and Father forever and ever. Amen," or "Let us give honor to our God our Father forever and ever. Amen." "We" should be inclusive.

The expression <u>Amen</u> is a Hebrew form of affirmation meaning "truly" or "so be it." It indicates solemn assent in prayers. The word may be transliterated if it is already known and used in the receptor language. Otherwise it may be translated as, for example, "surely this is true," "this is certainly the way it should be," or "so be it."

TEV	RSV
Final Greetings	
21 Greetings to each one of God's people who belong to Christ Jesus. The brothers here with me send you their greetings. 22 All God's people here send greetings, especially those who belong to the Emperor's palace.	21 Greet every saint in Christ Jesus. The brethren who are with me greet you. 22 All the saints greet you, especially those of Caesar's household.
23 May the grace of the Lord Jesus Christ be with you all. (4.21-23)	23 The grace of the Lord Jesus Christ be with your spirit.

(4.21-23) |

Following the conventional letter-writing custom of his time, Paul ends his letter with greetings and a benediction. However, he fills them with Christian content.

The section heading Final Greetings may be appropriately expressed in some languages as "Final words," "The last words of the letter," "Greetings to each one of God's people," or "Paul greets each one of God's people in Philippi." It is important to choose a term for "greetings" which would be appropriate to this kind of context. In many languages a term which would be appropriate enough in reference to oral greetings in personal encounter would be unacceptable in this form of written communication.

4.21   Greetings to each one of God's people who belong to Christ Jesus. The brothers here with me send you their greetings.

Paul begins his greetings by saying literally "Greet every saint in Christ Jesus." The verb "greet," a common word in the New Testament, is the word regularly used to convey greetings at the end of a letter. Its modern equivalent is "give my greetings to" (NEB NAB), "give my good wishes to" (Brc), "remember me to" (Gpd), or simply greetings to. In some instances one may translate greetings to each one of God's people as "I send these words to each one of God's people," or "I want each one of God's people to know that I remember them."

The word "saint" is not a description of the moral character of Christians; it refers rather to the fact that they belong to God. It is therefore usually best to render it as God's people (NEB; cf. Brc "God's dedicated people"). (See the discussion under 1.1.) Notice that the greetings are addressed to each one of God's people. Paul is careful to include the whole Philippian community in his expression of love and care.

The expression "in Christ Jesus" can be taken with greetings, so "give my greetings, in Christ Jesus" (NAB cf. FrCL GeCL SpCL), or "give my greetings in the fellowship of Christ" (NEB). It appears better, however, to connect it with God's people, thus God's people who belong to Christ Jesus, "all the people of God, fellow members of Christ Jesus" (Bruce cf. Mft JB TOB).

The word brothers (Brc "fellow-Christians") is often used synonymously with God's people ("saints"). It is impossible to determine who are included in this expression, but certainly Timothy would be one of them (cf. 1.1).

4.22 All God's people here send greetings, especially those who belong to the Emperor's palace.

The expression all God's people here would seem to indicate that
Paul has a wide circle of Christians in mind, including those who belong
to the Emperor's palace, literally "Caesar's household" (RSV). The word
"household" could refer to the Emperor's immediate family, but that is
not the likely meaning. The reference is probably to functionaries or servants in the palace who were Christian. Mft identifies them as "the Imperial slaves," but a broader rendering like that of TEV seems more suitable.
Who belong to the Emperor's palace may be difficult to translate literally,
since in some languages people are not regarded as belonging to a place.
One may need to say "those who work in the Emperor's palace."

4.23 May the grace of the Lord Jesus Christ be with you all.

Paul usually closes his letters with a benediction (1 Cor 16.23; Gal
6.18; Col 4.18; 1 Thes 5.28; 2 Thes 3.18). The central element in all ben-
edictions is the grace. It certainly means more than "favor" (NAB), as the
term is usually understood. It expresses the love and mercy which God
shows and gives through Jesus Christ to people who do not deserve it. The
grace of the Lord Jesus Christ is not to be thought of as something distinct from "the grace of God," but rather as an expression of it. In Paul's
letters, God and Christ are so identified that he can speak in one breath
of "the grace of our God and the Lord Jesus Christ" (2 Thes 1.12; cf.
Rom 5.15; 1 Cor 1.3). Since grace here refers essentially to an event, the
expression the grace of the Lord Jesus Christ must not be interpreted as a
character or quality of Jesus, but as something that he shows and does.
For this reason, it may be desirable to express this benediction in some
languages as "may the Lord Jesus Christ give you grace," "I pray that the
Lord Jesus Christ may continue to show you grace," "... show you his
great kindness," or "... be so kind to you."

The phrase be with you all is literally "be with your spirit." Since
the word "spirit" is often used in the sense of "person" or "oneself," the
TEV rendering is preferable. In the Greek text the pronoun rendered you
all is plural.

Some manuscripts conclude with an "Amen" (KJV). Most likely it
was not present in the original but was added by copyists in accordance
with liturgical practice. Otherwise it would be difficult to account for its
omission in many early manuscripts.

BIBLIOGRAPHY

BIBLE TEXTS AND VERSIONS CITED

(Unless otherwise indicated in the text, references are to the most recent editions listed. CL = Common Language Translation.)

Bibel, Die . . . nach der Übersetzung Martin Luthers. NT revised 1956. Stuttgart: Württembergische Bibelanstalt. Cited as Luther.

Bible, La. Traduction par Louis Segond. NT revised 1964. Paris etc.: Les Sociétés Bibliques. Cited as Seg.

Bonnes Nouvelles Aujourd'hui. Le Nouveau Testament traduit en français courant d'après le texte grec. 1971. Paris etc.: Les Sociétés Bibliques. Cited as FrCL.

Dios Llega al Hombre. El Nuevo Testamento de Nuestro Señor Jesucristo: Versión Popular. 2nd edition 1970. Asunción etc.: Sociedades Bíblicas Unidas. European edition 1971. Madrid: Sociedad Bíblica. Cited as SpCL.

Good News for Modern Man: The New Testament in Today's English Version. 4th edition 1976. New York: American Bible Society. Cited as TEV.

Gute Nachricht, Die: Das Neue Testament in heutigem Deutsch. 1971. Stuttgart: Württembergische Bibelanstalt. Cited as GeCL.

Holy Bible, The. American Standard Version. 1901. Cited as ASV.

Holy Bible, The. Authorised or King James Version. 1611. Cited as KJV.

Holy Bible, The. New International Version. The New Testament. 1973. Grand Rapids: Zondervan Bible Publishers. Cited as NIV.

Jerusalem Bible, The. 1966. London: Darton, Longman & Todd. Cited as JB.

Letters of Paul, The: An Expanded Paraphrase by F. F. Bruce. 1965. Grand Rapids: Wm. B. Eerdmans Publishing Co. Cited as Bruce.

New American Bible, The. 1970. New York: P. J. Kenedy & Sons. Cited as NAB.

New English Bible, The. 2nd edition 1970. London: Oxford University Press, and Cambridge: Cambridge University Press. Cited as NEB.

New Testament, The. A New Translation by William Barclay. Volume II: The Letters and the Revelation. 1969. London: Collins. Cited as Brc.

New Testament, The: A New Translation by James Moffatt. 1922. London: Hodder & Stoughton. Cited as Mft.

New Testament, The: An American Translation by Edgar J. Goodspeed. 1923. Chicago: University of Chicago Press. Cited as Gpd.

New Testament, The: Revised Standard Version. NT 1946. London, Edinburgh, and New York: Thomas Nelson & Sons. 2nd edition reprinted 1972 as part of The Common Bible. Cited as RSV.

New Testament in English, The, by Ronald A. Knox. 1944. London: Burns, Oates, and Washbourne. Cited as Knox.

New Testament in Modern English, The, translated by J. B. Phillips. Revised edition 1972. London: Collins; New York: Macmillan. Cited as Phps.

Traduction Oecuménique de la Bible: Nouveau Testament. Paris: Sociétés Bibliques / Éditions du Cerf. Cited as TOB.

Translator's New Testament, The. 1973. London: British and Foreign Bible Society. Cited as TNT.

GENERAL BIBLIOGRAPHY

Text

The Greek New Testament. Edited by K. Aland, M. Black, C. M. Martini, B. M. Metzger, and A. Wikgren. 2nd edition 1968. Stuttgart: United Bible Societies.

Metzger, B. M. 1971. Textual Commentary on the Greek New Testament. London and New York: United Bible Societies.

Grammars

Blass, F., and A. Debrunner. 1961. Greek Grammar of the New Testament and Other Early Christian Literature. Translated and revised by Robert W. Funk. Chicago: University of Chicago Press.

Moule, C. F. D. 1953. Idiom Book of New Testament Greek. Cambridge, England: Cambridge University Press.

Moulton, J. H. Grammar of New Testament Greek. Vol. 1, 1906; 3rd edition, 1908. Vol. 2, by J. H. Moulton and W. F. Howard, 1920; 2nd edition, 1929. Vol. 3, by N. Turner, 1963. Edinburgh: T. & T. Clark.

Dictionaries

Arndt, W. F., and R. W. Gingrich. 1956. Greek-English Lexicon of the New Testament and Other Early Christian Literature. Chicago: University of Chicago Press.

Buttrick, G. A., ed. 1962. The Interpreter's Dictionary of the Bible. 4 vols. New York and Nashville: Abingdon Press.

Commentaries

Barclay, William. 1959. The Letters to the Philippians, Colossians, and Thessalonians. The Daily Bible Study Series. Philadelphia: Westminster Press.

Beare, F. W. 1959. The Epistle to the Philippians. Harper's New Testament Commentaries. New York: Harper and Row.

Bonnard, Pierre. 1950. L'Épître de Saint Paul aux Philippiens. Commentaire du Nouveau Testament, X. Neuchatel and Paris: Delachaux & Niestle, S. A.

Grayston, Kenneth. 1967. The Letters of Paul to the Philippians and to the Thessalonians. The Cambridge Bible Commentary. Cambridge, England: The University Press.

Houlden, J. H. 1970. Paul's Letters from Prison: Philippians, Colossians, Philemon, and Ephesians. The Pelican New Testament Commentaries. Penguin Books.

Hunter, A. M. 1959. Galatians, Ephesians, Philippians, Colossians. The Layman's Bible Commentary, volume 22. Richmond: John Knox Press.

Johnston, George. 1967. Ephesians, Philippians, Colossians, and Philemon. The Century Bible, New Edition. London: Thomas Nelson and Sons.

Jones, Maurice. 1918. The Epistle to the Philippians. Westminster Commentaries. London: Methuen & Co.

Kennedy, H. A. A. 1956. The Epistle to the Philippians. The Expositor's Greek New Testament. Grand Rapids: Wm. B. Eerdmans Publishing Co.

Lenski, R. C. H. 1961. The Interpretation of St. Paul's Epistle to the Galatians, Ephesians, and Philippians. Minneapolis: Augsburg Publishing House.

Lightfoot, J. B. 1953. St. Paul's Epistle to the Philippians. Grand Rapids: Zondervan Publishing House.

Lohmeyer, Ernst. 1964. Die Briefe an die Philipper, Kolosser und an Philemon. Kritish-Exegetischer Kommentar über das Neue Testament. (Supplement by Werner Schmauch.) Goettingen: Vanderhoeck & Ruprecht.

Martin, R. P. 1959. The Epistle of Paul to the Philippians. The Tyndale New Testament Commentaries. Grand Rapids: Wm. B. Eerdmans Publishing Co.

Michael, J. H. 1923. The Epistle of Paul to the Philippians. The Moffatt New Testament Commentary. London: Hodder and Stoughton.

Moule, H. C. G. 1907. The Epistle of Paul the Apostle to the Philippians. The Cambridge Bible for Schools and Colleges. Cambridge, England: The University Press.

Müller, J. J. 1955. The Epistle of Paul to the Philippians and to Philemon. The New International Commentary on the New Testament. Grand Rapids: Wm. B. Eerdmans Publishing Co.

Scott, E. F. 1955. The Epistle to the Philippians. The Interpreter's Bible, Vol. 11. New York: Abingdon Press.

Vincent, M. R. 1955. A Critical and Exegetical Commentary on the Epistles to the Philippians and to Philemon. The International Critical Commentary. Edinburgh: T. & T. Clark.

Special Studies

Martin, R. P. 1967. Carmen Christi, Philippians 2.5-11 in Recent Interpretation and in the Setting of Early Christian Worship. Society for New Testament Studies, Monograph Series, 4. Cambridge: The University Press.

Nida, E. A., and C. R. Taber. 1969. The Theory and Practice of Translation. Leiden: E. J. Brill.

GLOSSARY

accusative case in Greek and certain other languages marks the immediate goal of the action or influence expressed by a verb or the object of the motion or tendency indicated by a preposition. The inflected forms "him," "them," and "whom" are some of the special accusative forms still found in the English language.

active voice   See **voice**.

adjective is a word which limits, describes, or qualifies a noun. In English, "red," "tall," "beautiful," "important," etc. are adjectives.

adverb is a word which limits, describes, or modifies a verb, an adjective, or another adverb. In English, "quickly," "soon," "primarily," "very," etc. are adverbs.

adverbial refers to adverbs. An *adverbial phrase* is a phrase which functions as an adverb. See **phrase**.

adversative expresses something opposed to or in contrast to something already stated. "But" and "however" are adversative conjunctions.

agency, agent   In a sentence or clause, the agent is that which accomplishes the action, regardless of whether the grammatical construction is active or passive. In "John struck Bill" (active) and "Bill was struck by John" (passive), the agent in either case is "John." See **secondary agency**.

ambiguity is the quality of being ambiguous in meaning. See **ambiguous**.

ambiguous describes a word or phrase which in a specific context may have two or more different meanings. For example, "Bill did not leave because John came" could mean either (1) "the coming of John prevented Bill from leaving" or (2) "the coming of John was not the cause of Bill's leaving." It is often the case that what is ambiguous in written form is not ambiguous when actually spoken, since features of intonation and slight pauses usually specify which of two or more meanings is intended. Furthermore, even in written discourse, the entire context normally serves to indicate which meaning is intended by the writer.

antecedent is the word, phrase, or clause to which a pronoun refers.

aorist refers to a set of forms in Greek verbs which denote an action completed without the implication of continuance or duration. Usually, but not always, the action is considered as completed in past time.

apposition (appositional construction) is the placing of two expressions together so that they both identify the same object or event; for example,

[157]

"my friend, Mr. Smith." The one expression is said to be the *appositive* of the other.

aspect is a grammatical category which specifies the nature of an action; for example, whether the action is completed, uncompleted, repeated (repetitive), begun, continuing (continuative), increasing in intensity, decreasing in intensity, etc.

attribution, attributive   An *attributive* is a term which limits or describes another term. In "the big man ran slowly," the adjective "big" is an attributive of "man," and the adverb "slowly" is an attributive of "ran." Attribution, therefore, is the act of assigning a certain quality or character to an object or an event. See **adjective, adverb**.

capitalize means to write or print the first letter of a word as a capital; for example, in the initial word of a sentence and in proper names. See **proper name**.

case is the syntactical relation of a noun, pronoun, or adjective to other words in a sentence.

causative (also **causation, causal relation**, etc.) relates to events and indicates that someone caused something to happen, rather than that he did it himself. In "John ran the horse," the verb "ran" is a causative, since it was not John who ran, but rather John caused the horse to run.

classifier is a term used with another term (often a proper noun) to indicate what category the latter belongs to. "Town" may serve as a classifier in the phrase "town of Bethlehem" and "river" as a classifier in "river Jordan."

cognates are words which are allied because of their derivation from a common source. The English words "love," "loving," "lovable," "lovely," and "lovingly" are cognates.

components are the parts or elements which go together to form the whole of an object. For example, the components of bread are flour, salt, shortening, yeast, and water. The components of the meaning (*semantic components*) of a term are the elements of meaning which it contains. For example, some of the components of the term "boy" are "human," "male," and "immature."

conditional refers to a clause or phrase which expresses or implies a condition, in English usually introduced by "if."

conjunctions are words which serve as connectors between words, phrases, clauses, and sentences. "And," "but," "if," "because," etc. are typical conjunctions in English.

connotation involves the emotional attitudes of both speaker and hearer (or writer and reader) to an expression (regardless of its specific meaning) and refers to associations and suggestions evoked by the expression which may be quite distinct from the thing named or described. A connotation may be colloquial, vulgar, old-fashioned, intimate, etc.

connotative refers to connotation.

connote means to suggest or imply a meaning which is not explicit in the term used. See **explicit**.

construction   See **structure**.

context is that which precedes and/or follows any part of a discourse. For example, the context of a word or phrase in Scripture would be the other words and phrases associated with it in the sentence, paragraph, section, and even the entire book in which it occurs. The context of a term often affects its meaning, so that it does not mean exactly the same thing in one context that it does in another.

contrastive means adversative.

coordinate structure is a phrase or clause joined to another phrase or clause but not dependent on it. Coordinate structures are joined by such conjunctions as "and" or "but," or they are paratactically related. See **subordinate structure, paratactic**.

copyists were men who made handwritten copies of books, before the invention of printing.

dative in Greek and certain other languages is the case which indicates the indirect or more remote object of the action or influence expressed by a verb. This is generally indicated in English by "to" or "for."

direct address   See **discourse**.

discourse is the connected and continuous communication of thought by means of language, whether spoken or writte. The way in which the elements of a discourse are arranged is called *discourse structure. Direct discourse* is the reproduction of the actual words of one person embedded in the discourse of another person; for example, "He declared, 'I will have nothing to do with that man.'" *Indirect discourse* is the reporting of the words of one person embedded in the discourse of another person in an altered grammatical form; for example, "He said he would have nothing to do with that man."

dynamic equivalence is a type of translation in which the message of the original text is so conveyed in the receptor language that the response of the receptors is (or, can be) essentially like that of the original receptors, or that the receptors can in large measure comprehend the response of the original receptors, if, as in certain instances, the differences between the two cultures are extremely great.

ellipsis (plural *ellipses*) or **elliptical expression** refers to words or phrases normally omitted in a discourse when the sense is perfectly clear without them. In the following sentence, the words within brackets are *elliptical*: "If [it is] necessary [for me to do so], I will wait up all night."

emendation is a correction or improvement in a text based on scholarly reasoning rather than positive evidence.

event is a semantic category of meaning referring to actions, processes, etc., in which objects can participate. In English, most events are grammatically classified as verbs ("run," "grow," "think," etc.), but many nouns also may refer to events, as, for example, "baptism," "song," "game," and "prayer."

exclusive first person plural excludes the person(s) addressed. That is, a speaker may use "we" to refer to himself and his companions, while specifically excluding the person(s) to whom he is speaking. See **inclusive first person plural**.

explicit refers to information which is expressed in the words of a discourse. This is in contrast to *implicit* information. See **implicit**.

finite verb is any verb form which distinguishes person, number, tense, mode, or aspect. It is usually referred to in contrast to an *infinitive* verb form, which indicates the action or state without specifying such things as agent or time.

generic has reference to all the members of a particular class or kind of objects; it is the contrary of *specific*. For example, the term "animal" is generic, while "dog" is specific. However, "dog" is generic in relation to "poodle."

genitive case is a grammatical set of forms occurring in many languages, used primarily to indicate that a noun is the modifier of another noun. The genitive often indicates possession, but it may also indicate measure, origin, characteristic, etc.

Gentiles signifies "the nations" or "foreigners" as opposed to the people of Israel. From this point of view, the human race is divided into two groups: Jews and Gentiles.

gnostic refers to the teachings of the Gnostics, teachers who mixed Greek and Oriental philosophy with Christian doctrines. They claimed possession of superior spiritual knowledge but were denounced as heretical by most Christians.

goal is the object which receives or undergoes the action of a verb. Grammatically, the goal may be the subject of a passive construction ("John was hit," in which "John" is the goal of "hit") or of certain intransitives ("the door shut"); or it may be the direct object of a transitive verb ("...hit John").

idiom or **idiomatic expression** is a combination of terms whose meanings cannot be derived by adding up the meanings of the parts. "To hang one's head," "to have a green thumb," and "behind the eight-ball" are English idioms. Idioms almost always lose their meanings completely when translated from one language to another.

imperative refers to forms of a verb which indicate commands or requests. In "go and do likewise," the verbs "go" and "do" are imperatives. In most languages imperatives are confined to the grammatical second person, but some languages have corresponding forms for the first and third persons. These are usually expressed in English by the use of "may" or "let." For example, "May we not have to beg!" "Let them eat cake!"

imperfect tense is a set of verb forms designating an uncompleted or continuing kind of action, especially in the past.

implicit refers to information that is not formally represented in a discourse, since it is assumed that it is already known to the receptor. This is in contrast to *explicit* information, which is expressed in the words of a discourse.

inclusive first person plural includes both the speaker and the one(s) to whom he is speaking. See **exclusive first person plural**.

indicative refers to a group of modal forms of verbs in which an act or condition is stated or questioned as an actual fact rather than a potentiality or unrealized condition.

indirect discourse   See **discourse**.

infinitive   See **finite verb**.

ironical   See **irony**.

irony is a sarcastic or humorous manner of discourse in which what is said is intended to express its opposite; for example, "That was a wise thing to do!" intended to convey the meaning, "That was a stupid thing to do!"

[161]

Judaism was, in New Testament times, the religion of the Jews, particularly as opposed to the teachings of Jesus and his apostles.

Judaize means to attempt to impose some of the distinctives of Judaism on the Gentile converts to Christianity. See **Judaism.**

linear refers to the continuous or repeated aspect of verbal action, in contrast with *punctiliar,* a completed aspect.

locative refers to a grammatical form or term which indicates a place in or at which an event occurs or an object or person is located.

metaphor (metaphorical term) is likening one object to another by speaking of it as if it were the other; for example, "flowers dancing in the breeze." Metaphors are the most commonly used figures of speech and are often so subtle that a speaker or writer is not conscious of the fact that he is using figurative language. See **simile.**

middle verb   See **voice.**

modal refers to forms of verbs in certain languages which indicate the attitude of a speaker to what he is saying; for example, wish, hesitancy, command, etc. The various categories of modal verb forms are called *modes* or *moods.* In English they are expressed by such auxiliary verbs as "can," "do," "may," "shall," etc.

mystery religion   See **gnostic.**

noun is a word that is the name of a subject of discourse, as a person, place, thing, idea, etc. See **proper name.**

optative means expressing desire or choice. This is indicated in some languages by certain verb forms.

papyri (singular *papyrus*) are, in the context of this Handbook, those texts of the Scriptures which were written originally on papyrus (an early form of paper) and which are representative of the earliest forms of the Greek text.

paratactic expression or relationship (*parataxis*) refers to two or more clauses of equal rank which stand together without being joined by a connective; for example, "I came, I saw, I conquered." See **conjunction.**

participial refers to participles.

participle is a verbal adjective, that is, a word which retains some of the characteristics of a verb while functioning as an adjective. In "singing waters" and "painted desert," "singing" and "painted" are participles.

particle is a small word whose grammatical form does not change. In English, the most common particles are prepositions and conjunctions.

[162]

passive voice   See **voice**.

perfect tense is a set of verb forms which indicate an action already completed when another action occurs. The perfect tense in Greek also indicates that the action continues into the present.

person, as a grammatical term, refers to the speaker, the person spoken to, or the person or thing spoken about. *First person* is the person(s) or thing(s) speaking ("I," "me," "my," "mine," "we," "us," "our," "ours"). *Second person* is the person(s) or thing(s) spoken to ("thou," "thee," "thy," "thine," "ye," "you," "your," "yours"). *Third person* is the person(s) or thing(s) spoken about ("he," "she," "it," "his," her," "them," "their," etc.). The examples here given are all pronouns, but in many languages the verb forms distinguish between the persons and also indicate whether they are singular or plural.

phrase is a grammatical construction of two or more words, but less than a complete clause or a sentence. A phrase may have the same function as the head word of the phrase. For example, "the old man" has essentially the same function as "man" would have. However, a phrase may have a function which is different from the function of any of its constituents, for example, "to town," "for John."

play on words in a discourse is the use of the similarity in the sounds of the words to produce a special effect.

pluperfect means, literally, "more than perfect" (see **perfect tense**) and refers to a verb form which indicates an action already completed when another action occurred. For example, in "the meeting had already ended when the speaker arrived," the verb "had ... ended" is a pluperfect.

possessive pronouns are pronouns such as "my," "our," "your," "his," etc. which indicate possession.

predicate is the part of a clause which contrasts with or supplements the subject. The subject is the topic of the clause, and the predicate is what is said about the subject.

primary agent   See **agency**.

preposition is a word (usually a particle) whose function is to indicate the relation of a noun or pronoun to another noun, pronoun, verb, or adjective. Some English prepositions are "for," "from," "in," "to," "with."

proper name or **proper noun** is the name of a unique object, as "Jerusalem," "Joshua," "Jordan." However, the same name may be applied to more than one object; for example, "John" (the Baptist or the Apostle) and "Antioch" (of Syria or of Pisidia).

[163]

pseudo passive (also called **false passive**) is a grammatical structure which is active in form but passive in meaning. For example, "John received the gift" is active in form, but semantically John is the goal of the giving; therefore the meaning is passive.

punctiliar is an aspect of an event regarded as a "point of time," in contrast with the continuative or durative aspect, which describes events as continuing over a period of time. See **aspect**.

purpose clause designates a construction which states the purpose involved in some other action; for example, "John came in order to help him," or "John mentioned the problem to his colleagues, so that they would know how to help out."

recast means the same as *restructure*. See **structure**.

Received Text   See **Textus Receptus**.

receptor is the person receiving the message. The *receptor language* is the language into which a translation is made. The *receptor culture* is the culture of the people for whom a translation is made, especially when it differs radically from the culture of the people for whom the original message was written.

relative clause is a dependent clause which qualifies the object to which it refers. In "the man whom you saw," the clause "whom you saw" is relative because it relates to and qualifies "man."

restrictive attributives are so called because they restrict the meaning of the objects which they qualify, while *nonrestrictive attributives* do not. In the expression "the soldiers who were retreating were commanded to halt and regroup" (no commas), the clause "who were retreating" indicates that the command was restricted to a particular class of soldiers, namely, those who were retreating. But in the expression "the soldiers, who were retreating, were commanded to halt and regroup," the same clause (this time set off by commas) qualifies all the soldiers referred to in the discourse and simply provides supplementary information about them. In the latter case, the clause is nonrestrictive.

rhetorical refers to special forms of speech which are used for emphasis or to create an effect on the receptor. A *rhetorical question,* for example, is not designed to elicit an answer but to make an emphatic statement.

root is the minimal base of a derived or inflected word. For example, "friend" is the root of "friendliness."

secondary agency (agent) involves the immediate agent of a causative construction. In the sentence "John made Bill hit the man," John is the primary agent and Bill is the secondary agent. John may also be regarded as the *responsible agent* and Bill as the *immediate agent*. Similarly, in the sentence "God spoke through the prophets," God is the primary agent and the prophets are the secondary agents. They do the actual speaking, but God is the real force behind the activity. See **agency**.

semantic refers to meaning. *Semantics* is the study of the meaning of language forms. *Semantic categories* (or *classes*) group words according to their meaning (objects, events, abstracts, etc.) in contrast to grammatical categories (nouns, verbs, etc.). A *semantic domain* is a definable area of experience which is referred to by a set of words whose meanings are in some way related. For example, kinship terms constitute a semantic domain. Similarly, the color terms of a language may be said to form a semantic domain. For *semantic components* see **components**.

Semitic refers to a family of languages which includes Hebrew. Greek belongs to quite another language family, with a distinct cultural background. In view of his Jewish ancestry and training, it is not surprising that some Semitic idioms and thought patterns (called *Semitisms*) appear in the Greek writings of the apostle Paul.

Semitism See **Semitic**.

Septuagint is a translation of the Old Testament into Greek, made some two hundred years before Christ. It is often abbreviated as LXX.

simile (pronounced SIM-i-lee) is a figure of speech which describes one event or object by comparing it to another, as "she runs like a deer," "he is as straight as an arrow." Similes are less subtle than metaphors in that they use "like," "as," or some other word to mark or signal the comparison. See **metaphor**.

specific See **generic**.

Stoics were people who followed the teachings of the philosopher Zeno (died 265 B. C.). He taught that happiness is to be found in being completely indifferent to both pleasure and pain.

structure is the systematic arrangement of the form of language, including the ways in which words combine into phrases, phrases into clauses, and clauses into sentences. Because this process may be compared to the building of a house or a bridge, such words as *structure* and *construction* are used in reference to this process. To separate and rearrange the various components of a sentence or other unit of discourse in the translation process is to *restructure* it.

subordinate structure designates a clause connected with and dependent on another clause. See **coordinate structure, paratactic**.

synonyms are words which are different in form but similar in meaning, as "boy" and "lad." Expressions which have essentially the same meaning are said to be *synonymous.*

syntactic refers to *syntax,* which is the arrangement and interrelationships of words, phrases, clauses, and sentences.

tense is usually a form of a verb which indicates time relative to a discourse or some event in a discourse. The most common forms of tense are past, present, and future.

textual refers to the various Greek manuscripts of the New Testament. A *textual reading* is the reading of a particular manuscript (or group of manuscripts), especially where it differs from others. *Textual evidence* is the cumulative evidence for a particular reading. A *textual witness* may be an ancient writing other than a New Testament manuscript which contains a quotation from or a translation of the text, thus lending support to a particular reading. *Textual problems* arise when it is difficult to reconcile or to account for conflicting readings.

Textus Receptus (Latin for "Received Text") is one of the earliest printed forms of the text of the Greek New Testament. Based on very late manuscripts, it contains a large number of readings which are untenable.

third person   See **person.**

transition in discourse is passing from one thought or group of related thoughts to another. In written discourse, the use of marks of punctuation and the division into paragraphs help to make the transitions. Transitional particles such as prepositions and conjunctions ("in," "so," "because," "furthermore," "however," etc.) and transitional phrases ("in other words," "in the meantime," "at last," etc.) serve a like purpose.

verbs are a grammatical class of words which express existence, action, or occurrence, as "be," "become," "run," "think," etc.

verbal has two meanings. (1) It may refer to expressions consisting of words, sometimes in distinction to forms of communication which do not employ words ("sign language," for example). (2) It may refer to word forms which are derived from verbs. For example, "coming" and "engaged" may be called verbals, and participles are called verbal adjectives.

voice in grammar is the relation of the action expressed by a verb to the participants in the action. In English and many other languages, the *active voice* indicates that the subject performs the action ("John hit the man"), while the *passive voice* indicates that the subject is being acted upon ("the man was hit"). The Greek language has a *middle voice,* in which the subject may be regarded as doing something to or for himself (or itself).

Vulgate is the Latin version of the Bible translated and/or edited originally by Saint Jerome. It has been traditionally the official version of the Roman Catholic Church.